Governing the
health care state

MANCHESTER
UNIVERSITY PRESS

Political Analyses

Series editors: Bill Jones and Michael Moran

Governing the health care state

A comparative study
of the United Kingdom,
the United States and Germany

Michael Moran

Manchester University Press
Manchester and New York

distributed exclusively in the USA by St. Martin's Press

Published by Manchester University Press
Oxford Road, Manchester M13 9NR, UK
and Room 400, 175 Fifth Avenue, New York, NY 10010, USA
http://www.man.ac.uk/mup

Distributed exclusively in the USA by
St. Martin's Press, Inc., 175 Fifth Avenue, New York,
NY 10010, USA

Distributed exclusively in Canada by
UBC Press, University of British Columbia, 6344 Memorial Road,
Vancouver, BC, Canada V6T 1Z2

British Library Cataloguing-in-Publication Data
A catalogue record for this book is available from the British Library

Library of Congress Cataloging-in-Publication Data applied for

ISBN   0 7190 4296 8 *hardback*
        0 7190 4297 6 *paperback*

First published 1999

06 05 04 03 02 01 00 99   10 9 8 7 6 5 4 3 2 1

Typeset
by Helen Skelton Publishing, London
Printed in Great Britain
by Biddles Ltd, Guildford and King's Lynn

For Jean and Stan Wainhouse

Most, maybe all, of the basic tenets of social science are truisms. Almost every-body agrees at first sight, almost everyone knew it all along – except that most people all along have also held the opposite to be true, without being bothered by the contradiction.

Abram de Swaan
The management of normality: critical essays in health and welfare
(London, Routledge, 1990), p. 3

Contents

List of tables

Series editors' foreword

The *Politics Today* series has been running successfully since the late 1970s, aimed mainly at an undergraduate audience. After over a decade in which a dozen or more titles had been produced, some of which have run to several new editions, MUP thought it time to launch a new politics series, aimed at a different audience and a different need.

The *Politics Analyses* series was prompted by a relative dearth of research-based political science series which persists despite the fecund source of publication ideas provided by current political developments. In the UK we observe, for example: the rapid evolution of Labour politics as the party seeks to find a reliable electoral base; the continuing development of the post-Thatcher Conservative Party; the growth of pressure group activity and lobbying in modern British politics; and the irresistibe moves towards constitutional reform of an arguably outdated state.

Abroad, there are even more themes upon which to draw, for example: the ending of the Thatcher–Reagan axis; the parallel collapse of communism in Europe and Russia; and the gradual retreat of socialism from the former heartlands in Western Europe.

The series seeks to explore some of these new ideas to a depth beyond the scope of the *Politics Today* series – while maintaining a similar direct and accessible style – and to serve an audience of academics, practitioners and the well-informed reader as well as undergraduates.

Preface

Like many books, this one originated in a small puzzle. During the 1980s and early 1990s the health care systems of most of the advanced capitalist nations were reformed. Casual inspection suggested that these reforms were in the main motivated by the desire to contain costs. That was no surprise. Many nations had greatly expanded their health care provision in the three decades after the close of the Second World War. The end, in the mid-1970s, of the 'thirty glorious years' of capitalist expansion created a more austere, cost-conscious environment. When the landmark British reforms finally arrived after 1989 they naturally greatly interested me both as a citizen and as a social scientist. The British soon emerged as international leaders in reform, notably in the construction of new kinds of health care markets. But the more I looked the more puzzled I became for, viewed in the light of cost containment, the British reforms made no sense. The National Health Service was bad at many things, but even the most cursory comparison of national experiences showed that it was actually very good at cost containment. Why fix something that didn't seem to be broken? Evidently casual inspection was not enough; something deeper was going on, and only comparative analysis promised to reveal it.

Early comparison only deepened the puzzle. At least as far as the control of consumption was concerned, Britain operated essentially a command and control health care economy. In that command and control system lay much of the clue to successful cost containment – and, indeed, the clue to the wider success of the NHS: we provided modest benefits to all citizens at modest cost. Other countries were conspicuously less successful. In particular the United States, which relied on private insurance markets to cover a large portion of the cost of health care, was a complete policy fiasco: health care was by British standards stunningly expensive, and a large section of the population did not have even the modest entitlements delivered as a right of citizenship in Britain. In these circumstances one might have expected a stream of American visitors to Britain intent on discovering the secret of British success; and one might have expected British command and control health care economics to set the international standard. The reverse was true. Some of the most distinguished American visitors – such as the famous health economist Alain Enthoven – came across the Atlantic to advocate reforms which were based on American innovations, while the British reformers of the late 1980s visited the United States in the hope of enlightenment. More generally, the diffusion of institutional innovation seemed to be from the system that was conspicuously failing at cost containment: it was the United States, not the United Kingdom or Scandinavia, that was state of the art as far as health care reform was concerned. In the international diffusion of health care reforms apparently nothing succeeded like failure.

There were two ways of making sense of this odd state of affairs: either there was grotesque perversity and stupidity in the policy process, or health care reform was shaped by forces deeper than the search for cost containment. Since I have lived all my adult life in the United Kingdom I was very ready to believe in the perversity and stupidity of the British governing class. I was nevertheless unwilling to assume that everyone else was equally stupid. The conclusion was inescapable: policy must be shaped by something more subterranean than the acknowledged search for cost containment. That conclusion dictated a book that would have four features: it would start by trying to make sense of how we understand health care policy; it would try to trace the historical routes by which states had arrived at their modern condition; it would place the British experience into a comparative setting; and that comparative setting would be dominated by the American presence since so much of what was happening was coming from America. That explains the broad shape of the book; the particulars are explained in later chapters, notably Chapter 1.

I accumulated many debts in writing this book. The research was part funded by small grants from the Nuffield Foundation and from the UK Economic and Social Research Council: I gratefully acknowledge their support. Elizabeth Alexander was a research assistant whose work went far beyond the normal call of duty. A number of friends and colleagues read earlier versions and offered numerous helpful suggestions: in particular, Martin Burch, Richard Freeman, Anders Lindbom, Calum Paton and Paul Wilding. I say 'offered' because I have sometimes been too stubborn to accept good advice, and therefore ought to stress my own full responsibility for what follows. I owe an extra debt to Richard Freeman for allowing me to quote in Chapter 6 from his work, which is presently in press, on European health policy. At a late stage in the research I was able to spend a month as a guest professor in Konstanz, invaluable for the passages of the book that concern Germany. I am grateful to the University of Konstanz for its hospitality. It is a particular pleasure to acknowledge the many kindnesses of Jens Alber, together with his numerous, often devastating, questions; and to thank Ellen Immergut for her comments on the manuscript. I must also acknowledge the very helpful comments of two anonymous readers for Manchester University Press. At the Press, the book would not have been started without the prompting of Richard Purslow and would not have been finished without Nicola Viinikka's kindness and encouragement. Helen Skelton's eagle-eyed copyediting greatly improved the final manuscript.

A special place in the pantheon is reserved for two figures. Steve Harrison's comments on the draft manuscript were invaluable, and his generosity in sharing information with me extraordinary. Bruce Wood read the entire manuscript with his usual sharp eye, and his comments improved it beyond measure. He also kindly allowed me to refer to his important comparative work in progress on the growth of political action among patient groups. Over the years we have taught both graduate and undergraduate courses together. I have stolen so many ideas from him that I am not even certain that he can be absolved from blame for any shortcomings in these pages. His generosity and encouragement are a constant reminder to me that there still exists in British universities a true community.

MJM, Manchester, 18 December 1998

1

Understanding the
health care state

Identifying the health care state

Health policy is about more than health, and its study is about more than
the study of health care. These truisms provide the starting point for this book.
Health care is indeed part of the welfare system of modern industrial societies.
It is a personal welfare service received, often, in our bitterest moments of
pain, despair and, finally, death: most of us will, after all, die in a health care
institution.[1] But modern health care systems are about much more than the
means of delivering a personal service. Health care facilities in modern industrial societies are great concentrations of economic resources – and because of
this they are also the subject of political struggle. We know this in our everyday
lives in numerous ways beyond any experience we might have as patients. In
our cities we can see huge health care institutions like hospitals which are both
important landmarks and major employers. Our high-street shops are full of
the products of modern health care industries – dental, optical, pharmaceutical. Those of us who are wage earners and tax payers know that, in one way or
another, a sizable slice of our income is taken to fund the costs of health care.

Our daily intuition that we are surrounded by huge and pervasive health
care institutions is not misplaced. The accompanying tables support the
evidence of everyday experience.[2] The tables assemble a statistical summary of
the scale of resources devoted to health care in the leading nations of the
advanced industrial world. These countries are conventionally identified as the
'G7' group, though similar trends are observable across all OECD nations.[3]
To provide a simple perspective figures are added for the Republic of Ireland,
one of the smallest, and until recently one of the poorest, members of the OECD
'club'. The figures begin in 1960 because that is as far back as reliable
comparative evidence goes. They give data for 1975 because, as we shall see at
numerous points later, the mid-1970s were a turning point in the history of
health care policy. And finally they give the latest available date of a series for
the whole group.

1

Table 1.1 *Total national expenditure on health as % of gross domestic product*

	1960	1975	1997
USA	5.2	8.2	14.0
UK	3.0	5.5	6.7
Germany	4.8	8.8	10.4[a]
Canada	5.5	7.2	9.3
Japan	na[b]	5.5	7.3
France	4.2	7.0	9.9
Italy	3.0	6.2	7.6
Ireland	3.8	7.7	7.0

Source: OECD, *Health data 98.*

Notes: [a]1960 and 1975 figures are for the former West Germany; 1997 figure is for the unified Federal Republic. [b]First available year, 1970: 4.4%.

Table 1.2 *Public current expenditure on health as % of general government expenditure*

	1960	1975	1995[a]
USA	4.5	9.7	18.6
UK	9.9	9.9	13.4
Germany	na[b]	13.3	13.6
Canada	7.2	13.1	14.1
Japan	na[c]	14.3	14.6
France	na[d]	11.4	13.8
Italy	10.1	12.7	9.7
Ireland	na[e]	13.5	13.4

Source: OECD, *Health data 98.*

Notes: [a]Latest year for which a complete series is available. [b]First available, 1970: 10.9%. [c]First available, 1970: 15.7%. [d]First available, 1970: 10.4%. [e]First available, 1970: 11.2%.

These tables show, for all the variations between nations, some remarkable similarities. In all the G7 nations health care is a large consumer of society's resources: that is the straightforward lesson of Table 1.1. But what is even more striking is the long-term rise in the share of resources taken by health care: as Table 1.1 also shows, all these nations have seen a substantial growth in the scale of resources given to health care since 1960, the year when reliable comparative evidence begins. Across the advanced industrial world, therefore, health care is not only big business; that size is a fairly recent phenomenon. But there is also a more distinctly political aspect to this state of affairs: as Table 1.2 shows, there has in most instances been a long-term rise

Table 1.3 *Public expenditure on health as % of total national expenditure on health*

	1960	1975	1997
USA	24.8	42.1	46.7
UK	85.2	91.1	84.5
Germany	66.1	79.1	77.4
Canada	42.7	76.4	68.7
Japan	60.4	72.0	77.4
France	57.8	77.2	78.4
Italy	83.1	84.5	69.9
Ireland	76.0	79.0	75.0

Source: OECD, *Health data 98*.

Table 1.4 *Coverage by publicly funded health care schemes*[a]

	1960	1975	1997
USA	20.0	40.0	45.0
UK	100.0	100.0	100.0
Germany	85.0	90.3	92.2
Canada	71.0	100.0	100.0
Japan	88.0	100.0	100.0
France	76.3	96.0	99.5
Italy	87.0	95.0	100.0
Ireland	85.0	85.0	100.0

Source: OECD *Health data 98*.

Note: [a]Measures the % share of the population which is eligible for medical goods and services that are included in total public health expenditure.

in the share of public spending taken by government expenditure on health care. Health care spending looms large in the budget of the modern state. Conversely, the modern state looms large in the wider health care economy. Table 1.3 shows that for a generation the largest share (in most cases the overwhelming share) of health care spending has come from the public purse. Even in the United States, the system commonly identified with market mechanisms of health care financing, the state was by the 1990s the biggest single contributor to the cost of health care.

The political significance of the rise of these huge health care institutions is in part obvious. At the most elemental level it increases the intensity of distributive struggles – over who should pay the enormous costs of health care, and over who should receive the resources that are being allocated. But another piece of evidence in these tables hints at a more subtle political significance for health care institutions – a significance that lies at the heart of this book. Table 1.4 shows that over a generation there has been a large growth in the proportion of populations with entitlements to medical treat-ment (either in or out of hospital) paid for by public schemes. 'Public schemes' mean different things in different nations, but everywhere their growth signifies one thing: the rising importance of states in the funding of health care systems. Indeed, with the exception of the United States we can see that by the 1990s all the states in our group had reached, or virtually reached, 'universalism' – complete coverage of populations by publicly funded schemes.[4]

Yet even these figures for entitlements give only a hint, and in some respects a misleading hint, of the state's significance. They give a misleading hint because, as the most casual observer of health care policy knows, the high tide of state involvement in directly financing entitlements to care was for the most part reached over twenty years ago. That high tide also swelled the volume of resources spent on health care. Since then, health care financing policy has been dominated by the language of cost containment, and part of that has involved trying to curtail entitlements funded by states. These developments have led to the widespread view that, across the industrial world, we are seeing a retreat by states from the health care arena – a view that seems to fit wider interpretations of the changing role of states in capitalist economies.[5]

These views are only half right. States have certainly been trying to disentangle themselves from funding obligations, but that is only part of the story of states and health care. States did indeed achieve prominence in health care by virtue of their role in its provision as a personal service. But health care policy is about more than health care as a personal service. Health care institutions are large-scale concentrations, and means of allocating, society's resources. The struggle to influence that allocation process is in part a political struggle. The health care state is the site for that political struggle. Across the capitalist world, health care institutions and the institutions of the state have penetrated each other so deeply that the notion of a 'retreat' by either makes no sense. It is this mutual penetration which makes it sensible to speak of the 'health care state'.[6]

'Health care state' is an obvious echo of 'welfare state', but health care politics are more than a subset of welfare politics and the health care state is more than a subsystem of the welfare state. Indeed, the best analogue is not the welfare state at all, but the modern industrial state, for as we shall see there are important connections between the industrial state and the health care state. States and health care systems pervade each other. It is precisely this pervading character which makes summary characterisations like 'retreat' so unconvincing. *There is more to health care politics than health care policy*; the scale of health care institutions means that they have ramifications for the modern state well beyond conventional health care arenas. Like any state, the health care state is about governing; and in the act of governing states shape health care institutions, and are in turn shaped by those institutions. The fact that influences run both ways – from states to health care institutions, and vice versa – is what gives sense to the notion of a health care state. Health care systems pose problems for statecraft; but they also offer ways of solving problems, often problems whose origins lie beyond health care systems themselves. Historically, indeed, concern for health was often a powerful force in the very development of the administrative state, creating new state instruments and cadres – a marked feature, for instance, of Britain in the 1840s.[7]

A summary definition of 'statecraft' is that it is about governing: about creating support for authoritative decisions, about making the decisions, about creating the means to put the decisions into effect. Statecraft in the health care state demands governing acts in three particularly important political arenas; the heart of the book examines those arenas. These three arenas are concerned with consumption politics, professional politics and production politics.

Governing consumption is a central responsibility of modern states, especially of democratic states in market capitalist economies, because competition for both material and positional goods is a key feature of those societies.[8] *Consumption politics* are particularly important in all modern health care systems – and the reasons are encapsulated in the data summarised in the tables given earlier. Health care is indeed a personal service, and it is provided on a quite extraordinary scale. Modern medical science has created huge demand for both the services of medical professionals and the technological artifacts which they control. 'Governing consumption' here means many things, but two are particularly important: governing the conditions under which populations have access to health care goods and services; and, the dominant theme of health care policy in recent years, governing the total cost of consumption in health care services.

These two tasks are connected because of the *collective* character of consumption in health care. The central feature of health care consumption across the advanced capitalist world may be expressed negatively: it is for the most part not purchased directly by the patient. Consumption can sensibly be described as collective because it is collectively financed, and access is collectively regulated. In some nations – of which the United Kingdom is a prime example – that collectivisation is expressed as an aspect of citizenship: in the words of the Act establishing the National Health Service, 'It shall be the duty of the Minister of Health ... to promote the establishment in England and Wales of a comprehensive health service ... The services provided shall be free of charge, except where any provision of this Act expressly provides for the making and recovery of charges.'[9] In Germany, collectivisation is expressed in an obligation on workers and employers to contribute to a health insurance fund, an obligation on the funds to meet the costs of care for their members, and an obligation on associations of contracted doctors to ensure that the services are delivered.

But perhaps the most revealing example of the collectivisation of consumption – because it is commonly pictured as an archetype of market individualism – is the United States. In truth, not far short of half of all spending on health care (to be exact, 46.7 per cent at the latest available estimate) is raised in the most emphatically collectivist way of all – from the public purse, to fund programmes like Medicare and Medicaid.[10] But beyond this public sphere, for the overwhelming majority of Americans care is collectively financed through insurance contracts, and increasingly it is collectively delivered.[11] The origins of that collective financing emphasise the way states and health care systems are intertwined. Health insurance in the US is mostly received as part of an employment package, and that is because historically the tax system, by generous allowances, has encouraged workplace-based insurance. Over 80 per cent of the non-elderly population is at any one time covered by health insurance, and the profiles of the uninsured show plainly that their status is not due to any individual choice, but to occupational stratification: the uninsured are uninsured because they work in particular kinds of firms and sectors.[12] Thus, even in the most 'marketised' of health care systems, consumption decisions do not turn on choices made by individual consumers; they involve collectively organised financing packages and collectively organised delivery systems. Even in the US struggles about consumption are thus collective struggles: about gaining access to these financing packages (for the uninsured); and about the content of entitlements (for the insured).

In sum: health care is in the main no longer individually purchased by patients at the moment of treatment. It is the collective character of consumption which gives consumption struggles their organised form, and which thus shapes consumption politics.[13] Some of the key groups include patients, in various guises as citizens, workers or insurance subscribers; and third-party payers, whether parts of the state, employers or parts of the insurance industry.

The state, then, pervades the health care system; but the groups involved in consumption struggles also pervade the state. The sheer scale of health care means that these groups are major institutional actors in the state system. In recent years, for instance, some of the largest contributing political action committees in the United States – a key channel for funding election campaigns – have come from the health care sector. One estimate of the money spent by health care interests in the Congressional lobbying over the Clinton reform proposals of 1994 – 'the most heavily lobbied initiative in recent U.S. history' – puts the cumulative cost in excess of $100 million; Federal Election Commission records show direct donations of $25 million to Congressmen from health-related interests in the period 1993 through the first quarter of

1994, the critical time when the Clinton proposals were killed.[14] As we will see in later chapters the interests organised in consumption have both reflected the changing pattern of democratic politics and have contributed to the way democracies are changing. The scale of health care spending also means that the outcomes of consumption politics have significant consequences for state-craft: they affect fiscal policy, the electoral fortunes of governments and even the competitiveness of nations. That explains why in each of the three countries examined in this book – and in a wider range, for that matter – the reform of health care systems has been a major preoccupation of high politics since the 1970s.

Governing consumption is a distinct sphere but it connects with *governing professionals*. Professions are central to the life of the modern state: as concentrations of expertise; as sources of legitimising ideologies; as institutional apparatuses through which state power can be transmitted; and, more simply, as important pressure groups.[15] Conversely, the modern state is central to the life of professions. Professionalism is a strategy pursued to defend occupational interests, involving the 'closure' of the occupation from market competition.[16] That closure is typically enforced by authority drawn, in the last analysis, from the state. As Wilding puts it, summarising a large body of work: 'What produces the privileges of professional status is a profession-state alliance.'[17] Thus professional government involves precisely the kind of mutual penetration which is a characteristic feature of the health care state.

Health care systems are highly professionalised. The delivery of care in modern industrial societies is done largely by groups that are attempting, with varying degrees of success, to use the strategy of professionalism in the defence of occupational interests. Some are historically well entrenched, like doctors and dentists; the largest of all, nursing, is a long-established, if insecure, claimant to professional status; others, like osteopaths in the United Kingdom, are only just climbing the ladder of professional privilege. As the examples of nurses and osteopaths show, the extent to which particular occupations have a secure place on the ladder of professionalism depends on contingent circumstances: it partly reflects the changing nature of the professional task, notably the extent to which it is surrounded by complexity and uncertainty; and it partly reflects the historical circumstances in which particular occupations first encountered the state.[18] Chapter 4 explores the government of professions through a study of a single group, doctors. There are many reasons for this focus, some to do with the substantive importance of the medical profession, some to do with more analytical considerations. Substantively, doctors have been recognised as historically dominant, both in the hierarchies of the health care system and in the sphere of professional politics. States have recognised this in making the government of the medical profession a centrepiece of their health care policies: as we will see, the government of the profession has been, and continues to be, a great preoccupation of health care statecraft. There are some well-known reasons for this preoccupation, mostly to do with the role of doctors in allocating health care resources. The primacy of doctors in the hierarchy of health carers means that they have an important say over health care spending: consider Kane's estimate that in the United States physicians control between 70–80 per cent of all health care spending decisions, even though they themselves only receive about 20 per cent of national health expenditures.[19] There is a good substantive case to be made, therefore, for saying that the government of the medical profession is the centrepiece of the government of professions in the health care state.

The analytical reason for organising a study of professional government around the case of doctors takes us back to one of the key features of the health care state – the way the institutions of the state, and those of the health care system, are bound together. In all the countries examined here the quintessential characteristics of medical professions – the nature of internal hierarchies, the strategies used to defend interests – have in large measure been shaped by relations with agencies of states. Nor have doctors simply been on the receiving end of state power; they have been important actors in the development of the modern state itself. Take the example of Britain: in the field of pressure group organisation the British Medical Association was a historical prototype, providing a model for the kind of pressure group organisation so important to the structure of policy making.[20] In the world of professionalism itself, doctors were among the pioneers of professional organisation as an occupational strategy – a strategy that large numbers of other occupations have sought to emulate.[21] In short, a key reason for concentrating on the government of the medical profession is that it demonstrates to perfection one of the key arguments of the book – that health care institutions are not just shaped by the state, but in turn help shape the wider features of the state system.

The way the institutions of the state and of the health care system pervade each other, fusing together in reciprocal relations of influence, is even more powerfully demonstrated by the third sphere examined in the book, that of *production politics*. When we look at health care systems we examine an important part of the modern industrial economy. Health care has been called 'the world's most successful industry'.[22] Whatever the difficulty of verifying such a sweeping claim the data summarised in the tables given earlier certainly show the great economic scale of modern health care institutions. Indeed, characterising health care as a distinct industry, however large, understates its significance, both in the modern industrial economy and in economic statecraft, for it is precisely the case that health is not a distinct industrial sector. Although in some jurisdictions there are discrete industrial classifications for particular groups of health care products, the really striking feature

Table 1.5 *Total health employment as % of total employment (full-time equivalents)*

	1960	*1975*	*1993*[a]
USA	2.6	4.7	7.0
UK	2.4[b]	4.2	4.5
Germany	na	3.7	6.4
Canada	3.3[c]	4.5[d]	5.6
Japan	1.5[e]	2.6	3.7
France	na	2.7[f]	6.8
Italy	0.8	2.5	4.8[g]
Ireland	na	4.1	5.4

Source: OECD, *Health data 98*.

Notes: [a]Latest year for which a complete series for whole group is available. [b]Figure is for 1961. [c]Figure is for 1961. [d]Figure is for 1976. [e]Figure is for 1962. [f]Figure is for 1976. [g]Figure is for 1992.

of health care as an economic phenomenon is the way it is woven into the fabric of the modern industrial economy.[23]

One measure of the growing importance of health care as an industry is given in Table 1.5, which charts the rise of health employment in the labour markets of the advanced industrial nations. But these are only the crudest, most direct measures of industrial significance. Behind them lies a story of the growth of complex industrial interests with big stakes in health care policy. An example from one of the countries examined in this book will illustrate the point. In the Federal Republic of Germany it is estimated that there are about 2.2 million people employed directly in some way in the health care system, and the employment creating indirect effects from their activities creates another 2 million jobs: in short, about 4.2 million jobs are directly or indirectly produced by the health care system. What is more, in recent years the growth of employment in health care has been particularly rapid: in Germany between 1976–92, numbers employed in health care rose 77 per cent, a rate almost certainly greater than in any other sector.[24]

Nothing better exemplifies the growing significance of production politics than those industries conventionally gathered under the label of 'medical technology'. The application of basic and applied science to clinical care was central to the historical process that created modern health care systems, for it produced a powerfully effective regime of curative medicine. At the intellectual base of these developments lay advances in fundamental science, notably in germ theory, in immunology and in physics. In the half-century or so after 1870 these advances produced a range of medical applications which in turn laid the foundations for the characteristic modern medical technology industries, of which two sorts are particularly important: the modern pharmaceutical industry, and the industries producing the range of medical devices that are applied in health care. The role of pharmaceuticals in health care systems will be obvious to any reader. The centrality of medical devices may need a little more explanation. Modern medicine is heavily reliant on the artifacts of modern technology. These artifacts range from the simple and mass produced (syringes, blood pressure machines) to machines, such as body scanners, whose cost and technological complexity are comparable to modern missiles or aircraft. (The comparison is not thoughtless: as we will see, medical technology and military technology are linked in important ways.)

Medical technology is the key to the connection between the health care system and the modern industrial economy – and thus the key to the place of medical technology in economic statecraft. There are three kinds of connection and they illustrate once again the critical feature of the health care state – the interpenetration of the institutions of the state and the institutions of the health care system. First, as we will see in Chapter 5, important features of the medical technology industries – structure, marketing strategies, even the very artifacts they deal in – are to a substantial degree the creations of states, albeit often unintended creations. Second, as we shall also see, the performance of these industries is a major independent influence on the success or otherwise with which national economies are managed. Finally, precisely because the medical technology industries are fused with a range of other industries, they are central to the modern industrial state. In brief, we observe here again a defining feature of the health care state: it is shaped by, but it also shapes, the institutions of the wider state system. There is a politics of technological production in health care, and it is twisted around the wider politics of industrial production; there is a production politics of medical technology, and it is twisted around the production politics of the wider industrial system. Medical technology poses problems for economic statecraft – but also offers opportunities for the more effective practice of that statecraft.

Consumption politics, professional politics and production politics provide the material for the accounts of the government of the health care state in the central chapters of the book. But that government is not conducted in a vacuum. Health care systems, like any other social constellations, are embedded in particular environments – social, temporal, even physical. Common sense suggests that we need to understand the significance of these embedded arrangements; but, as we shall now see, there is a good deal more to this than even common sense suggests.

The embedded nature of the health care state

'Embeddedness' is central to the idea of the health care state: the very conception involves the notion that health care institutions have been penetrated by, and have penetrated, their surrounding social environment. But that is to express the idea of being embedded only in a general way; it is the particulars of mutual penetration that matter. Those particulars are partly determined by the individual character of health care institutions, but they are also determined by the environment in which those institutions are embedded. Of these environmental factors, two are particularly salient in this study: the surrounding political and economic systems. The most obvious way to realise this is to think for a moment of the health care systems of the states of former communist Eastern Europe. Those health care systems were based on principles of command in their resource allocation and authoritarianism in their political practices. They were based on those principles because they were lodged in wider political and economic systems also based on principles of command economics and command politics. When those Marxist authoritarian regimes collapsed, their health care institutions were also transformed. The wider rise of market economics was reflected within health care in commercialisation, privatisation, the reduction of the state's role as a provider, and exposure to the direct influence of institutions like the World Bank and the European Union.[25] There could be no simpler, but more graphic, illustration of the significance of the political and economic systems into which health care institutions are embedded.

The command economies of communist Eastern Europe were a family of nations, and of health care systems, that have now vanished. The single most important existing 'family' of health care systems is that of the OECD nations; the leading members are the subject of the tables provided earlier. They can be thought of as a 'family' because they share important affinities. The most obvious are economic: this group covers virtually all the developed capitalist nations. A second affinity is political: most of these nations happen also to be pluralist democracies, albeit sometimes of a rough and ready kind. In summary, these health care systems are embedded in capitalist democracies.

The general implications of this state of affairs for health care government are so plain as to need only the most summary outline. The operations of market economics, and of competitive democratic politics, interact to provide both constraints and opportunities. Some of the most obvious constraints concern resource allocation. In democratic politics, distributive struggles are institutionalised through such means as electoral competition and competition between organised interests, and the resources available for health care consumption are in part a function of the outcomes of these struggles. More obviously still, the success with which market economies operate powerfully influences the resources available for consumption. That fact has been the single most important influence over the consumption of health care resources in the advanced capitalist world over the last half-century. For the first three decades after the Second World War the dominant feature of health care policy was the spread of entitlements to treatment among ever wider groups of citizens, and the growth in the resources allocated to consumption; since the middle of the 1970s consumption politics have been dominated by the search for cost containment and constraints on entitlements. The shift follows exactly the well-known historical trajectory of advanced capitalist economies, which for three decades until the middle of the 1970s experienced the 'long boom', and then entered decades of structural change, economic dislocation and new patterns of economic power and competition.[26]

In short, both the forms and the outcomes of consumption politics are heavily influenced by the fact that health care systems are embedded in wealthy capitalist democracies. It requires only the briefest inspection to see that the same is true of what I have termed *professional politics* and *production politics*. Abel has spoken of professions as walking a tightrope between the market and the state – simultaneously benefiting from a contract with the state, providing the foundation for professional authority, and practising competition (albeit highly regulated) in the market for professional services.[27] The tightrope act is an attempt to solve problems created by the twin forces of democratic politics and market competition: professional regulation 'closes' the occupation from some of the destabilising influences of market competition; the 'contract' confers the authority of the state while promising to preserve the profession's independence of public control. To anticipate: the growing difficulties faced by the medical profession in performing that tightrope act in modern capitalist democracies is one of the main features of professional politics explored in this book.

Production politics take us to the heart of modern democratic statecraft. Successful statecraft involves operation in two distinct arenas: democratic politicians have to compete successfully for the votes of electorates, and they have to manage powerful organised interests. Economic statecraft often fuses these two tasks together, since it is recognised that the ability to win elections depends heavily on popular perceptions of how well politicians have managed, or could manage, economic interests in the pursuit of prosperity.[28] Production in health care systems, when it takes place in capitalist democracies, is entangled with economic statecraft. The health care industries are major actors in the market economy, and are major actors in democratic politics. That is particularly true of the medical technology industries, for reasons which we have already aired: because of the scale of those industries, because of the way they are often part of the most technologically dynamic parts of economies, and because of the extent to which they are intertwined with other important parts of the industrial economy.[29] *Production politics* has important consequences for the wider economic statecraft of democracies, because the performance of the medical technology industries affects the wider performance of the capitalist economy; and economic statecraft, conversely, has important consequences for those industries.

Capitalism, democracy and health care

The propositions offered so far are unexceptional: that it makes sense to speak of a health care state because of the way in which, in modern health care systems, the institutions of the state and of health care penetrate each other; that there are distinct, though connected, spheres of consumption, professional and production politics; and that the way the most important modern health care systems are embedded in capitalist democracies has profound consequences for what happens in these three spheres. When we begin to look more closely at the way all these elements combine, some rather less obvious propositions appear.

Some of the most influential modern accounts of the connection between capitalism and democracy stress the tension between the two. The most distinguished modern interpretation of the link between politics and markets, that offered by Lindblom, argues that private ownership and the rules of market competition constrain the freedom of democratic government; influential theoretical accounts of the welfare state, such as that elaborated by Offe, picture a powerful tension between the constraints of competition in market economies and the universalism associated with welfare states; Marxist accounts of health care policy, notably that offered by Navarro, picture policy outcomes as the result of struggles between, on the one hand, popular movements and, on the other, elites entrenched by the unequal ownership structures of capitalist economies.[30]

The argument of this book is that the conjunction of capitalism and democracy does indeed produce powerful tensions in health care, but that these are more complex than, simply, an opposition between capitalist economics and democratic politics. At the most immediate economic level, indeed, the operations of the market can be both constraining and enabling. The simplest illustration of that is what the success or otherwise of particular capitalist economies does to the consumption sphere. The single best predictor of what any particular nation will spend on health care is not the character of democratic politics, nor the ideology of governing parties, but the level of national wealth, measured by standard per capita indicators of gross domestic product (GDP): the more successful is a particular capitalist economy the more are consumption struggles accommodated by increasing the volume of resources devoted to health care.[31] At the level of the whole population of capitalist nations that is also the story of the way the 'long boom' funded wider entitlements to free health care for more and more people.

Capitalist economics, then, is not simply in tension with pressures for popular provision; when capitalist economies do well they both stimulate and accommodate the pressure for provision. The impact of capitalist competition is both more benign and less benign than is suggested by a simple model of tension between capitalism and democracy. It is more benign because, as we have just seen, its impact can be as much enabling as constraining – and that is only to focus on the consumption sphere and to ignore professional politics and production politics. It is less benign because the single most important impact of capitalist competition is destabilisation. At any one moment the government of consumption, of professions and of production is the result of a particular political settlement reached between important interests. That point is perhaps most visible in the case of professional politics since professional authority is usually traceable to a particular set of institutional hierarchies embodied in an explicitly stated set of rules, often expressed as statute. One of the most obvious consequences of capitalist competition is constantly to disrupt any equilibrium between interests: it enriches some social groups and impoverishes others; it leads to technological innovations which undermine the economic position of some occupations, and advantages others; it destroys some large and powerful firms and creates others; it changes the internal structure of interests by likewise altering the balance of competitive advantage between different groups in the marketplace; it even profoundly alters the relationship between whole nations as economies rise and fall through international competition.

Capitalist competition is therefore a constant source of disturbance to any momentary institutional equilibrium reached for the government of consumption, professions or production – and this disturbance will be a constant feature of the accounts offered in the following pages. But competition does not reshape the interests mechanically. The disturbing effects of competition are transmitted both economically and politically: rising and declining interests struggle in markets, but they also struggle in the political system. A market economy contains nests of restrictive practices – that might be a summary, for instance, of the nature of professional organisation. As competition reshapes interests, those damaged by its effects try to use the political process to limit the damage, and those who gain try to press home their advantage by organising to change public policy. These effects are particularly important, as we shall see, in consumption and professional politics. But the significance of democratic political organisation is greater even than this account suggests, for democratic competition is more than a response to economic competition. The resources of the democratic state offer interests a chance to gain competitive advantages in markets by securing preferential policy outcomes. That, again, is a summary of the significance of professional regulation in the medical sphere.

In capitalist democracies, therefore, economic competition and political competition are intertwined: interests rise and fall in either sphere, and can use either sphere to moderate or to promote change. This is why it will not do to suggest that there is some sharp opposition between the results produced by capitalist economics and those produced by democratic politics. To take an example which will loom large in the following pages: market competition has often made it difficult to maintain health care 'universalism', the extension of

entitlement to free health care to whole populations; but democratic competition has also created problems in preserving the political coalitions that support universalism. That, in a nutshell, is the political cause of the problems of the consumption regime in the United Kingdom in recent years. If market capitalism produces both constraints and opportunities in the consumption sphere, the same is true of democratic politics. If capitalism and the welfare state are uneasy bedfellows, the same can be true of democracy and the welfare state.[32]

The tensions created by democratic politics are made more acute by the historical relationship between democratic politics and the institutions of the health care state. The health care state – that interpenetration of the institutions of the health care system and the institutions of the state – is not a democratic creation. Some important parts of the system of health care government – notably that of the medical profession – are in large part pre-democratic creations. Some systems of consumption politics originated explicitly as *anti-democratic* creations – the German case examined in the following pages is an important example. Some parts are the creation of industrial and professional oligarchies working separately from democratic politics: as we will again see, that is a summation of the historical origins of production politics. Thus the government of the health care state has had to adjust to institutions of democratic politics for which it was never designed. The significance of these historical tensions helps explain why, before we turn to the three spheres of politics that are examined in Chapters 3–5, we devote Chapter 2 to the process of state building in health care.

The severity of these tensions of course varies between different national systems, since each nation has its own distinct history of hierarchy and deference. But in every case examined in this book the gravity of the tensions between the established institutions of health care government and of democratic politics is magnified by common changes in the character of democratic politics over the last generation. We are attuned to the idea that long-term changes in the character of capitalism – the end of the post-war long boom, the growth of globalisation – have consequences for health care policy. Less obvious, but just as important, are the consequences of long-term changes in democratic politics. When the health care state encountered democracy it first encountered it in the distinct and restricted form of Schumpeterian democracy. Schumpeter's model of democracy, originally elaborated during the Second World War, pictured democratic politics as a competition between elites for the support of mass publics, who typically were mobilised into politics at infrequent intervals like elections.[33] Schumpeter's model enjoyed great influence over post-war democratic theory both because it was a convincing summary of how democratic politics had been practised, and because it prefigured post-war democratic systems, dominated as they were by electoral

competition between party elites and by policy making within stable, cohesive communities of policy actors.[34]

To anticipate a central argument of the following pages: we are witnessing the partial breakdown of the Schumpeterian system, and this breakdown is proving profoundly destabilising for the government of the health care state – whether we examine consumption, professional or production politics. The health care state fitted reasonably comfortably into Schumpeterian democracy because the Schumpeterian system, in its elitism, inherited a substantial legacy of hierarchy from a pre-democratic era. That legacy is now depleting and has left behind systems of democratic politics which are less hierarchical, more open and more unstable in their policy-making structures. The form and extent of national experiences differ; but in all three cases examined here the direction of change is the same. New interests are being mobilised; stable policy-making communities are being penetrated and transformed into more open, unstable networks of actors; and hierarchies that rested heavily on the deference of citizens are being transformed as that traditional deference declines.

The evidence to support these large generalisations is assembled in later chapters. It is assembled there for a reason which recalls one of the central themes of this chapter – the interpenetration of states and health care systems. In the transformation of Schumpeterian democracy the health care system is both a patient and an agent: it is both itself transformed by the altered character of democratic politics and is an agent of transformation. That health care government should be transformed as the wider democracy within which it is embedded is transformed will be readily comprehensible. To understand why health care politics itself contributes to the wider transformation we have to recall the scale of modern health care systems and the importance of so many health care institutions as prototypes of modern political institutions. Historically, for instance, doctors were among the pioneers of powerful professional organisation and of effective pressure group organisation in the modern state. The expansion of health care systems in the last generation has created within the modern state large, well-organised constellations of interests – reflected in electoral politics, in professional politics and in the world of pressure group organisation. The policy-making systems for health care are themselves large and important components of the whole policy-making system of the modern state. Consider, for instance, the implications of Morone's observation about the consequences of the introduction of Medicare (a federal-financed system of insurance for the old) in the United States: 'Medicare helped forge a powerful gray lobby – it was the legislation that made the interest group rather than the other way around.'[35] By the 1990s the effect was to produce a colossus of American pressure group politics: the American Association of Retired Persons has a membership of 33 million, a $300 million annual budget and represents half the US population

over the age of 50.[36] Thus any reshaping of health care government itself independently contributes to the reshaping of democratic government: health care government is both a victim of the problems of the Schumpeterian system and one of the sources of those problems.

Choosing the cases

Why choose to explore the issues sketched above through national cases? Why choose the particular cases examined here? Why choose three?

National cases are the focus of the analysis because health care states are still highly distinctive nationally. Health care systems, as Poullier says, are remarkable in their national institutional diversity. In his words: 'The delivery and finance of healthcare vary between nations more than any other public policy.'[37] These variations mean that the way states and health care institutions penetrate each other differs from nation to nation. This recognition of the significance of national institutional variation is what lies behind the recent interest in applying neo-institutional analysis to health care policy. This 'new institutionalism' argues that the structures of policy making, by their independent effect on the ability of interests to form coalitions, have an important influence on the capacity or otherwise of nations to change health care policy: the argument is made for nations as different as France, Switzerland and Sweden (by Immergut), the United States (by Morone) and Germany (by Döhler).[38] The globalisation of economic activity, far from reducing the influence of the particular national setting, actually makes it more important. The growth of globalised industries – a particularly important influence, as we shall see, in the sphere of production politics in health care – means the emergence of a global division of labour in which particular nations occupy distinct positions in that division.[39] We cannot make sense of health care states without placing them in that global division of labour, but the key to understanding a particular health care state will turn on understanding its particular place in the global system: that, for instance, is why in our chapter on production politics disproportionate attention will be paid to the United States and to its dominant place in the global medical technology industries.

The insight that we are here examining states in a world of globalisaton now helps explain the importance of the three systems examined in detail. In standard classifications of health care systems, the United States, United Kingdom and Germany are often selected as archetypes of three important variants: the first as market dominated; the second as a 'national health system' funded by general taxation; the third as an instance of compulsory insurance as a way of funding care.[40] But this classification is actually not particularly helpful in selecting cases for studying health care states – nor, indeed, for classifying health care systems. It bears only on one of the three spheres identified here, consumption politics, and gives us only incidental information about professional politics or production politics. The significance of the three cases lies not in providing some archetypical example of a wider population of health care systems; it lies in the particularly crucial place they occupy in a global state system.

Viewed thus, the case of the US virtually chooses itself. Its history and present global role make it both the key democratic state and the key capitalist economy; as we shall see, it also provides some of the best examples of the developments pressurising Schumpeterian democracy. More substantively, its health care system is the largest in the world, and, especially in the sphere of production politics, the giant American medical technology industries are powerful influences at both a global and national level. This reasoning departs from a common view of the US in the health care literature, a view which pictures it as a kind of bizarre deformation. Much of that literature, for instance, is concerned with trying to explain why the US has not developed the sort of access to free health care available to whole populations in so many other health care systems of the advanced capitalist world.[41] But picturing the US as a kind of laggard misses its significance. Far from being a laggard, the sheer size and technological development of the health care system, coupled with the central role of the American state and the American economy in the wider global system, mean that American institutions and innovations are driving developments in other health care states. Nor is this just a matter of the technological lead of the US. American institutions have been pioneers in the entry of multinational corporations into the hospital sector; the US system has pioneered a wide range of quality-enhancing mechanisms and ideas about appropriate case mixes, notions that dominated much health care reform in the 1980s and 1990s; and individual national systems, such as Britain's, were subject to extensive Americanisation through the diffusion of new administrative technologies, such as those associated with the managed-care revolution in the US.[42] At one stage, indeed, I considered exploring the themes of this book by a study of the US alone, but eventually rejected the implicit notion that other health care states could simply be viewed as satellites of an American sun.

Once we move beyond the obvious case of the US the decision to examine three cases in all is largely a limitation imposed by practical considerations. The argument outlined earlier – that health care states occupy particular places in a globalised division of labour – shows that a comprehensive study of health care government would have to encompass, at the very least, the health care systems of all the leading capitalist nations. The restriction to three cases is merely set by the limits to the competence of a single author and the limits to space in a single book. Germany's importance derives from the fact that it is the largest and most successful capitalist economy in Europe, the most powerful state in Europe and, especially after unification, has by any conceivable measure the largest health care system in Europe. All these considerations give it a special place in the global system, an importance reinforced by the special significance of Germany in the production and marketing of medical technology. I do not make a case that Germany is a more important health care state than some of those omitted here, like Japan; only that it is of first-rank importance.

The selection of the United Kingdom springs directly from the analytical issues that are at the heart of the book. Indeed, it was puzzles created by the British case that led in the early 1990s to the original idea for this study. The reforms heralded by the publication of the 1989 Thatcher government's White Paper *Working for Patients* marked, it became plain as the decade wore on, a profound change in the character of health care politics, and not just in the substance of health care policy itself.[43] The connection between those reforms and the wider efforts of Conservative governments to respond to British economic decline made it plain that understanding the British case depended on locating British reforms within the global system. It also became clear – and is demonstrated in the following pages – that Britain exhibited in a particularly serious form many of the stresses in the democratic character of the health care state sketched earlier: in particular, the tensions between a wider political system undergoing rapid cultural and institutional change, and a system of health care politics that still reflected political settlements made before the era of democratic politics, or outside democratic political arenas.

Reference to the tensions created by the historical legacy brings us to an obvious point: an examination of the way health care states were built. That is the purpose of the next chapter.

Notes

1 For instance, 80 per cent of deaths in the United States take place in a health care facility: L. Kass, 'Is there a right to die?', *Hastings Center Report*, 23:1 (1993) 34–43 at p. 43.

2 These tables are assembled from the most recently available (CD-ROM version) of the famous OECD health data set: OECD, *OECD health data 98: a comparative analysis of 29 countries* (Paris, OECD, 1998). The time series run from 1960 to 1997, with some some missing data. In general, data for the most recent years are provisional or estimated. There is a comprehensive discussion of the methodological issues involved in the assemblage and interpretation of the data set in the hard copy *User's Guide* to the CD, and in the software.

3 Similar patterns, though with some variations, are shown by the formerly successful 'tiger' economies of East Asia not covered by the OECD data set. For examples see: L. Chung-tung, 'Health care systems in transition II. Taiwan, Part 1. A general overview of the health care system in Taiwan', *Journal of Public Health Medicine*, 20:1 (1998) 5–10; and L. Meng-Kim, 'Health care systems in transition II: Singapore, Part 1. An overview of health care systems in Singapore', ibid., 16–21.

4 Note, however, that universalism does not imply completely free schemes nor universal coverage of all health care: it measures only the proportion of the population with entitlement to some medical care under a publicly funded scheme.

The case of Germany should also be noted in passing: the German figure is depressed by the exemption allowed high-income earners to buy health insurance in the commercial market.

5 For some characteristic, and only part right, views about the changing role of the state in health care, including my own, see: M. Moran, 'Reshaping the health-care state', *Government and Opposition*, 28:1 (1993) 48–63.

6 I have written at length elsewhere of the various meanings of this phrase, and here discuss it only in summary form. For elaboration see: M. Moran, 'The health-care state in Europe: convergence or divergence?', *Environment and Planning C*, 10:1 (1992) 77–90; and 'Three faces of the health care state', *Journal of Health Politics, Policy and Law*, 20:3 (1995) 767–81.

7 I owe this point to Paul Wilding (personal communication).

8 My debts to two writers in these passages will be obvious: F. Hirsch, *Social limits to growth* (London, Routledge, 1978), pp. 27–51; and C. Offe, notably his 'Competitive party democracy and the Keynesian welfare state', in his *Contradictions of the Welfare State* (London, Hutchinson, 1984), pp. 179–206; and 'Social scientific aspects of the regulation-deregulation debate', in his *Modernity and the state: East and West* (Cambridge, Polity Press, 1996), pp. 72–88.

9 *National Health Services Act, 1946*, reprinted in B. Watkin, (ed.), *Documents on health and social services: 1834 to the present day* (London, Methuen, 1975), pp. 140–1.

10 Medicare is a federally funded scheme to pay for the cost of care for the old; Medicaid is a set of programmes delivered at state level to pay for the cost of care for the poor. These are the two best-known publicly financed programmes, but there are numerous more piecemeal programmes, such as those for the Indian health service and for veterans: for a study of the former see, for instance, P. Cunningham, 'Access to care in the Indian health service', *Health Affairs*, 13:3 (1993) 224–33; for figures on the proportions contributed overall from the public purse, see K. Levit, H. Lazenby and B. Braden, 'National health spending trends in 1996', *Health Affairs*, 17:1 (1998) 35–51.

11 On delivery, by the mid-1990s nearly three-quarters of US workers with insurance coverage received that coverage through some system of managed care, rather than having the option of exercising their individual preferences in the choice of carers: see G. Jensen, M. Morrisey, S. Gaffney and D. Listow, 'The new dominance of managed care: insurance trends in the 1990s', *Health Affairs*, 16:1 (1997) 125–36.

12 For a profile of the uninsured see: D. Rowland, B. Lyons, A. Salganicoff and P. Long, 'A profile of the uninsured in America', *Health Affairs*, 13:2 (1994) 283–7.

13 Paul Wilding reminds me (personal communication) that, beyond the sphere of consumption described here, there is a well-established history of the collective politics of health care, dating back at least to the struggle for public health protection (sewers, water) in Britain in the 1840s. Such collectivisation is also a

central theme of A. de Swaan, *In care of the state: health care, education and welfare in Europe and the USA in the modern era* (Cambridge, Polity Press, 1988).

14 The source for this is: Centre for Public Integrity, 'Well-healed: inside lobbying for health care reform, Part 1', *International Journal of Health Services*, 25:3 (1995) 411–53, at p. 412, where the quotation also appears.

15 I take these generalisations to express a consensus from the existing literature and thus to border on the self evident, but for a summary of the scholarly literature on which they rest see, for instance, T. Johnson, 'Governmentality and the institutionalization of expertise', in T. Johnson, G. Larkin and M. Saks (eds), *Health professions and the state in Europe* (London, Routledge, 1995), pp. 7–24.

16 My debt to two works will be obvious here: T. Johnson, *Professions and power* (London, Macmillan, 1972); and R. Murphy, *Social closure* (Oxford University Press, 1988), pp. 186–8 and 246–8.

17 P. Wilding, *Professional power and social welfare* (London, Routledge, 1982), p. 12.

18 There is an excellent discussion of the significance of complexity and uncertainty in professionalism in G. Southon and J. Braithwaite, 'The end of professionalism?', *Social Science and Medicine*, 46:1 (1998) 23–8, to which this passage is indebted.

19 N. Kane, 'Costs, productivity and financial outcomes of managed care', in R. Saltman and C. von Otter (eds), *Implementing planned markets in health care: balancing social and economic responsibility* (Buckingham, Open University Press, 1995), pp. 113–33 (at pp. 117–18).

20 This obervation makes sense whether one uses the framework of pluralism that informs Eckstein's classic study, or the language of corporatism, as used by Cawson: H. Eckstein, *Pressure group politics: the case of the British Medical Association* (London, Allen and Unwin, 1960); A. Cawson, *Corporatism and welfare: social policy and state intervention in Britain* (London, Heinemann, 1982.)

21 Some of the forces creating this state of affairs are examined in A. de Swaan, 'The reluctant imperialism of the medical profession', *Social Science and Medicine*, 28:11 (1989) 1165–70.

22 S. Jencks and G. Schieber, 'Containing US health care costs: what bullet to bite?', *Health Care Financing Review*, Annual Supplement, 1991, pp. 1–12 (p. 1).

23 There is a complex debate about the industrial classification of medical artifacts: see, for instance, S. Foote, *Managing the medical arms race: public policy and medical device innovation* (Berkeley CA, University of California Press, 1992), pp. 9–18.

24 These figures are from D. Göppffarth and B. Milbrandt, 'Das Gesundheitswesen als Beschäftigungs und Wachstumsfaktor', *Zeitschriften für Gesundheitswissenschaften*, 6:3 (1998) 233–47.

25 There are good studies of these processes collected in C. Altenstetter and J. Björkman (eds), *Health policy reform, national variations and globalization* (Basingstoke, Macmillan, 1997), notably: G. Žarkovic and W. Satzinger, 'Politics and foreign involvement in reforming the health care systems of former Socialist countries', pp. 225–78; D. Duffy, 'State, economy, and civil society interdependency: lessons from Polish health systems', pp. 279–313; and M. Beckerman and J. Nemeč, 'Health care systems in transition in Eastern Europe: the Czech case', pp. 314–30.

For the penetration of Germanic insurance models see H.-U. Deppe and S. Oreskovic, 'Back to Europe: back to Bismarck?', *International Journal of Health Services*, 26:4 (1996) 777–802. For a fascinating micro-level study of what displacement from one environment to another does to professional outlooks see a study of the attitudes of Soviet doctors who emigrated to Israel: L. Remennick and R. Shtarkshall, 'Technology versus responsibilty: immigrant physicians from the former Soviet Union reflect on Israeli health care', *Journal of Health and Social Behavior*, 38 (1997) 191–202.

26 This summary of the recent history of both health care provision and of its connection to the fate of the wider capitalist economy is well established in the literature: for a characteristic account see, for instance, *Financing and delivering health care: a comparative analysis of OECD countries*, (Paris, OECD, 1987).

27 R. Abel, 'Between market and state: the legal profession in turmoil', *Modern Law Review*, 52:3 (1989) 285–325. I have been influenced by Abel more than is perhaps wise, so it is only right to quote his own words: 'Professions are unique social configurations, which flourished with the emergence of the liberal state and the rise of the bourgeoisie ... Professions persuade the state to protect them from market forces by arguing that commercialisation is inconsistent with their noble calling. At the same time, professions invoke market imperatives to resist state control, insisting that they must preserve their "independence" in order to serve their clients loyally' (at p. 285). The image of a tigthrope act from Abel is extensively explored in M. Brazier, J. Lovecy, M. Moran and M. Potton, 'Falling from a tightrope: doctors and lawyers between the market and the state', *Political Studies*, 41:2 (1993) 197–213.

28 The classic statement of the way the demands of economic statecraft hem in democratic politicians is C. Lindblom, *Politics and markets: the world's political-economic systems* (New York, Basic Books, 1977).

29 I select medical technology only because the illustration is particularly graphic. The production process ranges much wider: the core of the production process, after all, involves the creation of a personal service for individual patients; and even at the level of physical artifacts goes well beyond medical technology conventionally understood (consider the importance of hospital building in the construction industry.)

30 Lindblom, *Politics and markets*, p. 172, discussed at greater length in Chapter 6 of this book. C. Offe, 'Some contradictions of the modern welfare state', in his *Contradictions of the welfare state*, pp. 146–61. For Offe's gloomy view of the impact of democratic politics on welfare provision, a view that resembles the argument developed in these pages, see note 32 below. V. Navarro, *Dangerous to your health: capitalism in health care* (New York, Monthly Review Press, 1993), synthesises his well-known Marxist account.

31 A large literature establishes this relationship. For a detailed account of the data, as well as citation of supporting studies for earlier periods, see: *Financing and delivering health care*, pp. 79–86.

32 This argument is influenced by C. Offe: 'Democracy against the welfare state?', in his *Modernity and the state*, pp. 147–82.

33 J. Schumpeter, *Capitalism, socialism and democracy* (London, Allen and Unwin, 1976), pp. 269–83; the book was first published in the UK in 1943.

34 The intellectual orthodoxy to which Schumpeter gave rise is mercilessly examined in C. Pateman, *Participation and democratic theory* (Cambridge, Cambridge University Press, 1970).

35 J. Morone, 'Introduction', in J. Morone and G. Belkin (eds), *The politics of health care reform: lessons from the past, prospects for the future* (Durham NC, Duke University Press, 1994), pp. 1–7 at p. 2.

36 These details are from: Center for Public Integrity, 'Well healed: inside lobbying for health care reform, part III', *International Journal of Health Services*, 26:1 (1996) 19–46, at p. 24.

37 J.-P. Poullier, 'Managing health in the 1990s: a European overview', *Health Service Journal*, 27 April (1989) 6–8 (p. 6).

38 E. Immergut, *Health politics: interests and institutions in western Europe* (Cambridge, Cambridge University Press, 1992); J. Morone, *The democratic wish: popular participation and the limits of American government* (New York, Basic Books, 1990), pp. 253–321; M. Döhler, 'The state as architect of political order: policy dynamics in German health care', *Governance*, 8:3 (1995) 380–404.

39 The precise wider significance of globalisation is a vexed question: see in particular P. Hirst and G. Thompson, *Globalization in question: the international economy and the possibilities of governance* (Cambridge, Polity Press, 1995), especially pp. 170–94.

40 See, for instance, the classification offered in a standard and popular textbook on public policy: M. Harrop (ed.), *Power and policy in liberal democracies* (Cambridge, Cambridge University Press, 1992), p. 151.

41 This agonising was revived by the failure in 1994 of the Clinton health care reform plan. Many of the key historical and contemporary issues are ventilated in the essays in the collection edited by Morone and Belkin, *The politics of health care reform*; and in T. Skocpol, *Boomerang: Clinton's health security effort and the turn against government in US politics* (New York, Norton, 1996).

42 On hospital chains, see J. Mohan, *A national health service? The restructuring of health care in Britain since 1979* (Basingstoke, Macmillan, 1995), pp. 162–3; on quality, see *Health: quality and choice* (Paris, OECD, 1994); on Britain see D. Mechanic, 'The Americanization of the British National Health Service', *Health Affairs*, 14:2 (1995), 51–67; on the diffusion of particular techniques see L. Brown, 'Exceptionalism as the rule? U.S. health policy innovation and cross-national learning', *Journal of Health Politics, Policy and Law*, 23:1 (1998) 35–51.

43 *Working for patients*, Cm 555 (1989).

2

Building the
health care state

How states are built

States have to be built, but they do not have to be consciously designed – indeed, they rarely are.[1] 'State building' resembles not grand construction, but endless bodging: the institutional structures to hand are cut back, reshaped or extended in response to immediate contingencies. People make and remake states, but they are often not aware, or only half aware, of what they are doing. Skowronek catches the essence of all this in one of the finest modern studies of state building:

> State building is prompted by environmental changes, but it remains at all times a political contingency, a historical-structural question. Whether a given state changes or fails to change, the form and timing of the change, and the governing potential in the change – all of these turn on a struggle for political power and institutional position, a struggle defined and mediated by the organisation of the preestablished state.[2]

'The organisation of the preestablished state': this influence recurs constantly in the following pages. Dramatic developments there are in plenty: the crises of war; the trauma of national capitulation and occupation; breakthroughs in science and technology that transformed the curative capacity of medicine. But building the health care state – that constellation where the institutions of the state and the health care system are wound around each other – involved mostly trimming, reshaping and extending the organisation that already existed. Sometimes building was prompted by dramatic historical challenges, and those involved believed that they were indeed engaged in great institutional reconstruction – the case, for instance, with the creation of the National Health Service (NHS) in the UK and the introduction of Medicare and Medicaid in the US. More often, institutional creation was a matter of trying to shape what was to hand in the attempt to solve immediate policy puzzles. Even where there existed a sense of grand historical reconstruction, as in the UK in the 1940s, the task of building was constrained by the institutional inheritance: it involved reshaping what was to hand in order to solve immediate problems of statecraft created by the need to mobilise the support of affected interests for the new National Health Service.

The importance of institutional legacies arises, not because state builders are necessarily conservative in their ambitions, but because building is an exercise in statecraft. Statecraft is what governing elites do. In the case of institution building it involves managing key interests to support innovation. In the exercise of statecraft one elementary consideration has constantly to be confronted: institutions create interests. Since building never takes place on, so to speak, a vacant plot, but always involves reshaping existing structures, the interests created and advantaged by pre-existing institutions have in some way to be accommodated, circumvented or vanquished. And since institutions create interests, institutional innovation can damage old interests and create new ones. Thus the story of building health care states is a story of the tension between the ambitions of the new and the interests of the established. That unexceptional observation has a particular implication in the case of health care – an implication both for the history of state building and for the contemporary government of the health care state. As far as health care is concerned, 'the organization of the preestablished state' was not a democratic creation: the health care state was built out of pre-democratic and, in some instances, anti-democratic institutions. The point has an obvious relevance to understanding the history of institution building told in this chapter; but it will also prove relevant in exploring the contemporary stresses in health care policy explored in later chapters. (There is an echo here of Tilly's path-breaking work on state building in Western Europe: first states were created, often at the expense of rights; later states more-or-less successfully adapted to accommodate democratic rights; and these states in consequence have engrained within them tensions between modern democratic processes and the legacy of pre-democratic or even anti-democratic histories.[3])

Stressing the significance of the institutional inheritance is not at all the same as suggesting that outcomes are historically determined. State building is an exercise in statecraft precisely because the institutional inheritance is rather like a parable: its meaning is often unclear, 'enigmatical or dark'.[4] Statecraft consists partly in interpreting the parable: in the success with which different actors appropriate, and give a singular meaning to, different parts of the inheritance. What transpires is the result of an alchemy produced by the fusion of political creativity and the historical inheritance.

Historical reconstruction is conducted, we all know, under great limits: our vision is partial and our experience is indirect. But we have one great advantage over the original actors: we have a view of the outcomes which, for those involved, lay only in an unknowable future. The three sketches that follow try to take advantage of this. Unlike the actors I have a picture of the historical outcomes (though not necessarily a full or accurate picture). The accounts presented here try to make sense of these outcomes in the light of what went before. One consequence is that 'history' ends at different moments in the three countries examined here. In the case of the UK it 'ends' in 1948 with the creation of the NHS, which I characterise as the building of a 'command and control' state. There are limits to that characterisation, and the following pages try to recognise those limits; but my starting point is that the foundation of the NHS established a very special kind of relationship between the institutions of the central state and the health care system. In the German case, history stops in the middle of the 1950s. I try to show that by this date, after a period of uncertainty created by defeat in war, there was re-established a pre-Second World War pattern of corporatist government. In the American case, history, by my conventions, ceases in the mid-1960s with the legislation introducing the Medicare and Medicaid reforms. That moment marks the high point of what Jacobs has called the 'supply state' in American health care – where the state's role was largely shaped by the effort to maximise the supply of high technology curative medicine rather than to ensure popular access to health care.[5] Taking these national peculiarities as the starting point, each sketch tries to trace the roots of peculiarity.

The United Kingdom: building a command and control state

The health service that was established in 1948 was unusual – though not completely unknown – for a capitalist democracy. Several distinctive features are worth noticing. The system guaranteed free health care for the whole population, though with an escape clause allowing the imposition of some charges.[6] That guarantee was underwritten by resources derived from general taxation. Planning and resource allocation were done by administrative means where agencies of the central state (rather than the price mechanism) played a dominant part. The dominant position of the central state was reinforced by the fact that it owned most of the physical infrastructure of the health care system and was the main source of income for the medical labour force.

These innovations made the UK part of a small family of states whose health policy making was characterised by a distinct paradigm of policy making. Saltman and von Otter characterise the family as follows:

> The dominant policy paradigm during this post-war expansion [of health care provision] was a relatively rigid command-and-control planning model. Decision-making responsibility was vested in elected officials at national (the UK), national and regional (Sweden, Denmark, Norway) or national and municipal (Finland) levels, while day-to-day operating authority was delegated by these politicians to a corps of career administrators and planners. This

top-down planning model was conceptualised as a publicly accountable arrangement that could ensure provision of a necessary social good in a universal and hence cost-effective fashion.[7]

The emergence of this model in the UK demands some special explanation. As the passage above makes plain, the UK developed a particularly centralised version of the command and control system.[8] In Scandinavia, moreover, that system emerged as part of – to use Esping-Andersen's words – welfare regimes where 'universalism and de-commodification of social rights were extended also to the new middle classes'.[9] There is an obvious congruence, in other words, between the health care model and the wider welfare state regime. By contrast, the NHS was lodged much less congruently in a liberal welfare regime. In Esping-Andersen's words again, the welfare model 'typical of Great Britain and most of the Anglo-Saxon world was to preserve an essentially modest universalism in the state, and allow the market to reign for the growing social strata demanding superior welfare'.[10] The NHS at birth stood out from this welfare regime: it marginalised private provision and established common access as an implied principle of citizenship.[11]

The development of the command and control planning model in the UK is thus a considerable policy surprise. Understanding that surprise starts with our opening insight – that the nature of the building process depends in substantial part on the available institutional inheritance. In his official history of the founding of the NHS, Webster summarises the story thus: 'Although widely portrayed as a revolutionary departure, the National Health Service as a mechanism was in most respects evolutionary or even traditional.'[12] Continuity is evident in both the substance of policy and in the process by which institution building took place. It is tempting to think that the foundations were provided by the health services developed during the Second World War. That is only partly so. Substantively, the new service built on the extensive system of health insurance which had developed after the passage of Lloyd George's Health Insurance Act of 1911. At the outset of the Lloyd George reforms, 11.5 million workers (27.4 per cent of the population) were covered by his scheme; by 1938 the figure had risen to 20.3 million (43 per cent of the population).[13] The insured could claim treatment without extra cost by a family doctor, and drugs were available on free prescription. The insurance system dominated general practice: by 1936 three-quarters of general practitioners (GPs) in England and Wales were on the 'panel' of insurance doctors.[14] The insurance system profoundly shaped the economic and social character of the medical profession: insurance income became 'the economic bedrock of general practitioner medicine'.[15] This economic base was important in supporting the position of doctors as a prosperous, middle-class profession.

Impressive though the health insurance system was, it had two important limits: in the range of the population covered and in the range of services provided. Dependents did not generally have entitlements. Both children and wives were excluded – the latter exclusion a powerful source of gender bias in an age when the housewife as specialised homemaker was common. The services covered were only for ambulatory, not hospital, care. Profound changes nevertheless took place in the interwar years in the structure of the hospital service, and those changes anticipated key elements of the NHS. The power of the historically independent charitable hospitals had secured their exemption from the original 1911 National Insurance Scheme; but that exclusion from what turned out to be a substantial stream of income meant that after the First World War the hospitals were in financial difficulties. Those problems were rehearsed, inconclusively, in the report of an official committee of inquiry into their financial difficulties (the Cave Committee of 1921).[16] The problems led in turn to the development of an extensive voluntary hospital savings movement: by 1936, for instance, the London Hospital Savings Association had 1.75 million members extending benefits (covering dependents) to over 4 million persons.[17] But there was also a significant extension of free public hospitals. Neville Chamberlain's great Local Government Act of 1929 transferred control of poor-law infirmaries to local authorities, empowering them to transform these into municipal hospitals.[18] These twin shifts – the rise of the voluntary insurance sector in hospitals and the rise of the municipality as a hospital provider – accompanied continuing changes in the role of the hospital doctor. These changes could be summarised as progressive professionalisation and specialisation. Pickstone's account of the Manchester Poor Law Union in the second half of the 1920s is illustrative: 'Between 1924 and 1929 specialists in orthopaedics and dermatology were added, and facilities for x-ray, electrical therapy, heliotherapy and massage were extended.'[19] A powerful constellation of professional interests was thus being created in hospitals – a constellation that was to prove powerful in the struggles to create the NHS.

The institutional structure that developed in the interwar years shaped the key interests who had to be managed by statecraft in the wartime and post-war building of the NHS. But that institutional structure, with its associated interest configurations, was itself the result of an earlier exercise in statecraft – that conducted by Lloyd George and his allies in passing the legislation establishing National Insurance in 1911. That legislation, Hennock has shown, was heavily influenced by the desire to emulate the system already established by Bismarck's reforms in Germany.[20] But the British reforms involved a more generous role for the state in funding the scheme, and a more prominent role for the state in regulating the doctors' employment relations with the insurance funds.[21] The key to understanding this British distinctiveness lies in the critical interest that already occupied the landscape by the turn of the century – the institution of medicine. Some elite segments of the medical profession had already forged privileged connections with the pre-industrial state in Britain:

> London physicians became the first to acquire the more usual hallmark of modern professionalism by securing the charter in 1518 for the (Royal) College of Physicians which gave them 'self-government at the King's command'. Among those presenting the petition to Henry VIII, were the court physician and the Lord Chancellor. This grant not only made them autonomous of the emergent civil administration, but also made their authority ... independent of the universities.[22]

The critical event in creating the institutionally privileged position of medicine, however, was the passage of the 1858 Medical Act. Formally, it established a General Council of Medical Education and Registration (colloquially, the GMC). Entry onto the GMC's register was the mark of the qualified doctor. Substantively, it gave the profession a franchise to regulate itself. Membership of the Council was drawn from the profession. Although unqualified practice was theoretically possible, in reality the occupational boundaries of medicine were now drawn by the profession's own regulatory body. This control was reinforced by the decline in the nineteenth century of the 'apprenticeship' system of medical training and its replacement by education in a curriculum determined, first, by the teaching hospitals, and then by the universities.[23] These developments amounted to a bargain between the profession and a predemocratic state allowing the profession independent control of the key institutional domain of medicine. Every subsequent reform has had to accommodate this legacy and, as we shall see in later chapters, has had to manage the tensions between democratic politics and this pre-democratic inheritance.

Control of the domain of medicine had by the middle of the nineteenth century become a significant prize. The reasons are obvious. The industrial revolution created a large, propertyless, economically vulnerable working class. That working class in turn developed self-insurance – through, for instance, provident societies – as protection against insecurity. The chief threat to security was income loss through unemployment, and a significant source of that threat was sickness. Club practice – the employment of general practitioners by the provident societies to certify claims for benefit – developed as a major source of medical employment: by the end of the nineteenth century the friendly societies covered a third of the working class, with more informal club arrangements spreading the net wider; somewhere between 4,000 and 5,000 doctors depended largely on club fees for their income.[24]

There were powerful tensions between doctors and the societies who were third-party payers. A key part of the statecraft that created the insurance system in the 1911 Act was the invention of a contractual system that reconciled general practitioners, albeit after initial intense opposition, to the new arrangements. That contractual system involved greater reliance on state funding of the insurance system and a reduction in the representation of the friendly societies on the local insurance committees that administered the contractual system. The robustness of the arrangement is shown by the continuity in GP organisation when the NHS was established. For patients the NHS made a big difference, but in Eder's words:

> For the general practitioner in 1948, the differences [from the foundation of the NHS] were hardly noticeable. Patients continued to register themselves on a list and payment was made according to a fixed capitation fee. Furthermore, the basic administrative structure remained essentially unchanged. Local panel committees were simply renamed local medical committees. The general practitioner service was placed under the direction of local executive councils, which were no more than the old insurance committees without the approved societies.[25]

One reason for this continuity was that the epicentre of struggle for control over the domain of medicine had shifted from general practice to the hospital. That shift was in turn part of a deeper change in medicine's character, a change which also profoundly affected the financing system. At the end of the nineteenth century, health insurance was mostly to do with providing income maintenance in case of sickness, and the doctor's dominant role was certification to establish eligibility for benefit. In the first two decades of the century, medicine became increasingly effective in the *treatment* of disease, and health financing in turn shifted from income maintenance to directly financing the cost of curative care. Medical care was established as a distinct domain, not just a subset of social policy. In Fox's words: 'The priority of health policy in Britain changed within a few years from maintaining income to providing services.'[26] The shift was partly due to technological innovations which greatly increased the curative efficacy of medicine. In part it had to do with social innovations, especially those borrowed from the battlefields of the First World War, where the organisation of field hospitals showed the gains to be made from better specialisation of function and coordination of tasks.[27] The combined impact of technological and social innovation was to transform the hospital: once a dangerous resting place for the sickest of the poor, it now became the most important arena for the practice of advanced curative medicine. One of the most striking symbols of the change was the conversion, after the reform of local government of 1929, of the old poor-law hospitals – the classic receptacles of the poor – into local authority hospitals.[28] That was part of a process which made elected local government in the interwar years the kingpin of hospital medicine, its control spreading beyond the immediate sphere of domiciliary care into, for instance, maternity services and the school medical service. By the end of the 1930s the Labour-controlled London County Council was probably the largest hospital authority in the world, a veritable 'state within the medical state'.[29]

Managing medical hostility to the power of elected municipalities was one of the key problems tackled in the statecraft creating the NHS: 'By 1943, the doctors cared less about salary than they did about municipal control.'[30] That statecraft explains the single most distinctive feature of the new system, one that identifies it as based on a command and control planning model. It merged a highly heterogeneous mix of voluntary and local authority hospitals into a single national system, organised on regional lines, the 'direct responsibility of the Minister [of Health] and financed wholly from the exchequer'.[31] The story of the struggle within the Labour government after 1945 that led to that outcome has been told from a variety of historical positions. In essence it involves a largely unsuccessful defence in Cabinet of municipal interests by Herbert Morrison, the great leader the London County Council, and victory for Aneurin Bevan's solution of 'nationalising' the hospital system.[32] That outcome did not reflect some sharp philosophical differences between statesmen; it would be difficult to maintain a view of Morrison, the champion of the public corporation, as a representative advocate of decentralisation; nor to picture Bevan, the most iconoclastic of Labour leaders, as the unambiguous champion of centralisation. What we are observing here, rather, is the interaction between two influences: the contradictory nature of the institutional inheritance; and the phenomenon that Heclo calls 'puzzling' – the need imposed on policy makers to work out solutions to policy puzzles.[33] Municipal control represents 'a road not taken': a road of decentralisation, of democratic control of health service delivery and, probably, a road that would have seen a much less clear separation of general practice from hospital medicine than has subsequently characterised the NHS.[34]

That it was not taken in part represents the result of the 'puzzling' process, as Bevan and his advisers attempted the elementary job of statecraft: trying to put together an institutional package that would survive in the forums, like Cabinet, where it would be tested, and would survive in a world where doctor power had been historically entrenched. Some contingent factors shaped the outcome of the 'puzzling' process – for instance, the fact that the system of local government did not look sufficiently robust to support a municipally run service.[35] But what aided the puzzling process was the diversity of the institutional legacy that lay to hand: that diversity allowed political creativity to shape outcomes. There was a historical legacy of municipalism (albeit a brief one) and of course one of voluntary control, both in the hospital system and in the insurance system. But there was another very different legacy of central control over institutional provision. It could be traced in part to the original Poor Law Amendment Act of 1834, which realised Chadwick's vision of a locally administered poor law under the control of a central board. It was also well established in the sphere of mental health, one of the earliest fields of state involvement in the provision of care and, for obvious reasons, one of the areas where medicine, social control and the maintenance of public order intersect. As early as 1808 the County Asylums Act made public funds available for hospital accommodation.[36] Though they were nominally under local control, the establishment of the Lunacy Commissioners (1845) subjected these institutions to centralised systems of control and inspection.[37] By the end of the 1860s there was a large apparatus of hospitalisation for the mentally ill in institutions controlled and inspected by national boards; by 1869 there were 37,000 inmates in England and Wales.[38] In the early decades of the twentieth century the influence of the eugenics movement led to further centralisation, for instance through the Mental Deficiency Act of 1913.[39] The NHS reforms saw the final nationalisation of the county mental hospitals.[40] There was, thus, a legacy of central control upon which to draw. Beyond mental health there lay a more immediate institutional legacy of central control, the product of the crisis of the Second World War. The Emergency Hospital Service was created to cope with wartime air-raid casualties. It amounted to a unified service organised on regional lines, the regions in part following civil defence requirements. There is even a striking correspondence between the regional hospital boundaries in the NHS and the boundaries of civil defence regions.[41]

Klein has neatly summarised the political settlement that founded the NHS in the phrase 'the politics of the double bed':

> it created a situation of mutual dependency. On the one hand the state became a monopoly employer: effectively members of the medical profession became dependent on it not only for their own incomes but also for the resources at their command. On the other hand the state became dependent on the medical profession to run the NHS and to cope with the problems of rationing scarce resources in patient care.[42]

The state did create a command and control planning system, but that planning system could only run with the cooperation of the medical profession. At the heart of the matter lay an issue central to any command and control mechanism: how were resources to be rationed? The rhetoric of a National Health Service promised access to health care as a more-or-less unqualified right of citizenship. How could this be realised in a democratic polity without entangling politicians in choices about patient care that might be electorally disastrous? The special status and institutional authority of the medical profession were resources in solving this problem. The status and authority, we have seen, were pre-democratic in origin. The relationship between the profession and democratic politics in the foundation of the NHS was therefore not simply one of tension between democratic and pre-democratic institutional interests. The very independence of the medical profession was a resource for democratic government: it allowed the creation of institutional mechanisms which could make rationing decisions on 'non-political' grounds by doctors.

Part of the key to this was the referral system in British medicine, an unusual (though not unique) arrangement. The origins of the referral system lay in what Honigsbaum has called 'the division in British medicine' between general practice and hospital care, a division that originated in struggles at the start of the twentieth century.[43] The structure of the NHS institutionalised and stabilised this referral system: on one side lay GPs acting not as employees, but as professionals contracted with the NHS; on the other lay the hospital, the domain of the salaried professional and, of course, of the most expensive parts of the health care system. The GP was the critical figure in this arrangement. The most important entitlements extended by the new service were the right to register with, and to receive appropriate care from, the GP. Direct access to hospital or to specialist care was highly restricted.[44] The restriction was enforced mostly through the referral system. GPs provided a simple, low-technology consulting and treatment system – and, by the same token, a low-cost system; access to more sophisticated, expensive care depended on referral by the GP.[45] The structure of the NHS ruled out the opportunistic use of the referral system on either side: specialists in hospitals did not depend for resources on referrals from GPs, and GPs had no economic incentive to refer. Referrals were on medical grounds, judged at the professional discretion of the GP.

The key role of the GP as a gatekeeper thus converted the citizenship entitlements into something which, while valuable, were much more constrained than a right to health care. The 'politics of the double bed' involved an accommodation between democratic and pre-democratic forces from which both sides drew advantage. It is obvious that the viability of this arrangement depended heavily both on the authority of medicine, and on the preservation of a stable relationship between organised medicine and the state. The history of the politics of consumption, and the politics of professional government, in the latter-day NHS is a history of the difficulty of preserving these historic accommodations.

But that is for later pages. For the moment we turn to an account of the building of the health care state in Germany.

Germany: building a corporatist state

In the mythology of post-war Germany, 1945 is sometimes referred to as 'Stunde null' – zero hour. The implication is that, matching the physical destruction suffered by the country in the moment of defeat, there occurred a corresponding institutional destruction, thus clearing the ground for the fresh construction of a Western-style capitalist democracy. The emergence of democratic institutions is actually more mysterious.[46] The detailed histories of reconstruction often suggest something less than a fresh start: they stress continuity, and particularly the extent to which there occurred in the early years of the Republic a reconstruction of key pre-war institutional patterns.[47] That mode of reconstruction is particularly marked in health care. By the middle of the 1950s an institutional structure had been rebuilt that strikingly resembled that created before 1939; indeed it even included some features which were added in the Second World War. In short, in the years up to the mid-1950s a health care state on corporatist lines was rebuilt in the Federal Republic. Where did that original state come from, and why was it rebuilt?

The origins take us back once more to Skowronek's remark that exercises in state building draw on 'the organisation of the preestablished state'.[48] The most important origins lie in Bismarck's exercise in pre-democratic, indeed anti-democratic, statecraft which in the 1880s laid the institutional foundations of the corporatist system. The landmark health reform law of 1883, which introduced the principle of compulsory insurance, was a defensive response to the emergence of a politically and industrially organised proletariat. It was part of the the wider Bismarckian strategy of 'tying workers to the state by providing welfare benefits'.[49] The fundamental principle of the Bismarckian health care reforms involved compulsory insurance, based on contributions from workers and employers, to state regulated funds. Bismarck's reforms did not, however, create the funds. They built on and extended an existing institutional structure, endowing pre-existing institutions with new powers and functions: in 1881 there were already in existence over 1,300 *Krankenkassen* (sickness funds).[50] Nor did Bismarck's reforms invent the principle of compulsion: even before the creation of the Reich some groups of workers in Prussia (notably miners) had been subject to compulsory health insurance.[51] Bismarck turned to the existing institutional legacy of self-administered insurance because absorbing the self-administered system into the law was a means of controlling these already politicised working-class institutions.[52] Indeed, health insurance was only a by-product of Bismarck's wider scheme of accident insurance for workers, and the compulsory character of the insurance arrangements had mainly political rather than social ends. In the Chancellor's own words:

> Accident insurance in itself is for me a secondary consideration. My chief consideration is to use this opportunity to attain corporative associations that must be extended gradually to include all productive classes of the population. In this way we will establish the basis for a future representative body that will become an important participant in the legislative process.[53]

The key original steps in building the corporatist health care state in Germany involved the characteristic stages we identified in the British case: extending and reshaping existing structures, and a statecraft which appropriated existing practices – in this case, compulsory insurance – to new ends.

The post-Bismarckian history of health insurance is a history of its expansion.[54] That expansion took two forms, both of which were to be momentous for the history of the system. There occurred, first, an expansion in the numbers and the social range of workers covered by the insurance system: in 1885 there were 4.29 million insured; by 1914 the figure was 15.61 million.[55] As far as the political history of the German health care state was concerned, the second kind of expansion was even more momentous. In the system that existed before 1883, where there already existed of course an extensive network of insurance institutions, the funds generally paid benefits in cash to members. The cash could be freely used by members either for income maintenance or for a wide range of health care, including the services of carers other than doctors, like apothecaries. In the statutory system the funds were obliged to pay doctors directly for the health care services provided to insured members.[56] This shift was momentous because it entangled the funds with the medical profession; and in this entanglement lies a key to the subsequent historical development of the whole system. The dominant issue in medical politics until the middle of the 1930s was the struggle for control of the market in medical labour. The struggle was vital because the expansion of the health insurance system into a mass system of funding for health care meant that large resources were at stake. One index of this is the growth in the size of the medical profession itself: there were about 15,000 doctors in 1880 and 27,000 by 1900.[57]

Two themes can be traced through the half-century following the Bismarckian reforms: the struggle over employment relations between doctors and the health insurance funds; and a parallel struggle over the shape of the regulatory institutions that would govern medicine. The expansion of the statutory health insurance system, and the switch to direct payment for health care instead of distributing cash benefits to members, created significant new income for doctors. Under what conditions could doctors have access to this stream of income from the statutory insurance system? The question was laden with potential conflict, a potential increased by powerful political currents: doctors were *petit-bourgeois* professionals; the funds were dominated by trade union members and were closely tied to the institutions of social democracy, notably following a sharp surge in politicisation after 1890.[58] As far as doctors were concerned, two matters were vital: patients, not funds, should be able to choose freely between doctors; and doctors, in turn, should be able to bill the funds for services which their clinical judgements led them to give patients. The funds, by contrast, wanted to treat doctors as their employees. The funds' model, especially in those institutions most influenced by social democratic ideology, would at the extreme have turned doctors into *angestellten* – fairly low-level paid officers of the funds. Some funds wanted to run their own clinics for members, where a wide range of health care services would be provided under one roof by their own paid employees.[59] Most medical professionals in local practice, by contrast, wanted access to the considerable income now flowing from the statutory insurance system, while maintaining medicine's status as a 'free profession'. In particular, the doctors demanded the right to charge according to collectively bargained scales regulating fees for service, rather than having to negotiate as individuals with funds.[60]

The conflicts about these issues in the early years of the century considerably collectivised the health care system. In order to press their demands, doctors organised, notably in the body named, variously, the *Hartmannbund* (after its founder) or the *Leipziger Verein* (after its main place of foundation.) The membership of the *Bund* rose from under 1,000 at the start of the century to 23,000 a decade later.[61] The early years of the century saw a series of industrial disputes between the doctors and the funds. These were partly resolved in the Berlin Agreement of 1913 – an agreement only achieved at the cost of bringing in the state as a mediator between the parties. The *substantive* significance of the Berlin Agreement was that it reduced the control wielded by the statutory funds over the medical labour market by requiring them to maintain a fixed ratio of doctors to fund members. The *procedural* significance of the agreement was that it greatly strengthened the corporatist character of the system: it 'established committees with equal representation of sickness funds and physicians for the accreditation of sickness fund affiliated doctors. In this way, the fundamental principles were elaborated in a law-free area by self-governing bodies.'[62]

The institutional relationships established by the Berlin Agreement were tested to the point of destruction in the political and social turmoil of the Weimar years. There were severe tensions inside the medical profession between those registered with the funds (and thus with access to the income streams of the statutory system) and a growing army of (mostly younger) doctors waiting to get on the fund lists. There was conflict, in the years of mass unemployment, between accredited doctors and the funds as the. latter responded to their increasingly desperate financial circumstances by pressing doctors more and more for savings. And there was more conflict still between the medical profession and the funds because the funds were directly organising and supplying health care services to their members. The 1920s were years of industrial disputes, made more bitter because doctors increasingly viewed both the insurance funds and the whole Weimar regime as signifying 'socialised medicine'.[63]

Weimar's intensified economic and political crisis after 1930 produced both a pronounced rightward shift in government policy and a profound financial crisis for the health insurance system. The combination of a dramatically changed political climate and intense economic crisis led to a major structural reform of the system by the Brüning government at the end of 1931. The reforms were a great victory for the medical profession over the insurance funds. They removed individual doctors from the control of the funds by establishing a new category of statutory public body, the *Kassenärtzlichen*

Vereinigungen. These were the associations of insurance doctors that, mediating between individual doctors and the funds, were henceforth to negotiate payment rates with funds and to distribute payments to doctors.[64]

The reforms at the end of Weimar greatly strengthened the medical profession and greatly weakened the insurance funds; but radical though they were, they were only a prelude to the even-more fundamental transformation in the balance of power that took place in the wake of the Nazi takeover. In right-wing demonology the funds were pictured as subject to Marxist and Jewish domination. The Nazis destroyed the funds as independent political actors: their officers were purged, state-appointed officials being imposed in their place. The associations of insurance doctors, created at the end of Weimar, were considerably strengthened: their organisation was centralised nationally and they were given total control in regulating relations between the funds and doctors, a control previously shared with the funds.[65]

The Nazi assault on the funds can be seen as completing an item which had been high on the agenda of the medical profession for the half-century since the initial establishment of the Bismarckian system in the 1880s: breaking the influence of the funds in the management of the health care system, and establishing medical control over the resources created by compulsory insurance. But the rise of the Nazis also allowed the medical profession to complete a second part of a long-term agenda: that part which involved reshaping the regulatory relationship between the profession and the state. The way that reshaping was achieved still deeply influences the character of the German health care state.

The historical problems faced by the medical profession in Germany resembled in some important ways those encountered by doctors in Britain. Many of these problems had to do with the impact of the rise of scientific medicine, which created divisions within the profession between hospital-based medicine and doctors working in local practice, and stimulated attempts by the profession to try to force older, lay therapeutic traditions from the market.[66] The response in Britain, we have seen, was to create a regulatory structure where the profession could control markets independently of the state – the essence of the system created after the Medical Act of 1858. Professional authority in Germany was shaped by a different historical tradition, where states had a much longer history in licensing professional authority and in explicitly distinguishing professional occupations from others. The key to professional status lay not in the sort of *ad hoc* solution represented in Britain by the Medical Act, but in appropriating an already available ideological and institutional legacy: that legacy which had, since the eighteenth century in the separate states eventually unified by Bismarck, identified various occupations as professions, as distinct from trades, and had organised them into public law 'chambers'. The chamber system conferred self-government on an occupation backed by the powers of the state. It allowed restrictive control of entry and regulation of the terms of competition between members. National unification in 1871 was soon followed (in 1873) by the establishment of a national association (the *Deutsche Artzesvereinbund* (DÄV)) to campaign for a national chamber and for a national professional code for doctors. Stone has summarised the subsequent history:

> the overriding goal of the DÄV was to promote a national physicians' code and to secure chamber status for the profession nationwide. Despite constant pressure by the DÄV, the national government refused to create a national physicians' code, and insisted instead that regulation of medical practice was the responsibility of the different states. Eventually, several of the states did grant chamber status to their physicians ... [but] it was not until 1935 that a national physicians' code was finally achieved. This first code ... declared that medicine is not a trade, but by its very nature, a free profession. The question of professional status of physicians was thus not completely resolved until the 1930s.[67]

It will be obvious that the closing months of Weimar and the early years of the Nazi dictatorship were critical for the German health care state. Four elements of that change are particularly important. The first is the series of reforms, begun in the closing days of Weimar and completed in the early months of Nazi rule, which removed doctors completely from the control of the insurance funds, by establishing the associations of insurance doctors, and then handing to those associations a monopoly of control over ambulatory medical care. The second was the (literally) murderous attack on the funds by the Nazis, removing their leadership and subjecting them to state control. This destroyed the institutional resource which had been possessed by the funds in their historic struggles with the medical profession and obliterated their independence and their distinct political cultures. The third element of critical change involved the final, full incorporation of the medical profession into the privileged sphere of professional self-government – the code of 1935 referred to in the passage from Stone quoted above. The fourth element was one of the key preconditions for all these changes that plainly so advantaged the medical profession: the creation of a close alliance between medicine and Nazism. The medical profession had from the start a particularly close connection with the Nazi dictatorship: by 1935, one-third of all non-Jewish doctors were members of the ruling party's association for Nazi doctors, and over 7 per cent were members of the SS – a level of participation markedly higher than for other professions.[68] Part of the origin of this connection lay in the political economy of medicine under Weimar: in the way control over entry to the lists of licenced insurance doctors created a long waiting list of ageing doctors; in the way a crowded medical labour market set up intense competition within the profession, partly along generational lines; and in the way the tensions created by this competition intersected with the culture of anti-semitism. (In 1933, 13 per cent of German doctors were Jewish, and the figure for Berlin was estimated at 52 per cent.[69]) The alliance with the Nazi regime purged the profession of Jews and left-wing radicals, established medicine as a free profession with independent control over its markets – and laid the foundations, in consequence, for the post-war shape of the German health care state.

Perhaps the single most remarkable feature of the German health care system that developed in the decade after the Second World War was the way it recreated pre-war institutions and practices. Reconstruction can be considered accomplished by 1955 with the passage of the law which finally reestablished the arrangements, made in late Weimar and the early period of Nazi rule, giving the associations of insurance doctors the central role in negotiating with the insurance funds and in managing the payments of doctors in local practice. Deppe sums up the impact of the 1955 law thus:

> Thereby the medical profession has since 1955 had as good as a monopoly in the supply of ambulatory care once more securely in its control. It could also enforce its economic interests and main political aim, to secure free professional status under the guardianship of the state.[70]

In the post-war debates about the shape of the health care system, the issue of financing was critical. It resolved itself into one key choice: should there be created a single, unified health insurance system, or should the old divided system, with its mix of funds organised along lines of territory, occupation and status, be reinstated? The creation of an *Einheitsversicherung* (a unified social insurance system) had both ideological and institutional implications: ideological, because it would weaken the link between health insurance and an unequal system of occupational stratification; institutional, because a unified system posed a potential threat to the dominant position which the medical profession had secured in the reforms passed at the end of Weimar and in the early period of Nazi rule. The coalition supporting a radical reconstruction of health care financing was potentially impressive: the forces of social democracy that had been revived by the defeat of Nazism; some important parts of the old statutory system, particularly the district funds; and some at least of the occupying powers, notably the Soviets and the French. Indeed, a unified system was initially established in Berlin, in the French zone and, of course, in what came to be the German Democratic Republic.[71]

That this radical reform project failed was due to a variety of circumstances, of which the most important was the richness of the institutional inheritance. One of the most remarkable features of the immediate post-war period was the speed with which, despite the destruction of Nazism, old organisations were recreated. As early as 1946 in Bavaria a state-wide doctors' chamber (*Ärztekammern*) was created as a public law organisation.[72] By 1948, associations of insurance doctors – the linchpin of the system created at the end of the Weimar period – were already established as public law institutions in individual states, for example Bavaria.[73] The year of the foundation of the Federal Republic, 1949, also saw the refoundation of the *Hartmannbund*, the main interest group representing doctors in local practice.[74]

The decade after 1945 is therefore central to understanding the German health care state. Institutionally it re-established the system created in the dying days of Weimar and the early months of Nazi rule. Ideologically, it actually represented a further development of the logic of those changes: it finally removed any political component from the insurance funds, turning them into apolitical institutions governed by bureaucratic oligarchies.[75] It thus inaugurated the characteristic style of health care policy making in the post-war German welfare state: the supremacy in policy language of a technocratic discourse where concerns with organisational efficiency and medical effectiveness were the dominant mode; a policy-making world dominated by decentralised networks of policy actors drawn, mostly, from the oligarchies of public law organisations; and a power structure where the medical profession was dominant.

Understanding why this route was taken, in preference to others such as a national system of social insurance, demands understanding the range of forces, domestic and international, that shaped the post-war character of the German state. The support for an alternative system of unified, nationally organised insurance was fatally weakened from the start by differences between the most important parties who could have imposed a new system, the occupying powers. Webber likens them to a coalition government trying to agree on a common policy – an agreement that proved impossible.[76] Nor was the division only the obvious one between the Soviets and the Western powers. As we have seen, there were other differences over the shape of health care financing: the French actually created a unified system in their zone, while American advisers were powerfully opposed to any unified system. Nor was division confined to the allies. There were powerful institutional and class interests in the old statutory insurance system which opposed a unified system of health insurance: the substitute funds, which organised for the most part white-collar workers, saw a unified system as a danger both to their institutional autonomy and to the sectional interests of their contributors.[77]

The absence of any agreed solution in the immediate aftermath of the war was one of the factors allowing the rapid reconstruction of the old regulatory institutions. The differences between key actors were magnified by the intensification of the Cold War. This had a range of important consequences for the reconstruction of the health care state: it led, of course, to the foundation of the separate German Democratic Republic and the establishment of a command and control health care state in the East which endured until the collapse of the Communist regime at the end of the 1980s; and it encouraged the re-emergence of traditional interests, especially in the medical profession, in West Germany as the allied powers began to look for support in the construction of an anti-communist Federal Republic.

The political colour of the government that dominated the early years of the Federal Republic further strengthened the hands of those who wanted to re-establish the old system, notably the hands of the leading sections of the medical profession. Not only was the dominant governing party Christian Democratic, but the minority partner, the Free Democrats, had inherited from Nazism the role of articulating the sectional interests of the most powerful section of the medical profession, those doctors in local office practice who wanted to retain the status of a free profession.[78]

The history of the German state in the seven decades after the introduction of the Bismarckian welfare reforms is a story of extraordinary tumult. Two world wars, the collapse of three separate regimes (Imperial, Weimar, Nazi), division into two separate states: these are only the most obvious benchmarks of upheaval. Yet the health care state is marked by a profound continuity: by institutional continuity, notably in the system of health care financing: by enduring institutional fragmentation of the statutory funds; and by the way the funds followed the contours of occupational stratification. It is also marked by a different kind of continuity: the gradual realisation of a historical project by the medical profession, which freed the profession from control by the funds and stripped them of their historic political character. By the middle of the 1950s this historical project had been fully accomplished.

The United States: building a supply state

The institutions built in the UK and Germany were different, but they shared a common feature: they were shaped by the pressure to provide universal access to a package of health care provision. Jacobs has identified a very different imperative in the American case:

> the general sequence and form of health policy in the United States diverge from those of all other industrialized nations. The U.S. government's first and most generous involvement in health care focused on expanding the supply of hospital-centered, technologically sophisticated health care ... In contrast to the United States, however, other Western countries have made the expansion of access their first and primary priority; governments have accelerated the expansion of supply in response to widening access and growing demand for care.[79]

Understanding this very different state structure has to begin by unravelling the connections between politics and medicine in the later decades of the nineteenth century, when some of the key institutional features of the American health care system developed. Medical power in Britain and

Germany originated in undemocratic and hierarchical societies. The consolidation of medical authority relied heavily on the power of traditional hierarchies (reflected, for instance, in the links between medicine, the royal court and the ancient universities in Britain) and on the power of the state. In the second half of the nineteenth century the American medical profession, by contrast, was struggling for authority in a society with a weak central state and a democratic political culture: federal regulatory power was weak; federal resources were scarce; many of the institutional marks of democratic politics (such as a mass franchise) were already highly developed; and there were powerful egalitarian components to popular culture. In an egalitarian culture with a weak state, how could medical authority be maintained? For much of the century, the answer was: with great difficulty. Medicine was divided into sects, often overlapping with religious sects led by charismatic figures.[80] Some strands of populism amounted to a rejection of medical authority wholesale: consider the Thomsonians, closely allied to Jacksonian democrats, and their slogan: 'every man [sic] his own physician.'[81] There was widespread reliance on domestic medicine administered in the home, mostly by women using traditional, herbal, remedies.[82]

In a society with an egalitarian culture and a weak federal government, the problem of controlling and legitimising medical authority could only be tackled at the level of individual states, and by working to some low common denominator of medical competence. That common denominator was provided by a rudimentary system of licensing, in particular by the stipulation that the authority of a doctor should reside in those with a qualification from a licensed medical school. From the 1870s, the licensing movement spread through individual states. That had a number of important results. It greatly decentralised the regulatory structure, for the key bodies were now the licensing boards in the separate states. The control of these licensing boards was obviously a critical matter, and this gave a great spur to the organisation of the American Medical Association (AMA). By the turn of the century the boards were controlled by AMA members, in part because other potential regulators – like the universities – abdicated responsibility.[83] The early years of the century saw the transformation of the AMA into the dominant national actor in health care. Its national constitution was reformed, and state and substate associations were organised into a unified national structure. Membership rose rapidly: from 8,000 members nationally in 1900 to 70,000 a decade later.[84] These developments had profound consequences for the long-term government of health care. State institutions had weak authority and few resources. A private association had now emerged as a key influence in licensing, in the dissemination of professional knowledge (through its journals, for instance) and as the only well-organised national institution in health care. As for licensing, medical domination of the state licensing boards meant that, despite the institutional surroundings of democratic politics, the key decisions were now taken by a *de facto* system of private interest government.

A weak, decentralised state and private interest government: to these features were added a critical role for medical education. That role grew from the resort to licensing as the key instrument of occupational control, but after 1870 it became entangled in the building of an American higher education system. That building process was heavily influenced by German models of research-driven, scientific universities, involving a struggle to displace traditional 'collegiate' conceptions of university life inherited from the ancient English institutions.[85] The prototype was the medical school at Johns Hopkins University in Baltimore, which opened in 1893 and which created a powerful fusion between medical practice, medical education and medical research. More generally, through a generation of young American medical researchers who received part of their scientific training in German institutions, a Germanic, research-driven model was imported to the US: Bonner estimates that between 1870 and 1914 at least a third, and perhaps a half, of the leading figures in American medicine received part of their training in a German university.[86] The closing decades of the nineteenth century were also the years that saw the establishment of associations catering for many specialised branches of medicine.[87] In the first two decades of this century the education of the profession, the organisation of the hospital and the organisation of medical research were all subjected to similar reform pressures – pressures leading to more scientific rigour, specialisation and an emphasis on research-based medicine. The landmark reforms succeeded the Flexner Report (published 1910) on medical education, the result of a study jointly sponsored by the AMA and the Carnegie Foundation. The effect of Flexner was to make medical education more scientifically rigorous and more intellectually and socially elitist.[88] The pattern laid down by Flexner – reforms produced by an alliance between sections of the medical elite and a powerful private foundation funded from a great capitalist fortune – was repeated in the case of medical research, where the instrument was the Rockefeller Foundation.[89]

These developments combined to produce the power structures which marked the American 'supply state'. Although the surrounding political system was democratic, and the political culture egalitarian, the health care system was dominated by private interests: by the professionals organised in the AMA; by an elite of researchers in the newly reformed medical schools; and by supporters in the great capitalist foundations. In Morone's words: 'A single pattern dominated American health care politics for most of the twentieth century: public power was ceded to the medical profession.'[90]

This mix helps explain the 'supply' mentality which has dominated US health care: it was the suppliers of care, and the providers of technology, who were from the beginning in the saddle. It also helps explain the central historical puzzle of US health care policy. The puzzle is put thus by Rothman:

There are some questions that historians return to so often that they become classics in the field, to be explored and reexplored, considered and reconsidered. No inquiry better qualifies for this designation than the question of why the United States has never enacted a national health insurance program. Why, with the exception of South Africa, does it remain the only industrialized country that has not implemented so fundamental a social welfare policy?[91]

Over a period of nearly eighty years to the 1990s there were six major attempts to create some system of health insurance in the US. All failed.[92] Separate accounts of each failure turn in part on the contingencies of particular historical moments. In explaining the failure of the movement for compulsory insurance which swept through Progressive politics in the years after 1912, for instance, Stevens argues that the surge in the influence of private insurance companies in the aftermath of the 1919 influenza epidemic mobilised a powerful interest against compulsory insurance.[93] For Skocpol, the same failure is part of the story of the arrested development of the historically precocious American welfare state, an arrested development which had to do with the failure of Progressive intellectuals to penetrate the labour movement and with the transformation of the reforming spirit of social enquiry into a professionalised social science that had lost its moral drive.[94] Hirshfield's account of 'the lost reform' – the failure to extend the reforming social agenda of the New Deal to the health sphere – stresses the lobbying skill of the AMA within the Roosevelt administration and the failure of reformers to convey their case for change to a wider public.[95]

Behind all these contingencies, however, were inherited features that first shaped, and then reinforced, the powerful private interests that dominated the health care arena for the first six decades of the century. The reorganisation of medicine in defence of professionalism at the close of the nineteenth century was a successful defensive response to the corporatization of American economic life – to the displacement of an older, rural America of agriculture and commerce by an industrial America where capitalist monopoly and labour organisation were increasingly important. The extent of that success can be gauged by what it did both to the practice of medicine by individual doctors and to the organisation and structure of the hospital sector. The profession not only appropriated control of the health care arena; it fashioned an ideology which rejected collectivism and placed the solo practitioner, the family doctor practising as an independent professional, at the centre of the health care system. The AMA had the power to block reform, and it judged reforms by what they might do to the solo practitioner. The dominant feature of AMA policy in the first three decades of this century was the refusal, as Hirshfield shows, of rank-and-file doctors to abandon traditional individualism in the face of the collectivisation and urbanisation of the US in these decades.[96]

If the dominant feature of medical practice was the supremacy of the solo

44

practitioner, the dominant institutional feature was the rise of a hospital system independent of state control and ideologically hostile to state financing of health care. 'Between 1870 and 1917 the American hospital was transformed from an asylum for the indigent into a modern scientific institution.'[97] And between 1910 and 1917, the basic rules of a standardised national system were developed, not by the state but by medical school professors: 'the standardisation process – the system of industrial government – was largely independent of the state.'[98] By the 1930s, the voluntary hospital as an institution, and 'voluntarism' as an ideology of hospital organisation, had emerged as the dominant alternative to 'socialised' medicine.[99]

But this ideological resistance to systems of public health insurance was not the same as a resistance to the *collectivisation* of health care payment. The very success of the sort of technological medicine that the new hospital represented also meant that traditional financing, without some third-party support, was by the 1930s beyond the pockets of many citizens. The expense of care could not be met fully from direct out-of-pocket payments; it had to be collectivised. The Great Depression caused a sharp drop in doctors' incomes, and the early 1930s saw a sustained debate about the problems of financing health care.[100] The decade also saw, partly as a response to the crisis of financing, a start to the collectivisation of health care financing, by the spread of pre-payment insurance organised through the Blue Cross schemes. At the close of the decade 9 per cent of the American population had some form of private health insurance.[101] The achievement of the Blue Cross has been well described by Rothman. It collectivised the single greatest cost of medical care, that incurred by hospitalisation. It creamed subscribers from the middle class, neglecting the poor. And it did this on a huge scale: by 1945 it insured 2 million Americans; by 1950 the figure was 40 million.[102] The rise of Blue Cross as a vehicle for voluntary insurance in the middle class helps explain why by the end of the 1930s the medical profession, and its most powerful voice, the AMA, had swung in favour of voluntary health insurance.[103]

The political significance of this partial collectivisation of consumption is that it helped mute for a generation potentially powerful voices that might have supported publicly financed health insurance. It solved the financing problems of the middle class, and it solved for doctors the problem of treating patients who could not afford to pay out of pocket the growing costs of care. The popular voice was further weakened by the incorporation, during and after the Second World War, of the best-organised sections of the working class into systems of private insurance. The origins of this development lay in the wage controls imposed on the economy in the war. One way of circumventing wage controls was to include welfare, including health care, benefits in collective bargaining agreements. After the war there was an expansion of two types of collective health care financing in the organised working class: an expansion of historically established union administered plans and, following a landmark court case in 1948, the spread of joint union-employer administered plans. By the mid-1960s, the miners' welfare fund, for instance, was the country's biggest single buyer of health services, while joint plans had been created in the core sectors of the industrial economy, like automobiles, construction and steel.[104]

Until the 1960s the historical configuration of interests in American health thus marginalised the state's role in providing access to health care. The supplier domination of the system meant, conversely, powerful support for the development of a 'supply state' – for state support to provide the sort of technological infrastructure on which the authority of modern medicine had been founded. Two signs of the significance of the supply state were public support for hospital construction and for medical research. After the passage of the Hill-Burton Hospital Construction Act in 1946 the federal government became a major source of finance for hospital building. As Morone puts it: 'The legislation was emblematic of postwar health policy. The state financed the industry's workshops and laboratories, while it studiously avoided meddling with professional decisions.' Over the succeeding thirty-five years the programme disbursed $3.7 billion of federal money.[105] Federal support for medical research was even more enthusiastic, since large-scale state involvement was possible without threatening the ideological core of the health care system – the autonomy of the solo practitioner. In the words of Congressman (later Defense Secretary) Melvin Laird: 'Medical research is the best kind of health insurance.'[106] The remark typified the supply mentality which dominated thinking about the appropriate role of the state in the health care system. The state's role in securing the health of the nation lay not in regulating access to care, but in promoting the supply of technologies which could conquer disease. 'Conquer' was precisely the sort of quasi-military language used in discussions about the need to produce produce dramatic advances in the treatment of diseases like cancer.[107] That quasi-military mentality was strengthened by the direct connection between war and federal support for medical research. The medical demands of military combat in the Second World War, coupled with the more indirect effects of technological innovation resulting from military conflict, boosted both the volume of medical research and the federal government's role as its funder.[108] In the two decades after the Second World War the American medical research community rose to a position of world dominance, both in numbers and in quality of work. Those decades also saw the supply state at its height, for the money welded together an elite of medical researchers, actors in the federal government and the medical technology industries in the private sector.

The introduction of Medicare and Medicaid in the middle of the 1960s was both the product of the established politics of the supply state, and the harbinger of a different political order. Medicare and Medicaid grew out of the success of Kennedy's presidential election campaign of 1960, though they were largely shaped by bargaining within Congress and by the mandate delivered to Johnson in 1964 by his landslide victory a year after Kennedy's assassination. Although the reforms contributed to a long-term transformation of both the role of the state in health care, and of the wider health care system itself, they mark, not a point of revolutionary change, but a moment of transition between a new and an old politics of health care. They consisted, and still consist, of three elements: Part A of Medicare, a compulsory hospital insurance program for the old (and disabled) built onto the old New Deal social security system; Part B of Medicare, a programme of government subsidised voluntary insurance to cover doctors' bills, inserted largely as a result of compromise with Republicans in Congress; and a third part, Medicaid, which 'expanded assistance to the states for the medical care of the poor'.[109] The very different influences at work are well summarised by Starr:

> Though adopted together, Medicare and Medicaid reflected different traditions. Medicare was buoyed by popular and acknowledged dignity of Social Security; Medicaid was burdened by the stigma of public assistance. While Medicare had uniform national standards for eligibility and benefits, Medicaid left the states to decide how extensive their programs would be. Medicare allowed physicians to charge above what the program would pay; Medicaid did not and participation among physicians was far more limited. The objective of Medicaid was to allow the poor to buy into the 'mainstream' of medicine, but neither the federal government nor the states were willing to spend the money that would have been required.[110]

Part A of Medicare – that establishing the compulsory health insurance programme for hospitalisation for the old as part of social security – epitomises the way the reforms of the 1960s were shaped both by a newly emergent health care political order and by the old politics of health care. The stimulus for Medicare legislation lay not within the health care system, but in the wider sphere of competitive democratic politics. As Jacobs has shown, it originated in commitments made by Kennedy in fighting the 1960 presidential election, commitments made as part of a strategy of establishing the candidate's 'liberal' credentials. In turn, the particular strategic commitment to reform of health care insurance for the elderly was shaped by increasingly sophisticated 'soft' technologies of democratic politics. The most important of these was the growing sophistication of opinion polling in detecting the public mood, and the increasing use of polls by candidates to shape their platforms.[111]

We see here the beginnings of what was to become a characteristic feature of health care politics over the next three decades: the intrusion into the health care arena of actors with interests beyond the specialised world of health care, and the reshaping of that arena by the changing technologies of democratic politics. But Medicare also ushered in a new kind of health care politics in a more obvious sense: it transformed both the interests and the significance of the federal government. After the reforms of the mid 1960s, the federal government became, mostly through Medicare costs, the largest third-party payer in the health care system: in 1960 it accounted for only just over 10 per cent of national health spending; thirty years later the figure exceeded 30 per cent.[112] Its interest in policy was thus transformed, since to its historical regulatory roles, and its roles in funding medical research, it now added a very direct interest in the cost of care. This transformation was accompanied by a change in institutional capacities. Historically, as we have seen, the federal state was a weak institution in health. The establishment of Medicare also demanded a regulatory body to administer the Medicare system, in the form (eventually) of the Health Care Financing Administration (HCFA).[113] As we shall see in later chapters, the HCFA was to become a major institutional actor in health care policy.[114]

Yet Medicare was also deeply influenced by the old politics of health care. The most obvious sign of this was the way the politics of the supply state still shaped the content of policy. The reimbursement procedures extracted by the medical profession as the price of cooperating with Medicare meant that physicians retained control of charges – with inflationary consequences for health care costs during the succeeding decade as access, and thus patient numbers, increased.[115] For hospitals, by the 1960s the organisations at the centre of the supply state, Medicare proved an engine of transformation. In Stevens' words, 'Medicare gave hospitals a licence to spend'.[116] In fact for all the traditionally dominant provider interests – doctors, hospitals, drug firms, medical equipment manufacturers – the reforms of the mid-1960s created a cornucopia. But this very generosity destabilised the old world of medicine. It exposed health care to the full force – creative and destructive – of competitive markets; it led to rampant inflation and huge industrial growth; and finally it led to federal regulation.

The passage of Medicare marks a historical point of change, the moment at which the supply state began to experience extraordinary pressures. Those pressures lie at the heart of the contemporary politics of health care government examined later in this book.

Democratic politics and health care states

The three countries examined here each had different experiences of building a health care state, and the differences have some obvious roots. These roots lie in the particular historical contingencies of medical politics and in the wider forces, both national and global, shaping the fate of nations. The result, as we will see in the chapters that follow, was that each country experienced different patterns of health care politics in the spheres of consumption, professional government and production. The *differences* are what are most obvious. But what is less obvious, and therefore in need of emphasis, is the way historical trajectories launched all three countries onto paths which created tensions with democratic politics. The health care states described here are not democratic creations; they were built before, or apart from, or even in opposition to, the wider institutions of democracy.

That separate trajectory is most obvious in the German case. The system was the product of anti-democratic statecraft: of the Bismarckian strategy of incorporating working-class insurance institutions into the state system, simultaneously offering workers security and controlling their institutions; of the succesful realisation of the medical profession's great historical project, which involved giving access to the income streams produced by mass compulsory insurance while assigning control of the resource to an oligarchic profession; and of finally creating, under the patronage of Nazism, a system of government-backed control led by the profession itself.

In the case of the UK the key feature was not an alliance with anti-democratic forces; it was the way some of the most important institutions of the health care state had been built before the rise of democratic politics, and the way the culture of the health care state continued to be permeated, even after the advent of democratic politics, by pre-democratic notions. Institutionally, the heart of all this was the system of medical government established by the Medical Act of 1858, which allowed the profession not only autonomy in its own affairs, but also placed it at the heart of the whole health care system. Culturally, the creation of the NHS, although plainly a response to the pressures of democratic politics, also involved using traditional deference to the medical profession to solve problems of rationing that were too delicate for democratic politics. The division of labour that allowed the medical profession to make practical decisions about the allocation of clinical resources, coupled with the central role played by the referral system, meant that democratic politicians were able to establish a command and control system on modest funding levels without becoming entangled in the politics of rationing. Of course, it is only in the 1990s that we have come routinely to describe this process as 'rationing' with all the delicate implications that the word conveys. But that was part of the essence of the system: what were truly decisions about the rationing of health care were not conceived as such, but as the outcome of the customary exercise of clinical authority.

The British and the German cases make plain that the health care state was anything but a democratic creation; at best, its insitutions had an ambiguous relationship with democracy, and at worst they were the conscious creation of forces hostile to democratic politics. The American case reveals a similar history of tension, though from a different starting point. In Germany and the UK the institutions of medicine originated in societies which were institutionally undemocratic and culturally hierarchical. But in the American case the institutions of medicine had to find a solution to the problem of how to construct authority in a society where democratic practices were quite well

established, and where there did not exist that culture of hierarchy and deference that characterised European societies. For much of the nineteenth
century the medical profession struggled to establish medical authority in a
society where populism was a powerful political force and where charismatic
leadership, frequently allied to religious appeals, could often substitute for
clinical competence. It achieved this in the half-century or so after 1870
through an alliance with science and with industrial capitalism that was itself
built on scientific advance and technological innovation. In so doing it also
managed to establish the characteristic of the American health care state as a
supply state: the way the driving force in resource raising and allocation was
not the needs of citizens to gain access to medical care, but the demands of
professional and research elites. Institutionally, it created a system marked by
striking imbalances in the distribution of political resources: a system where
suppliers – notably medical professionals and corporate interests – were by far
the best-organised and best-informed participants in health care debates. The
result insulated health care policy making from the wider influences of democratic politics.

The three health care states built here were very different in their institutional structures, but they shared, we now see, an important feature: they
all had a problematic relationship with democratic politics. The unfolding of
that problematic relationship is, in essence, what the succeeding chapters
are about. Consumption politics, professional politics, production politics: all
have had to operate in a democratic political environment. That democratic
environment, in turn, was not fixed: the institutions of democratic politics; the
technologies available in democratic politics, both 'hard' and 'soft'; the nature
of deference and hierarchy: all these features have greatly changed over a
generation. It will be one of the key arguments of the rest of this book that
this developing character has made more acute still the problematic relationship between the health care state and the democratic state. To explore the
problems, we turn first to the government of consumption.

Notes

1 Even when they are, in post-colonial circumstances, they commonly use a
   colonial institutional dowry: see as an example R. Barrington, *Health, medicine
   and politics in Ireland, 1900–1970* (Dublin, Institute of Public Administration,
   1987).
2 S. Skowronek, *Building a new American state: the expansion of national administrative capacities, 1877–1920* (Cambridge, Cambridge University Press, 1977),
   p. 285.
3 C. Tilly, 'Reflections on the history of European state-making', in C. Tilly (ed.),
   The formation of national states in western Europe (Princeton NJ, Princeton
   University Press, 1975), pp. 3–83, especially pp. 21–5 and 34–8.
4 The phrase is from the account of the word in the Oxford English Dictionary.

5   L. Jacobs, 'Politics of America's supply state: health reform and technology', *Health Affairs*, 14:2 (1995) 143–57.

6   See the original Act reprinted in B. Watkin (ed.), *Documents on health and social services: 1834 to the present day* (London, Methuen, 1975), pp. 140–1: 'The services shall be provided free of charge, except where any provision of this Act expressly provides for the making and recovery of charges.'

7   R. Saltman and C. von Otter, *Planned markets and public competition: strategic reform in northern European health systems* (Buckingham, Open University Press, 1992), pp. 4–5.

8   A key phrase in the quotation is 'dominant policy paradigm'. In the NHS, as in any other complex system, there were alternative paradigms: as Steve Harrison points out to me (personal communication) some elements of corporatism were important and – in part connected to this – there was a long established emphasis on clinical autonomy.

9   G. Esping-Andersen, *The three worlds of welfare capitalism* (Cambridge, Polity Press, 1990), p. 27.

10   Esping-Andersen, *Three worlds of welfare capitalism*, p. 26.

11   I stress *implied* and *principle* for two reasons: because nowhere in the Act is the language of citizenship used, there being only a statutory duty on the Minister to ensure the provision of a comprehensive service; and because we know that in practice both service consumption and health outcomes were heavily influenced by prevailing patterns of inequality which cut across the equality principles of citizenship. The classic document concerning the latter is the Black Report, originally published as *Inequalities in health: report of a research working group* (London, DHSS, 1980). The research was commissioned in 1977 and the report was viewed with disfavour by the Conservative Administration returned in 1979 – witness the foreword to the 1980 edition by the Secretary of State. Only a tiny number of copies of the report were printed, and wider circulation awaited republication by Penguin Books.
     My account also ignores the rise of private financing and private provision as the NHS developed. Our focus is on 1948, when the private sector was residual. In 1985, for instance, 4.5 million persons were covered by some private health insurance, whereas in 1950 the figure was only 120,000: E. Papadakis and P. Taylor-Gooby, *The private provision of public welfare: state, market and community* (Brighton, Wheatsheaf, 1987), p. 58 and pp. 40–70.

12   C. Webster, *The health services since the war, volume 1, problems of health care: the National Health Service before 1957* (London, HMSO, 1988), p. 2.

13   Webster, *Health services since the war*, vol. 1, p. 11.

14   The details are from B. Armstrong, *The health insurance doctor: his role in Great Britain, Denmark and France* (Princeton NJ, Princeton University Press, 1939), pp. 10 and 31.

15   The quotation is from N. Eder, *National health insurance and the medical profession in Britain, 1913–39* (New York, Garland, 1982), p.141.

16   *Ministry of Health: voluntary hospitals committee. Final Report*, Cmnd 1335, 1921. (Chairman: Viscount Cave.)

17   Armstrong, *The health insurance doctor*, pp. 89–93.

18 This relies on B. Watkin, *The National Health Service: the first phase, 1948–1974 and after* (London, Allen and Unwin, 1978), p. 9.

19 J. Pickstone, *Medicine and industrial society: a history of hospital development in Manchester and its region, 1752–1946* (Manchester, Manchester University Press, 1985), p. 257. I have been heavily influenced in my general account of the changing institutional shape of care by Pickstone's monumental history.

20 E. Hennock, *British social reform and German precedents* (Oxford, Clarendon Press, 1987), pp. 176–84.

21 Hennock, *British social reform*, p. 193 is particularly clear on how the final legislation produced a system involving less self-government than in Germany.

22 A. Heidenheimer, 'Professional knowledge and state policy in comparative historical perspective: law and medicine in Britain, Germany and the United States', *International Social Science Journal*, 61 (1989) 529–53 (at p. 535).

23 These passages rely entirely on the work of Waddington: I. Waddington, *The medical profession in the industrial revolution* (Dublin, Gill and Macmillan, 1984), esp. pp. 135–52 and pp. 201–2; and 'The movement towards the professionalisation of medicine', *British Medical Journal*, 301 (1990) 688–90 (3 October).

24 These figures are from F. Honigsbaum, 'The evolution of the NHS', *British Medical Journal*, 301 (1990) 694–9 (3 October).

25 Eder, *National health insurance*, pp. 361–2.

26 D. Fox, *Health policies, health politics: the British and American experience, 1911–1965* (Princeton NJ, Princeton University Press, 1986), p. 5

27 This is drawn from Fox, *Health policies, health politics*, pp. 8ff, who is particularly revealing on the impact of battlefield medicine on hospital organisation.

28 Watkin, *The National Health Service*, p. 9.

29 Webster, *Health services since the war*, vol. 1, p. 6 and p. 78 (the last for the quotation).

30 F. Honigsbaum, *The division in British medicine: a history of the separation of general practice from hospital care 1911–1968* (London, Kogan Page, 1979), p. 191.

31 The words in quotation marks, from Webster, *Health services since the war*, vol. 1, p. 82, are themselves a quotation from official papers.

32 Morrison was actually leader of the LCC until 1940, at which point he entered the wartime coalition government. The best account of the divisions about the shape of the NHS in the post-war Labour Cabinet is in K. Morgan, *Labour in power* (Oxford, Oxford University Press, 1985), pp. 151–63.

33 H. Heclo, *Modern social politics in Britain and Sweden: from relief to income maintenance* (New Haven CT, Yale University Press, 1974), p. 305: Heclo actually uses the phrase 'collective puzzlement on society's behalf'.

34 Honigsbaum, *Division in British medicine*, pp. 190–4 is instructive on the role of the municipally controlled clinic as a bridge between general practice and the hospital.

35 Webster, *Health services since the war*, vol. 1, p. 83 cites this as a consideration for Bevan.

36 Webster, *Health services since the war*, vol. 1, pp. 9–10.

37 K. Jones, *Mental health and social policy 1845–1959* (London, Routledge, 1960), p. 38.

38 R. Hodgkinson, *The origins of the National Health Service: the medical services of the New Poor Law 1834–71* (London, Wellcome Historical Medical Library, 1967), p. 590.

39 Webster, *Health services since the war*, vol. 1, p. 10.

40 Jones, *Mental health and social policy*, p. 149.

41 Webster, *Health services since the war*, vol. 1, pp. 22–4 and p. 265.

42 R. Klein, 'The state and the profession: the politics of the double bed', *British Medical Journal*, 301 (1990) 700–2, at p. 700 (3 October).

43 Honigsbaum, *Division in British medicine*, pp. 9–21, where the connection with the Liberal government's insurance reforms is stressed.

44 The areas of specialist care which were beyond the referral system – notably dental and optical care – turned out to be among the most difficult in which to practice rationing in a politically uncontentious way: famously, the occasion for the resignation of Aneurin Bevan and Harold Wilson from the Attlee Cabinet in 1951 was a dispute about the imposition of charges for dental and opthalmic services: there is an authoritative account in Webster, *Health services since the war*, vol. 1, pp. 157–78.

45 The prescribing system meant that access to free or subsidised drugs was like-wise at the GP's discretion.

46 The emergence of a democratic Federal Republic within the western sphere is a central research question in post-war German history. It is discussed, in partic-ular, in H.-P. Schwarz, *Vom Reich zur Bundesrepublik* (Stuttgart, Klett-Cotta, 2nd edition, 1980) – which contains a bibiographical essay, pp. xxi–xxiv, discussing the historiography of the period, and which raises the character of the transi-tion to Western-style democracy as a key research question, pp. 1–10.

47 Among the studies in this mode: V. Berghahn, *The Americanization of West German industry, 1945–73* (New York, Berg, 1986); M. Moran, 'The state and the reform of the securities industry in Germany', in S. Bulmer (ed.), *The chang-ing agenda of West German politics* (Aldershot, Gower, 1989), pp. 110–27; J. Diefendorf, A. Frohn and H.-J. Rupieper (eds), *American policy and the reconstruc-tion of West Germany* (Cambridge, Cambridge University Press, 1993).

48 Skowronek, *Building a new American state*, p. 285.

49 D. Zöllner, 'Germany', in H. Köhler, H. Zacher and M. Partington, *The Evolution of social insurance 1881–1981* (London, Pinter, 1982), pp. 1–92 (at p. 13).

50 F. Tennstedt, *Soziale Selbstverwaltung: Geschichte der Selbstverwaltung in der Krankenversicherung, Band 2* (Bonn, Verlag der Ortskrankenkassen, 1977), p. 35. Of course, as I show later, the effect of the reforms was greatly to expand the funds.

51 G. Ritter, *Social welfare in Germany and Britain*, trans. K. Traynor (New York, Berg, 1986), pp. 21–2.

52 For this I rely heavily on: G. Göckenjan, 'Verrechtlichung und Selbstverant-wortlichkeit in der Krankenversorgung', *Leviathan*, 9:1 (1981), 8–38; and 'Die Unbekannte Geschichte: Die Absicherung der Proletarischen Existenz als Ansatzpunkt Organiserte Arbeiterbewegung', in E. Hansen *et al.*, *Seit über einem Jahrhundert ... Verschütte Alternativen in der Sozialpolitik* (Düsseldorf, Bund Verlag, 1981), pp. 27–60.

53 Quoted, O. Pflanze, *Bismarck and the development of modern Germany: volume III, the period of fortification, 1880–1898* (Princeton NJ, Princeton University Press, 1990), p. 156. I have also relied on this source for my account of the general origins of the Bismarckian reforms.

54 Only on checking the source did I realise that this remark is a crib from Zöllner, 'Germany', in Kohler, *Evolution of social insurance*, p. 81 –'The history of social insurance in Germany is a history of its expansion'.

55 From Ritter, *Social Welfare in Germany and Britain*, p. 187.

56 B. Rosewitz and D. Webber, *Reformversuche und Reformblockaden im deutschen Gesundheitswesen* (Frankfurt, Campus Verlag, 1990), p. 15.

57 D. Stone, *The limits of professional power: national health care in the Federal Republic of Germany* (Chicago IL, University of Chicago Press, 1980), p. 41.

58 On this last, Tennstedt, *Soziale Selbstverwaltung*, pp. 50ff.

59 It is striking that in Eastern Europe after the fall of Communism in 1989 a similar pattern emerged: doctors favoured financing through insurance and wanted fee for service payment arrangements.

60 P. Rosenberg, 'The origin and development of compulsory health insurance in Germany', in D. Light and A. Schuller (eds), *Political values and health care: the German experience* (Cambridge, Mass., MIT Press, 1986), pp. 105–25, esp. at pp. 116–17.

61 H. Schadewaldt, *75 Jahre Hartmannbund: Ein Kapitel deutscher Sozialpolitik* (Bad Godesberg, Verband der Ärtzte Deutschlands, 1975), p. 163.

62 F. Schwartz and R. Busse, 'Germany', in C. Ham (ed.), *Health care reform: learning from international experience* (Buckingham, Open University Press, 1997), pp. 104–18, at p. 109.

63 The words in quotation are from M. Kater, 'Physicians in crisis at the end of the Weimar Republic', in P. Stachura (ed.), *Unemployment and the Great Depression in Weimar Germany* (London, Macmillan, 1986), pp. 49–77 (at p. 67), on which I have relied for this whole passage about Weimar.

64 This passage is based on: D. Webber, 'Krankheit, Geld und Politik: Zur Geschichte der Gesundheitsreformen in Deutschland', *Leviathan*, 16:2 (1988) 156–203, esp. pp. 171–5.

65 Tennstedt, *Soziale Selbstverwaltung*, pp. 212–14; and Webber, 'Krankheit, Geld und Politik', p. 177.

66 These passages rely on two sources: G. Göckenjan, 'Nicht länger Lohnsklaven und Pfenningskulis? Zur Entwicklung der Monopolstellung der niedergelassenan Ärzte', in H.-U. Deppe, H. Friedrich and R. Müller (eds), *Medizin und Gesellschaft*, Jahrbuch 1 (Frankfurt, Campus Verlag, 1987), pp. 9–36; and E. Hansen *et al.*, *Seit über einem Jahrhundert*, pp. 27–60.

67 Stone, *Limits of professional power*, pp. 39–40.

68 This account relies on: S. Leibfried and F. Tennstedt, 'Health-insurance policy and Berufsverbote in the Nazi takeover', in Light and Schuller (eds), *Political values and health care*, pp. 127–84; the figures quoted are on p. 174.

69 Leibfried and Tennstedt, 'Health-insurance policy', pp. 164–5. There is some difficulty in reconciling Nazi categories of 'non-Aryan' with 'Jewish', and this is also discussed in these pages.

70 H.-U. Deppe, 'Zum gesellschaftlichen Charakter der gesetzlichen Kranken-
   versicherung', in Deppe (ed.), *Vernachlässigte Gesundheit: Zum Verhältnis von
   Gesundheit, Staat, Gesellschaft in der Bundesrepublik Deutschland* (Cologne,
   Kiepenheuer and Witsch, 1980), pp. 85–138, at p. 101.
   The English translation quoted in the text is mine; the original text reads:

   > Damit hatte die Ärtzteschaft seit 1955 praktisch das Angebotsmonopol für
   > die ambulatne ärztliche Versorgung sowie dessen wirtschaftliche Kontrolle wieder
   > fest in eigener Hand. Sie konnte also ihre ökonomischen Interessen und ihre
   > politisches Hauptziel nach Freiberuflichkeit unter Aufsicht des Staates durchsetzen
   > und festigen.

71 This passage relies heavily on Tennstedt, *Soziale Selbstverwaltung*, pp. 227–61.
72 Deppe, 'Zum gesellschaftlichen Charakter der gesetzlichen Krankenversicherung', p. 99.
73 H.-U. Deppe, 'Zulassunssperre: Ärtze in den Fesseln der Standespolitik', in Deppe
   et al. (eds), *Medizin und Gesellschaft*, pp. 37–67, at p. 43.
74 Schadewaldt, *75 Jahre Hartmannbund*, pp. 146ff.
75 The remark about the removal of political components is virtually a direct
   quotation from Hansen *et al.*, *Seit über einem Jahrhundert*, p. 93.
76 Webber, 'Krankheit, Geld und Politik', p. 182.
77 This relies on Hansen *et al.*, *Seit über einem Jahrhundert*, pp. 86–96.
78 Webber emphasises the significance of the FDP connection for the subsequent
   history of reform: see D. Webber, 'Zur Geschichte der Gesundheitsreformen in
   Deutschland – II. Teil: Norbert Blüms Gesundheitsreform und die Lobby',
   Leviathan, 17:2 (1989), 263–300; and 'The politics of regulatory change in the
   German health sector', in K. Dyson (ed.), *The politics of German regulation*
   (Aldershot, Dartmouth, 1992), pp. 209–34, at p. 221.
79 Jacobs, 'Politics of America's supply state', pp. 144–5.
80 P. Starr, *The social transformation of American medicine* (New York, Basic Books,
   1982), pp. 30–59, 'Medicine in a democratic culture, 1760–1850' is authoritative on this. Readers of Starr will recognise the extent of my intellectual debt to
   his account. I also rely on S. Shryock, *Medicine in America: historical essays*
   (Baltimore MD, Johns Hopkins Press, 1966), esp. pp. 1–45.
81 There is a wonderfully perceptive account of the Thomsonians in Starr, *Social
   transformation of American medicine*, pp. 51–5; the slogan is quoted by
   Heidenheimer, 'Professional knowledge and state policy' p. 537.
82 On this domestic medicine and its eclipse, R. L. Caplan, 'The commodification of
   American health care', *Social Science and Medicine*, 28:11 (1989) 1139–48.
83 R. Stevens, *American medicine and the public interest* (New Haven CT, Yale
   University Press, 1971), p.60.
84 Starr, *Social transformation of American medicine*, p. 110.
85 For the spread of the German model, and the struggles it encountered, I rely on
   F. Rudolph, *The American college and university: a history* (New York, Alfred Knopf,
   1962), for instance pp. 99–100, 233–4, 268–75.
86 T. Bonner, *American doctors and German universities: a chapter in the history of
   international intellectual relations 1870–1914* (Lincoln NB, University of
   Nebraska Press, 1963), p.23.
87 Stevens, *American medicine and the public interest*, p. 46, has the details.

88 This relies on J. R. Hollingsworth, *A political economy of medicine: Great Britain and the United States* (Baltimore MD, Johns Hopkins Press, 1986), pp. 90–2.

89 That part of the story is told in E. Brown, *Rockefeller medicine men: medicine and capitalism in America* (Berkeley CA, University of California Press, 1979).

90 J. Morone, *The democratic wish: popular participation and the limits of American government* (New York, Basic Books, 1990), p. 254.

91 D. Rothman, 'A century of failure: class barriers to reform', in J. Morone and G. Belkin (eds), *The politics of health care reform: lessons from the past, prospects for the future* (Durham NC, Duke University Press, 1994), pp. 11–25 (at p. 11).

92 This is Mark Peterson's estimate: the Progressive proposals, 1912–17; Roosevelt's Committee on Economic Security, 1935; Truman's health insurance proposals in the latter half of the 1940s; proposals to provide cover for the elderly in the late 1950s and early 1960s; proposals in the 1970s stemming from both the Nixon and Carter Adminsitrations; and the Clinton proposals of the 1990s. This is from the version of Peterson's chapter, 'Congress in the 1990s: from iron triangles to policy networks', in Morone and Belkin (eds), *Politics of health care reform*, pp. 103–47, at p. 105.

93 R. Stevens, *In sickness and in wealth: American hospitals in the twentieth century* (New York, Basic Books, 1989), p. 102.

94 T. Skocpol, *Protecting soldiers and mothers: the political origins of social policy in the United States* (Cambridge, Mass., Belknap Press, 1992), pp. 194–204.

95 D. Hirshfield, *The lost reform: the campaign for compulsory health insurance in the United States from 1932 to 1943* (Cambridge, Mass., Harvard University Press, 1970), pp. 42–70.

96 Hirshfield, *The lost reform*, p. 38.

97 Stevens, *In sickness and in wealth*, p. 17. The remainder of this paragraph relies on Stevens' account.

98 Stevens, *In sickness and in wealth*, p. 52 and pp. 115–16.

99 Stevens, *In sickness and in wealth*, pp. 140–1.

100 The most important product of this was the report of the deliberations of a committee of experts on the problems of meeting the costs of medical care, reported in: *Medical care for the American people: the final report of the committee on the costs of medical care* (Chicago IL, University of Chicago Press, 1932).

101 Stevens, *In Sickness and in wealth*, ch. 7 on the genesis of Blue Cross; the figure is from p. 259.

102 D. Rothman, *Beginnings count: the technological imperative in American health care* (Oxford, Oxford University Press, 1997), p. 19 for the figures and pp. 18–21 for its class preferences.

103 The evolution of the views of the medical profession, especially in the 1930s, is described in R. Numbers, 'The third party: health insurance in America', in J. Leavitt and R. Numbers (eds), *Sickness and health in America: readings in the history of medicine and public health* (Madison, University of Wisconsin Press, 1985), pp. 233–47.

104 These details from R. Munts, *Bargaining for health: labor unions, health insurance and medical care* (Madison WI, University of Wisconsin Press, 1967), esp. pp. 12, 30 and 101.

105   Morone, *The democratic wish*, p. 259 for the quotation and p. 260 for the figure.
106   Quoted in S. Strickland, *Politics, science and dread disease: a short history of United States medical policy* (Cambridge, Mass., Harvard University Press, 1972), p. 213.
107   Strickland, *Politics, science and dread disease*, pp. 13ff, is very good on the origins of hysterical campaigns to combat particular dramatic diseases in the 1930s.
108   The impact of war on the role of the American state in funding medical research is discussed in more detail in Chapter 5.
109   The quotation is from Starr, *Social transformation of American medicine*, p. 369, from which this summary is also taken. For Medicare I rely on the standard political science study: T. Marmor, *The politics of Medicare* (London, Routledge, 1970).
110   Starr, *Social transformation of American medicine*, p. 370.
111   L. Jacobs, *The health of nations: public opinion and the making of American and British health policy* (Ithaca NY, Cornell University Press, 1993), pp. 85–107.
112   K. Levit, C. Cowan, H. Lazenby, P. McDonnell, A. Sensenig, J. Stiller, D. Won, 'National health spending trends, 1960–93', *Health Affairs*, 13:5 (1994) 14–31, at p. 25.
113   Initially regulatory responsibility was divided; the HCFA was not itself established until 1977.
114   On the HCFA see D. Mechanic, 'Sources of countervailing power in American medicine', *Journal of Health Politics, Policy and Law*, 16:3 (1991) 485–98.
115   The standard detailed account of the passage is in Marmor, *Politics of Medicare*, pp. 42–78.
116   Stevens, *In sickness and in wealth*, p. 285.

3

Governing consumption

Consumption and commodification

To govern is to control – or at least to attempt the task. In the last generation the government of consumption in health care has been about the problem of control. At the root of this preoccupation lies a key feature of the modern consumption of health care: it is predominantly collective in character. The direct purchase of health care by individual patients from their own pockets accounts for only a minor proportion of what is consumed. Consumption is collectivised through third-party payment systems. It could hardly be otherwise; the cost of modern health care means that only the super-rich could contemplate its purchase off the shelf as a normal commercial service. Only by pooling risks, and the assumption by a third party of an obligation both to cover costs and to regulate the conditions of consumption, can the mass of patients get access to most health care services.[1] This makes third-party payers central to the control of consumption, and in turn explains why government is important. In some cases government is itself the third-party payer: that is true in Britain, where most health care is funded from general taxation. Even in the US the public sector now pays for more than 40 per cent of the cost of care.[2] In other cases government is the regulator of third-party payers and simply cannot separate itself from the issues of control that they face: that, in a nutshell, is the situation in Germany's statutory health insurance system. But even when, as is the case in the US, a large part of consumption is collectivised by risk pooling in the commercial insurance market, government is not absolved of responsibility for control. On the contrary: as we shall see the growth of public regulation of consumption is one of the most distinctive features of the consumption regime in the US over the last generation.

The extent to which consumption has been collectivised varies: it varies across different parts of national health care systems; it varies by social group; it varies between nations. But even the nation where the market remains most powerful, the US, has seen a sharp decline in the last generation in direct out-of-pocket payments by patients: between 1960 and 1993 the contribution of this source of revenue fell from 56 per cent to 20 per cent.[3] The rise of collective consumption is central to the politics of consumption because it provides the two key issues on which consumption struggles have turned in the health care arena: what should be the boundaries of collectivisation; and on what principles should collectivisation be organised? No health care system has fully collectivised payment. The struggle over the boundaries of collectivisation is important because, while only a minor proportion of the total cost of care falls on the individual patient, to the extent that it does so fall the burden on the third-party payer is lightened. There is thus a direct conflict of interest, and it emerges sharply in all three systems examined in these pages. The existence of that direct conflict of interest in turn helps makes sense of a distinctive feature of the language used to debate health care policy. That language has been strongly shaped by theories of consumer moral hazard – by the notion that consumers, faced with a free good, will consume it irresponsibly. Thus, out-of-pocket contributions – co-payments, in the jargon – are commonly resorted to not only to shift costs but in the belief that they restrain consumption. The shape of health care consumption also means that issues to do with the boundaries of collectivisation greatly test solidarity as a principle of collectivisation. The case of the US makes the point. In the US, the most expensive 1 per cent of the population accounts for 30 per cent of all health care spending; the least expensive 50 per cent accounts for only 3 per cent. The rewards of risk selection – if the least expensive can exclude the risky and expensive sick – are huge; the temptations to reject solidarity correspondingly great.[4]

Intersecting with the issue of the collectivisation of consumption is therefore a second point of struggle, concerning the principles of collectivisation. Granted that collectivisation is inevitable, how should it be organised? At the heart of this lies a struggle about the extent to which consumption should be *decommodified*.[5] The general character of decommodification has been described thus by Esping-Andersen: 'De-commodification occurs when a service is rendered as a matter of right.' Its significance therefore is that it can 'emancipate individuals from market dependence'.[6]

It is easy to see that commodification and decommodification are best talked about in the language of a continuum. At one end are goods widely treated as pure commercial commodities. Consider the large market in patent medicines bought over the counter from the pocket or purse of individual citizens in most industrial countries, in exactly the same way as most goods and services are exchanged in a market economy. (The example is particularly pertinent. There is an international movement to deregulate controls over many drugs formerly issued on prescription, precisely to turn them into pure commodities purchased over the counter for full price.[7]) At the other end of the continuum picture health care goods and services where access is entirely a right of citizenship independent of market location or contribution history. All the health care systems examined here contain instances where this latter principle is applied, and in some cases it is their dominant organising principle. Thus, in the British case, access to the services of a GP is available as a right to every member of the community. (Note, though, that the actual services to be rendered are at the professional discretion of the GP.) Beyond this particular British case, we encounter complex mixes. In the German insurance case, for instance, although the everyday experience of most citizens is of precisely the sort of decommodified entitlement which marks Britain, the creation of those rights, through the system of compulsory insurance linked to the work-place, is shaped partly by market forces through its connection to the system of occupational stratification. In the American case, there are even closer connections with commodification. The collective organisation of American health care, beyond provision for the old, is now dominated by the private insurance industry: just about 70 per cent of the population not old enough to be covered by Medicare have some private health insurance cover.[8] Even private insurance, however, is not identical with thoroughgoing commodification. Much depends on the terms under which insurance cover is bought. Since the vast bulk of private health insurance is bought by employers for workers as part of the employment benefit package, the extent of commodification for the individual worker depends on the terms of the package: how far access is affected, for instance, by rules governing deductibles, co-payment and personal financial or health circumstances. Regulation may likewise modify the link with the market: the most obvious instance is where regulation insists on community rating, thus obliging companies to charge the same premiums, and offer the same benefits, to all members of a defined community, independent again of their financial circumstances or health record. Thus, although the involvement of private insurance connects consumption closely to market location, it is by no means the same as complete commodification; much depends on the regulatory framework and the nature of the link between insurance and the labour market.

The collective character of consumption has consequences, therefore, for the kinds of issues around which consumption struggles turn. But it has also consequences for the way those struggles are conducted. Collectivisation means that particular kinds of organisations dominate the consumption process, and the struggles that take place have these organisations at their centre. The kinds of institutions that are important depend heavily on the way collectivisation is organised. To take an obvious example from the UK: the commercial insurance companies, which had been important political actors in the health insurance system established by the Liberal reforms before the First World War, were almost completely marginalised by the kind of consumption regime established by the post-war NHS. The conclusion is

obvious, but of great importance in what follows: making sense of the government of consumption has to start by making sense of the organisational world
within which consumption takes place. That lies at the heart of what follows.

The United Kingdom: consumption and the limits of citizenship

The foundation of the NHS in 1948 was an important episode in the extension
of the rights of social citizenship in the UK. It established a formally generous
set of entitlements: Britain's health service became, in the words of Klein, 'the
first health system in any Western society to offer free medical care to the
entire population'.[9] It may thus be said to have offered a consumption regime
based on the principles of citizenship. The language of citizenship is nowhere
mentioned in the establishing legislation, but when Marshall gave his famous
lecture on citizenship one year after the foundation of the service, he plainly
was thinking of the NHS in characterising social citizenship as a set of equal
entitlements for all citizens to a 'guaranteed minimum' of service.[10]

Marshall's phrase exactly catches the double edge of the entitlements
offered by the NHS: the 'guarantee' catches the historic generosity of Bevan's
reforms; 'minimum' catches what is less often declared – that the guarantees
were tightly circumscribed, and that the history of the NHS combined formal
generosity with tight control over the actual consumption of services. The
early years of the Service were accompanied by anguish about its unexpected
expense, but when reasonably reliable statistics of comparison were finally
compiled they actually showed the UK to be a low spender by the standards of
most advanced industrial nations.[11] A uniquely generous entitlement philoso-
phy went with parsimonious practice. The reasons for this juxtaposition of an
apparently open-ended consumption commitment with tight budgeting lie in
both the way the entitlement regime was actually expressed, and in the institutional means by which it was put into effect. The tension between formal
generosity and the reality of tight control lies at the heart of the politics of
consumption in the UK.

The distinctiveness of the UK entitlement regime has been well put by
White. In discussing the UK he draws a contrast between *insurance for care* and
access to a system of care. In the former, insurance creates entitlements to identifiable services, and 'the insurer pays for services that are bought from
competing hospitals, physicians and other suppliers'. The UK, by contrast,
created an entitlement to access. The British system 'said in essence "Your
taxes have built an organization to provide you with care. That organization
will serve you to the best of its ability".'[12] Taxes built the NHS; the entitlement
amounted to a claim to the treatment that the service could afford to provide
out of its share of tax take. One of the few absolute rights was to register with,
and consult, a provider of primary care, usually a GP. This arrangement
created great tensions, between the reality of a highly parsimonious system

and the formal generosity of one based on citizenship rights. The political history of consumption is about how those tensions were managed – and, as we shall see, how the system of management broke down.

From the very foundation of the NHS there was both a high politics and a low politics of management, though they intersected: the high politics often involved furious debates, organised around the party battle, about the level of resources to be allocated to health care, and about the status of some of the entitlements offered; the low politics was a politics of routine and discretion through which resources were in practice allocated. The workings of this low politics underpinned the high politics; and the moments of great change in the system – such as the review in the late 1980s which led to the major reforms of the 1990s – mark moments when the low politics of routine and discretion broke down.

The most important matter at issue in the high politics of health care for most of the post-war years was the sort of service taxes would provide – in other words, what the total funding of the service should be. That was an issue in the domain of high politics precisely because health care was funded by taxation – a striking contrast, we shall see, with conditions in Germany. The story of this high politics has been well documented in histories of the early years of the NHS. Initial expectations about the level of demand for the new service turned out to be underestimates, especially as far as demand for some forms of primary care were concerned. The reason this impinged on high politics was due to a structural feature of the service which was to condition the whole history of high politics in health care until the 1990s: although the central state soon devised ways of constraining the consumption of resources by the hospital sector (for instance, control over establishment, over capital spending), it managed no similar feat with the providers of primary care. The origins of the problem lay in the historical bargain which had brought the service into existence. The critical providers of primary care (GPs, dentists, opticians) were at 'arms length' from the service: not employees, but independent professionals contracted to provide care. The resources required of the Service depended on what level of demand they accommodated. It is extraordinary to reflect that, in the first decade of the NHS's life, the share of GDP it consumed actually fell (from 3.75 per cent to 3.01 per cent).[13] Those figures are in some degree a measure of the successful relegation of the problem of resource allocation to the domain of low politics and routinisation – a relegation that in some degree was the result of early painful lessons about just how explosive health service resource allocation could be if it entered high politics.

As far as primary care was concerned, government was obliged to try to manipulate the level of demand – the very task which, given the symbolic representation of the NHS as providing free care as a right of citizenship, proved to be politically explosive. The first explosive intrusion into high politics was enough to demonstrate just how disturbing the politics of health care consumption could be: in 1951 the decision by the Labour Cabinet (after fierce infighting) to support its Chancellor in imposing charges for some dental and optical services led to the resignation of two Cabinet ministers, including the architect of the NHS, Aneurin Bevan, and contributed to the collapse of Mr Attlee's Labour government.[14] The explosive nature of the NHS in high politics was well understood by the Conservative government that replaced Labour in 1951: in its first months in office it gradually whittled away proposals to impose charges and economies on the NHS.[15] The history of attempts to use the price mechanism to restrain consumption of pharmaceuticals shows the circumstances within which politicians were trapped. Over the post-war years periodic public spending problems caused the imposition of prescription charges, but the political sensitivities of charging 'vulnerable' groups (like the chronically sick, the old, the very poor) forced the concession of exemption clauses: by the 1990s 50 per cent of the population were exempt from charges, and 80 per cent of consumption was from exempted prescriptions.[16]

The immensely troublesome problem of matching the rhetorical promise of a National Health Service founded on citizenship entitlements to the reality of a service constrained by what could be extracted from the taxation system explains the key feature of the politics of consumption in health care for the post-war period: the way the important allocation decisions were pushed into the sphere of low, routine politics. The gap between rhetoric and reality created a need to ration resources. The task of doing this rationing was too explosive for open, democratic politics.

What did pushing the rationing problem to the domain of low politics entail? As far as the primary-care sector was concerned the key actor was the GP. The historical development of the system of medicine had, in the GP system, endowed the NHS with a powerful mechanism for routinising rationing. In one sense the GP was a problem: as we have seen, the status of the GP as an independently contracted professional meant that the NHS constantly encountered difficulties because of the resource commitments arising from the clinical decisions made by the GP. But the status of the GP was not only a problem; it was also an opportunity to routinise resource allocation. The GP system presented this opportunity for both historical and cultural reasons. As we saw in Chapter 2, the historical development of British medicine created what was, by international standards, an unusual separation between primary care and hospital care. The single most important consequence was the way it established the GP as a gatekeeper regulating health care consumption, for the GP was in the majority of instances both the first port of call for the citizen to the NHS and the authoritative figure who decided whether that first port of call should be the only one, or whether the patient should be referred further.[17] The *consumption* implications of this gate-keeping role became more significant over the post-war years, as medicine became more technologically sophisticated and expensive. For the most part, this world of expensive, technologically driven medicine was in Britain located in the hospital. Hence the referral decisions were a key part of the process of governing consumption.

This institutional mechanism was reinforced by a cultural characteristic of GPs as a group. They not only controlled the gate to expensive consumption in the hospital; they used remarkably little high technology in their own surgeries. For most of the post-war years the primary-care system was dominated by solo practitioners or by practices with very small numbers of partners. Solo practitioners in particular practised low technology medicine: the typical GP's surgery contained little that was more technologically sophisticated than a blood pressure measuring machine.[18] Thus not only did the routinisation of consumption decisions use the GP as a gatekeeper, it also directed the patient in the first instance to a low-tech, inexpensive, area of health care.

But the routinisation of the government of consumption was not confined to the GP's surgery. It extended into the hospital sector, where the most expensive consumption decisions were taken. It was here that Klein's 'politics of the double bed' came into its own. The domain of clinical decision making in the hospital was assigned to the doctor, especially to the consultant. Decisions about scarce resource allocation – decisions that in different circumstances could be politically explosive rationing choices – thus appeared to be the result of clinical judgement. Aaron and Schwartz's study of the allocation of hospital resources describes in helpfully concrete terms what typically happened, using the example of dialysis:

> By various means, physicians and other health care providers try to make the denial of care seem routine or optimal. Confronted by a person older than the prevailing unofficial age of cutoff for dialysis, the British GP tells the victim of chronic renal failure or his family that nothing can be done except to make the patient as comfortable as possible in the time remaining. The British nephrologist tells the family of a patient who is difficult to handle that dialysis would be painful and burdensome and that the patient would be more comfortable without it; or he tells the resident alien from a poor country that he should return home, to be among family and friends who speak the same language – where, as it happens, the patient will die because dialysis is unavailable.[19]

Here was the basis for the routinisation of rationing. Resources passed to those who controlled the hospital sector, which in effect meant the consultants; and the consultants also made the key allocations governing consumption. This process had various effects on the government of consumption, overt and covert. The covert effect was to 'depoliticise' rationing – in other words, to relegate it to the level of daily clinical decisions by doctors.[20] It literally put the power of life and death into the hands of the medical community. The more overt effect was to prove one of the key points of tension in the whole arrangement – arguably the point where the mechanism for governing consumption created after 1948 finally proved untenable. Rationing by consultants led to a highly visible sign of resource scarcity: waiting lists.

As we saw in Chapter 2, the NHS was a variant of a command and control health care system. It raised and allocated resources by centralised administrative means and was largely insensitive to market mechanisms as a way of allocating those resources. In such systems the rigidities of command and control allocation can produce a number of adaptations: corruption and black markets, for instance, both of which seem to have been unimportant in the NHS; and queuing, which was very important indeed. The history of waiting lists in the NHS is contentious and difficult. There has long been argument about the exact meaning of the very long queues, especially for elective surgery. In particular, there is argument about how far the lists have been manipulated by the medical profession in its struggle for resources. But the reality of the lists, and the reality of waiting, is not in question. The connection between the routinisation of rationing and the exercise of clinical power has been well summarised by Salter in his account of what we know about how the waiting-list system operated when clinical authority was still secure:

> Waiting lists are a temporal extension to the private professional world of the clinician. Traditionally they have been regarded as purely medical territory which others enter at their peril. It is instructive to explore how they work since it is this long-established practice which is at the heart of the profession's power to control demand. Taking surgery as an example, each surgeon has a waiting list composed of two sequential queues for out-patient consultations and in-patient treatment. Each queue has a fast and a slow stream (urgent and non-urgent patients). In theory, the admission to each queue and the designation as urgent or non-urgent within each queue are decisions made by the surgeon on the basis of his/her clinical judgement. In practice, the waiting list is used to structure and manipulate patient demand to satisfy numerous non-clinical criteria – including the criterion of available resources.[21]

The government of consumption for the first forty years of the life of the NHS might therefore be summarised as being heavily dependent on two mechanisms: gatekeeping in the surgery of GPs, and queuing in the hospitals.[22] With the benefit of hindsight it is now possible to see – especially in view of the fate of the other command and control health systems examined by Saltman and von Otter – that this state of affairs could only be sustainable under very particular conditions.[23] Three should be highlighted, since they were the very ones which were eroded as time passed: they relate to medical technology, to the outlook of patients, and to the separation of high and low politics.

The first condition was a stable system of medical technology. In fact, over the post-war years the pace of technological change in medicine continued unabated. That had important destabilising effects. The expanded treatment possibilities created by medical technology were a source of intensified demand on the NHS; in other words, they made more problematic over time the workings of the twin mechanisms of gatekeeping and queuing. Even to list only some of the best-known technological developments is to see the scale of destabilisation: heart by-pass procedures, organ transplants, joint replacements – all became available and, just as important, knowledge of their availability became widespread. The direction of technological advance also helped erode one of the crucial control mechanisms in the system – the way the GP's surgery was a gateway barring access to high-technology medicine. One of the effects of technological advances in surgery, for example, produced innovations in 'cold' surgery that made it possible to perform elective procedures using day surgery without hospitalisation.[24]

To the technological condition for the successful maintenance of the NHS's consumption regime we should add a cultural condition: it demanded deferential patients/citizens, especially deference in the face of medical authority. Since there was a constant gap between demand and supply, and since alternative mechanisms like markets or corruption could not bridge the gap, the system could only be stable if patients were prepared to accept without dissent what doctors decided they were entitled to. Although it is difficult to assemble reliable longitudinal evidence about either patient attitudes or behaviour, all the circumstantial evidence points towards change in this state of affairs. One of the most important pieces of circumstantial evidence concerns the relationship between the health care system and women. Women are disproportionately important as patients in their own right, notably because of the very special experience of childbirth; but they are also disproportionately significant because they play a more important role than men within families as carers, for the young and for the old. It requires only a few moment's observation to see that the women whose consumption demands were being 'managed' in the NHS at the end of the 1940s were very different from the women of a generation later when the major reforms of the service began to gestate. Two very obvious changes are noticeable: there was a great rise in the formal educational attainments of women, and therefore we can be fairly certain in their sense of competence in dealing with professionals like doctors; and there was a sharp rise in the proportion of women in paid employment, including increases in the proportions employed in white-collar and professional occupations.[25] The picture we can assemble, in other words, is of male doctors being confronted by increasingly well-educated women patients whose range of experience was being widened well beyond the home; and, in some celebrated cases, notably involving childbirth, of confrontation intensified by challenges to male professional hierarchies by women physicians.[26]

A more direct piece of evidence about the changing role of the patient in the government of consumption is provided by evidence about patient organisation. In part patients were acquiescent and deferential because they were not organised. By contrast, the health care system they encountered was dominated by professions with a powerful sense of continuing identity, and that sense was embodied in professional organisations that were, among other things, the dominant pressure groups in the making of health care policy. One of the most striking institutional changes in the NHS is the way this imbalance has been partially redressed by the spread of patient organisations, characteristically disease related, in recent years. Wood's pathbreaking work on patient organisation makes this clear: in his national survery of patient associations, 88 per cent had been founded after 1960.[27]

In short, the picture we assemble here suggests the passing away of the second important condition for the effective functioning of the sort of consumption regime practised from the foundation of the NHS: an acquiescent and deferential population of patients.[28]

The third condition, although procedural rather than substantive, was the very cornerstone of the whole consumption regime: the routinisation of rationing decisions depended on a consensus between government and the medical profession about the proper boundaries between high and low politics. This consensus was what helped create the original 'politics of the double bed', in Klein's graphic phrase: the state was 'dependent on the medical profession to run the NHS and to cope with the problems of rationing scarce resources in patient care'.[29] But the cornerstone – the one part of any structure that needs to be rock solid – was inherently unstable. Government could relegate particular rationing decisions to low politics; but that could never silence the wider argument about the resourcing of the NHS, especially in conditions of continuing technological change and declining deference. One route taken incessantly by governments involved the search for the philosopher's stone of increased efficiency through managerial reorganisation – an obvious route since it seemed to hold the promise of squeezing more health care out of existing resources. In part, the history of reorganisation is another version of the effort to shift delicate rationing decisions away from the centre, as in the various cycles of decentralisation in the NHS.[30] An even more important part of this history involved increasing efforts to 'manage' the service in the search for more efficiency. But these efforts threatened, or even damaged, the barriers between high and low politics. Management reforms in 1974 introduced 'consensus management', a practice that retained a clinical veto in decisions but institutionalised consultation between clinicians and other parties, such as professional administrators. Nearly a decade later consensus management was dismissed as institutionalised stagnation by Roy Griffiths in his NHS Management Inquiry, an inquiry which led to the establishment of a cadre of professional managers with executive authority.[31] By the late 1980s the search for efficiency, in the words of Harrison and his colleagues, had produced 'a battery of centre-driven, top-down initiatives and controls, including a regional review system, performance indicators, policy scrutinies, cost improvement programmes, competitive tendering, and changes in management structures and processes'.[32] The list shows just how far the occupants of Klein's 'double bed' now disagreed about who should lie where.

This was the background to the major institutional changes which fundamentally altered the consumption regime in the NHS in the early 1990s. These changes are associated with the reforms originally outlined in the White Paper *Working for Patients* in 1989,[33] and usually summarised as involving the introduction of an 'internal market' into the service. In fact, three sets of linked changes should be highlighted: the wider use of market mechanisms; the alteration in the power and significance of important gatekeepers; and the shift towards a more explicit rationing regime.

The consumption regime established after the foundation of the NHS allowed markets only an insignificant role. Charging patients directly was, we have seen, heavily constrained by political sensitivities. Although there has been a long-term growth in the numbers covered by private health insurance, this insurance was normally only used to supplement the care offered by the NHS, especially to allow quick (and conveniently timed) access to elective surgery. And while by the late 1980s some competitive tendering and market testing was going on, this was concentrated on non-clinical services such as cleaning. That was to alter in a number of ways. The most obvious was the introduction of an internal market between key institutions of the NHS itself: a separation of purchaser and provider designed to make explicit the terms on which health care was allocated. There also occurred an extension of what had for most of the history of the service been marginal: the use of market forces (charges) directly to govern the consumption decisions of individual citizens. There were many signs of this, but perhaps the most important were in areas of primary care which had been among the most difficult to control over the post-war history of the service because they were not passed through the traditional gatekeeping process, dental care and optical care.[34] That development made more significant still the long-term growth in numbers covered by private health insurance. Perhaps more important than the sheer growth in numbers was the way insurance cover was concentrated among those in professional and managerial jobs, and in the south east: between 1982 and 1987, for instance, private insurance coverage of manual workers showed no advance at all, while the numbers of managers/employers insured recorded an increase of 21 per cent.[35] These developments greatly altered the government of consumption from the principles of equal, minimal entitlements established by the NHS. Mohan summarised the change thus:

> There is an emergent spatial division of welfare here: the distribution of employer-paid benefits, such as medical insurance, is skewed between the north and south of the country. Access to such benefits depends increasingly on one's position within the division of labour, with key personnel within firms being able to avail themselves of a range of subsidies in the health, housing, educational

and transport fields ... The presence of large numbers of branch plants carrying out largely routine assembly tasks in the regional economies of Scotland, Wales and north-east England, may mean that few employees in such locations receive perks such as medical insurance as part of their salary package. In contrast executives, management and research and development staff in areas where most corporate headquarters are located, such as South East England, will be more likely to receive such fringe benefits.[36]

The developments summarised here – the introduction of the institutional internal market, the partial recommodification of dental and optical services, the spread of private health insurance – are thus all part of the first big change in the consumption regime identified earlier: the rising importance of market mechanisms in consumption.

A second key change – the relative importance of gatekeepers – was probably an unintended outcome of reform, or at least the magnitude of the change was much greater than originally envisaged. This change was associated with the introduction of GP fundholding. The precise institutional meaning of the fundholding system was that it created a category of GPs (who rapidly became the most numerous and the most innovative parts of the primary-care system) who controlled an independent budget for secondary care and who, within that budget, could provide or purchase a wider range of services for their patients than could the traditional GP. The wider significance of the innovation was that it hastened the transformation of the gatekeeping system in the NHS. These new fundholders were anything but the low-technology, low-innovation barriers to expensive health care typified by the old GP. They were able to use their fundholding resources to change the balance of power between the GP and the hospital system, since for the first time in the history of the NHS the primary care doctor was not now referring patients for the authoritative decision of the consultant in the hospital. More important still, the mechanics of the fundholding system encouraged fundholding GPs to expand the range of services they offered, and to exploit the new technologies which allow a range of elective surgical procedures, once only feasible in hospital, to be performed in surgeries. The development of fundholding teams offering an increasingly wide and complex range of services thus widened what was once a narrow 'gate' to the range of health care.[37] The return of a Labour government in May 1997 produced superficial institutional discontinuity but fundamental policy continuity. The GP fundholding system is a casualty of the new government's reform intentions. Its replacement – intended to be in place by the spring of 1999 – is a network of primary care groups.[38] The creation of the primary care groups is intended to do two things: to honour the rhetoric of the Labour Party's pre-election opposition to fundholding, while accommodating the powerful new interests created by the wide spread of the fundholding system.[39] Gatekeeping has been transformed and there is no reversing that transformation.

This account presents a fairly benign picture of how the system has responded to the decline of the original mechanisms governing consumption of health care. But not all the changes have been so benign. Perhaps the most difficult change is the third identified here, the altered significance of rationing mechanisms. As we have seen, the single most important feature of consumption politics under the old NHS was the way rationing decisions were pushed to the level of low politics – they were routinised as part of the continuing process of clinical decision making, notably by consultants in hospital. But both the long-term changes that broke down this system, and some of the responses to the change, like the introduction of the internal market, have forced the development of more open discussion of rationing. The rise of rationing as an issue encapsulates the tensions that now exist in the consumption regime in the UK. Half a century of technological, cultural and political change are inexorably forcing the issue of rationing into the open. Despite the formal ideology of universal citizenship which underpins the NHS there are great variations between health authorities in what treatments they are prepared to fund.[40] Yet few health authorities are willing to engage in open proscription of services in the language of rationing.[41] Nor is that surprising: managers have learnt that to attempt openly to deny treatment in the name of rationing is to raise a storm of popular argument, often orchestrated by the tabloid press.[42] The intrusion and manipulation of individually tragic cases into general election campaigns have frightened democratic politicians away from the rationing issue: it is reported that when Virginia Bottomley was Secretary of State for Health she even banned the very use of the word 'rationing'.[43] As the NHS enters into its second half-century of life, the rationing issue is the most graphic demonstration of the fragility of the consumption regime bequeathed by its founders.

Germany: consumption and the limits of corporatism

By the middle of the 1950s the fundamental features of the German health care consumption regime had been established. That regime involved all but the highest paid in compulsory health insurance, based on premiums levied equally on workers and employers. History and institutional structure combined to ensure that this consumption regime was firmly relegated to the sphere of low politics. The insurance institutions themselves were fragmented along a number of lines: there were funds based on local communities, on national occupations and on individual firms. The institutional fragmentation was made more extreme by the sheer number of funds, over 1,200 for most of the post-war period. This extreme fragmentation went with a requirement that each fund be both a self-governing institution and be an independent budgetary unit – in other words, charge such premiums as were required, given the demands made by members, to balance its books. These requirements were important in pushing consumption to the level of low politics, because they converted issues about the range of benefits and the charges to be levied into the separate decision-making systems of over 1,200 funds.[44]

A highly routinised consumption regime was also integrated into the system of occupational stratification. This made the regime more routinised still by transforming issues about contributions and benefits into outcomes produced by the division of labour. The fragmented system corresponded to the wider occupational hierarchies in society. The part of the population allowed to make its own private insurance arrangements, and thus exempted from the statutory system, was the elite of the highest paid. Key privileged groups, notably established civil servants, had their own nationally organised funds offering, in general, a wider range of benefits than those available to manual workers.[45] The history of the funds also contributed to this process of routinisation. The Nazis had destroyed the culture of social democratic activism that had historically characterised many of the funds. Those that emerged after the war, though formally democratic institutions controlled by their members, were in reality for the main part under the control of bureaucratic oligarchies.[46]

The most obvious political consequence of these arrangements was to marginalise the state, notably the central state, in the government of consumption. By contrast with Britain, 'high politics' had nothing to do with resource raising and only touched in a tangential way on the state's responsibilities as the regulator of the system. That marginalisation was accentuated by the character of the state that emerged in West Germany after the Second World War. Authority was widely dispersed, key roles in health care being reserved for the governments of the individual *Länder*.[47] Perhaps more important still, the reaction against the Nazi dictatorship led to an especially strong emphasis on the character of the Federal Republic as a *Rechtstaat*, one where state authority was circumscribed by a written constitution and the courts. In practice, this 'juridified' a whole range of policy issues, giving the courts a key role in deciding the boundaries of policy, and shifting issues outside the domain of partisan politics.[48]

These patterns, mostly established (or re-established) in the first five years of the life of the new *Bundesrepublik* after 1949, shaped the early history of the government of consumption. By the late 1990s, however, that original consumption regime had been altered in key ways. Understanding that alteration is central to understanding consumption politics in Germany; and a start to understanding obviously has to start with a sketch of the changes that occurred.

There are three major alterations which are noticeable when we compare the late 1990s with the mid-1950s. The first lies in the structure of the system. While the basic outlines of the insurance funds remain the same, there has been considerable consolidation: in 1949 there were over 1,800 funds; by

1993 that figure was down to about 1,200; since then, it has fallen to around 700, with most of the fall occurring through mergers between *Ortskran-kenkassen* (district sickness funds).[49] At the same time, one of the key principles, that each fund should be an independent budgetary unit, has been breached by the development of arrangements for cross-subsidisation between funds.[50] That change in turn is allied to an even more important institutional development, which might be summed up as a sharp increase in the degree to which the insurance system is centralised. There are many signs of this, but easily the most important is the extent to which the federal government has increasingly intervened, and has developed some of the tools to intervene, in steering the consumption system: in Döhler's striking phrase it has assumed a role as 'the architect of political order' in governing health care consumption.[51]

The growing significance of state, especially central state, intervention in turn flags a second major change in the character of consumption politics. A generation ago many consumption issues were relegated to the domain of low politics, within the routinised, bureaucratic world of the separate insurance funds. In the 1990s, although the state still largely stands aside from direct financing, consumption issues are part of the stuff of high politics. A simple but telling indicator of that is the fact that within the last decade there have been two major attempts (in 1989 and 1993) to reform the health care system, and even after the second of these reform remains a major preoccupation of the federal government.

That move in turn is connected to the changing *content* of the consumption system: one of the most important alterations that has taken place in the consumption regime in the last generation is the end of a consensus about the content of the rules governing consumption. The most obvious way in which this has manifested itself is in the rise of co-payments imposed on patients, a virtually continuous trend since 1977.[52]

There have thus been long-term changes of three linked kinds in the German health care consumption regime: the basic institutional structure of the system has become more centralised; the key consumption issues, once decided in a routine and dispersed way, are now part of the high politics of the Federal Republic; and there is a drift from a system where most services were provided free of charge to one where co-payments by patients have spread. In explaining this shift we need to take account of a range of factors: the changing shape of health care consumption itself over the last generation; the kind of link that exists in the German system between consumption and funding; and the economic and political environments in which health care institutions are embedded.

The most obvious (though, as we shall see, not in the end the most revealing) place to begin is with the 'headline' rate of health care consumption. If in Britain the most commonly highlighted headline figure in health care is some measure of aggregate national consumption, in Germany it is the contribution rate levied in the insurance system. When the compulsory insurance system was re-established at the foundation of the Federal Republic, the contribution rate was around 6 per cent, about the same level as that of the mid-1920s; by the mid 1970s, when pressure for change first became significant, it was over 10 per cent; a decade later it exceeded 12 per cent.[53] By 1998 it was 13.5 per cent.[54]

As this litany shows, the upward trend can be made to look inexorable and threatening. But in truth the focus on the headline rate is not especially revealing because it misleads about the post-war experience of German health care consumption. It is certainly true that health care costs, and consumption, have risen markedly over the last generation. That is an experience Germany shares with the health care systems of all advanced industrial economies. Yet while the German experience has been more 'inflationary' than that of Britain, it has been less so than that of many others. This is symptomatic of a quite fundamental feature of both the health care system and the wider German welfare state: as a spender Germany is, in international terms, a consistently 'average' performer. An important common structural influence driving up health care consumption has been the growing wealth of nations. There is a powerful statistical relationship between standard measures of national wealth and national health spending. The relationship is entirely unsurprising: health care is a 'merit' good, consumption of which tends to rise with wealth. Growing wealth provides the means to accommodate increased demand. We should therefore expect nations that have been above-average economic performers over the post-war period, like Germany, to have a more inflationary health care spending history than nations with a below-average record of economic performance, like Britain.[55] The general expansionary force produced by increasing prosperity has then been mediated by various institutional and cultural factors. The result is that countries have experienced upward movement to different degrees. Thus in any scatter diagram charting the correlation between wealth and health spending, countries are typically dotted around – some above, some below – the trend line. The most striking feature of the comparative analyses of the German experience has been their revelation that the country's experience has been 'average': in other words, Germany has usually been about on the trend line, indicating that its spending is just about what would be predicted given its growing prosperity. To put it a little crudely: health care consumption was accommodated by economic advance (in a way that it was not in, for instance, France and the US).[56] The persistence of this 'average' performance is remarkable: it can still be observed, for instance, in Alber's most recent comparative analysis of patterns of welfare spending in the European Union.[57]

An even more striking consideration in this argument is the German experience since the 1980s. Germany, like a range of other industrial nations, developed a variety of cost-containment mechanisms following the economic recession produced by the rise in oil prices in the mid-1970s. The result was that the German experience in the 1980s and early 1990s was actually one of successful cost containment: for instance, whereas the share of health expenditure had risen from 5.5 per cent of GDP in 1970 to 7.8 per cent five years later, the figure in 1990 was still only 8.1 per cent.[58] Yet it was precisely in the era of *successful* cost containment that efforts at reform accelerated. If cost inflation in health care was the driving force alone we might expect the most serious efforts at reform to coincide with the peak of health care cost inflation and to slacken as inflation abated. In short: forces other than the straightforward pressure to consume more health care must be at work refashioning the government of health care consumption in Germany.

One influence might be thought to be the mechanism by which resources are raised. The argument becomes obvious if we compare Germany with the UK. In the UK the resources for health care spending have to be squeezed out of the taxation system, and the cost of health care to the individual citizen is not transparent because it is bundled into the total package of taxation. In Germany, although the insurance system by no means pays for the total cost of care, that proportion produces a highly visible 'headline' figure which is deducted half from the paypacket of workers and half from the employers, and which is regularly alluded to in public debates about health care reform.[59] The key may thus lie, not in the size of the bill, but in its visibility.

There is no doubt that the 'headline' national insurance rate does provide part of the staple diet of argument about health care costs in Germany. It is less certain, however, that the insurance rate is for workers a highly visible source of discontent. Survey evidence suggests, for instance, that insurance fund members tend to have vague and incorrect information about contribution rates and entitlements. It also suggests that they accept that they will for most of their lives be net contributors to the funds – on the understanding, of course, that should sickness strike they can be net beneficiaries. An ideology of solidarity, rather than a calculus of financial advantage, seems to shape their beliefs.[60] It is thus difficult to see the mechanism by which resources are raised as a significant source of popular pressure to reform the consumption system. What is more, the sheer scale of health care employment means that not everyone by any means has an interest in dampening the growth of health care premiums. The huge health care workforce has a powerful interest in maintaining, indeed increasing, spending. The 4.2 million who owe their jobs either directly or indirectly to health care constitute a formidable constellation of interests with a stake in continuing investment in health: a study commissioned by the main corporatist forum in health care estimated that every 1 per cent increase in the insurance rate created an additional 35,000 jobs in the sector.[61]

If we are to identify the source of upheaval in the consumption regime we must therefore look beyond the consumers, and indeed beyond the producers of care. Insurance premiums are not only a levy on workers; they are also a levy on employers. Viewed thus, the rise in the political sensitivity of the insurance rate from the mid-1970s becomes more explicable. The economic upheaval of the mid-1970s was not only associated with the short-term impact of the rise in oil prices. It began a long period of structural change in the world economy, which had particularly serious effects on Germany as a leading industrial exporter. These changes included the rise of new sources of international competition, especially in Asia, a sharp increase in the global mobility of capital and, with the increasing pace of globalisation, major changes in the competitiveness of different economic locations. At a policy level this was reflected in an incessant pressure for the liberalisation of markets and the intensification of competition.

The period after the onset of these major structural changes in the world economy saw great debates in Germany: about the capacity of the German economy to adapt to new patterns of world trade and competition; about the adequacy, in a more globalised and liberalised world, of '*Modell Deutschland*', based as it was on a generous social security net below the market economy; and about the ability of the German economy to sustain these generous social welfare provisions.[62] Leaman, in his history of the post-war German economy, summarises the position in the immediate aftermath of the oil price rises at the mid-1970s:

> The West German economy was also subject to critical structural developments within the world economy, apart from cartellised oil supplies. The emergence of new developed economies in the Far East and to a lesser extent in South America coincided with rapidly improved world communications, far shorter lead-in times for industrial and commercial innovations and an increasing mobility of international capital, all of which demanded rapid and flexible responses from private competition as well as effective national and transnational political action. The combination of the Bretton Woods system of fixed exchange rates and liberal exchange controls could not survive the pressures of unequal national economic development or the anarchic behaviour of vast amounts of rogue capital.[63]

A major reason for the rising political salience of health care costs in the German case, therefore, was the way the financing system impacted directly on the cost structure of the business community. That feature was reinforced by another powerful influence: the growing structural instability of the insurance institutions themselves. The health consumption system was built on a foundation of inequality, since it was linked to the occupation system. But because of economic change that occupation system itself was not stable. Even before the great climacteric of the mid-1970s the German economy was experiencing the sort of structural changes familiar across a wide range of industrial nations. They were reshaping the occupation system, a process accelerated by the recession that brought an end to the long boom and produced the ensuing structural changes sketched above. Among the most important of these structural changes were the decline of the old manufacturing industries of the industrial revolution – the occupations that had been at the historical centre of the health insurance system in Germany. There was a corresponding expansion in white-collar and professional employment, and sharp changes in the geography of prosperity: the traditional industrial areas of the Federal Republic, such as the Ruhr, suffered disproportionately, and new areas of economic dynamism, especially in parts of Bavaria and Baden-Württemberg, experienced a new prosperity.[64]

One effect of these changes was to make more acute what had always been intrinsic to the system: the inequalities between different occupational groups. Since under the unreformed system insurance funds were independent budgetary units, their 'domestic economies' were very different: the taxation base was larger or smaller depending on the incomes of members; and their liabilities to pay for the care of members varied with the consumption demands made by those members, demands which were in part at least a function of the health risks and life chances of contributors. The result was to intensify class inequalities in the consumption system: by the end of the 1980s, on the eve of the first of the two most momentous attempts to reform the system, around a national average contribution rate of 12 per cent there existed a range stretching from 7.5 per cent to 16 per cent.[65] Some of the newly dynamic sectors of the economy were seeing the formation of firm-based sickness funds which were in practice engaged in risk selection, thus delivering attractively low rates to members.[66]

The origin of this problem was structural: it was rooted in the way the German health care consumption regime was bound to the division of labour and therefore tied to occupational inequality. But it was made worse by contingent circumstances, such as the world economic recession and restructuring after the mid-1970s. At the end of the 1980s another contingent event, German reunification, intensified the problem, and provided one of the main circumstances for changes in the system. The command and control health care economy of the defunct GDR was displaced by a modified version of the system in the *Bundesrepublik*. In particular, an attempt was made to replicate two key features of the West German system: compulsory insurance based on a payroll levy, and a system of health care delivery founded on the primacy of the private medical practitioner.

The wider economic outcome of reunification is well known: integration of the old GDR economy into that of West Germany proved disastrous for the chronically inefficient East German industries, especially heavy manufacturing industries employing large numbers of manual workers. The results were bankruptcy, closures and mass unemployment. In the health care sector, an attempt to replicate the contribution system on traditional West German lines would have led to the collapse of the consumption system, since the funds would have been unable to meet their obligations. In the immediate aftermath of reunification the federal government was obliged to depart from a cardinal principle of the West German system, in establishing a uniform contribution rate for all the separate funds in the new *Länder*.[67] The decision was significant for two reasons. For the first time, it recognised that embedding the insurance system in an unequal occupational hierarchy could not be reconciled with one of the key institutional features of the system since the original Bismarckian reforms: that each fund should be considered an independent budgetary unit. Second, it marked a considerable jump in central state intervention in the consumption system, and was to be a precedent for more extensive intervention in the 1990s.

The distinguishing feature of the consumption politics of the German system for most of the post-war period was a special kind of corporatism, which marginalised both the state, notably the central state, and the market. The stability of that system was undermined by economic change, by the political upheaval of reunification, and by incessant change within the health care system itself emanating, for instance, from technological innovation. The reforms begun in the wake of the passage of the Health Care Structure Act of 1993 (for shorthand, the Seehofer reforms, after the health minister responsible for the legislation) are significant because they mark a decisive turn towards both more market and more state. From 1996 a key feature of the compulsory system was abolished, with the introduction of free choice of sickness fund by members. The significance of the change lies less in the immediate substance of the rule than in the behaviour which it stimulates. It has greatly destabilised the historically established institutions. Freedom of choice has, not surprisingly, encouraged workers to move to funds charging lower premiums. The culture of solidarity which was for so long part of the bedrock of the system is thus being eroded. The biggest losers have been some of the district funds, historically the funds that in the old system of compulsion insured high risks, like the low paid, and because they insured high risks had to charge higher premiums. The biggest winners have been *Betriebskassen* (funds catering for workers in a single enterprise) which, practising *de facto* risk selection, offer lower premiums.[68] The movement of members in turn helps account for other institutional changes: the considerable recent merger movement between funds alluded to earlier, which has mostly involved the district funds; and changes in the internal management practices of funds as they seek to organise themselves on more 'business-like' lines to squeeze more efficiency out of the system. There is now increasing pressure from some of the funds for further liberalisation to allow individual funds more freedom in negotiating competitive contracts with providers.[69]

Of potentially even greater importance than these structural changes is the growing significance of the state as a regulator, a significance enhanced by the Seehofer reforms. The principle that each fund is an autonomous budgetary unit has been abandoned: the state now redistributes finances between funds, according to a formula determined by the sociodemographic characteristics of their members.[70] In his account of the reforms, Hinrichs summarises their consequences for the place of public authority in the German system. The reforms represent:

> the state's recovery of strategic capacities and autonomy against the priority of self-government in the health-care sector ... The immediate savings of the 1993 reform resulted from direct state intervention into self-government: Remuneration for most benefits was frozen at the 1991 level, and budgets could not be increased beyond the growth of the sickness funds' revenues until 1995. Providers, especially physicians, will face remuneration decreases if the volume of their services and prescriptions exceeds certain thresholds. Furthermore, the pharmaceutical industry was forced to lower some prices of prescription drugs and encountered more price competition. Excess hospital capacity (and inefficient hospitals) will be addressed more rigorously (by something resembling the United States' diagnosis-related groups). Patients' co-payments for dentures and prescription drugs were increased again.[71]

The reason for this sharp increase in the state's strategic capacities has been convincingly explained by Döhler as a breakthrough resulting from an accumulation of institutional change over a period of twenty years. One legacy of preceding reform attempts, despite their failures to control the growth in insurance premiums, was to endow the state with greater institutional capacities and to weaken the internal solidarity of some of the most powerful corporatist institutions, notably among providers.[72]

One of the most striking instances of the growth of state capacity is provided by the Concerted Action in Health Care, an institution established in 1977 as a corporatist forum for all the major interests. Through a kind of 'drip feed' contribution to the policy process, the Concerted Action has become an increasingly significant instrument of public authority. In part this is because of its role in negotiating indicative targets for the total resources to be allocated to health care; and in part through its machinery of expert advisers, whose reports have been increasingly central to the debates about the allocation of resources to health. This latter growth in public capacity to help shape debate is well illustrated by one of the most important initiatives taken in the wake of the 1993 reforms by the expert advisers to the Concerted Action. In commissioned reports on *Health Insurance 2000* they have raised the question of the rationing of health care – in particular, the possibility of replacing the presumption that every possible treatment is covered by membership of an insurance fund by adopting instead a 'basic' core of universally available services. This would be to adopt the 'basket of services' principle which is being canvassed in several different health care systems.[73] These ideas have led to a difficult debate – difficult because Germany's health care history under the Nazis means that any attempt at explicit discrimination in the allocation of health care resources arouses troubling historical memories. The problem is illustrated by one suggestion made by the expert commission, which was that some illnesses which patients might be presumed to have a capacity to prevent – the obvious instances are diseases linked to tobacco and alcohol consumption – could in some circumstances be excluded from any package of treatment entitlements. That suggestion has probably foundered, in part because of the argument that it represented a thin end of a wedge which might lead to the exclusion of those suffering from culturally stigmatised diseases, like Aids.[74]

The fatal flaw in the consumption regime established in the UK after 1948, we have seen, was that it relied on control mechanisms which were eroded by social change and technological innovation. But the German system was also vulnerable to change, since the corporatism on which it rested relied on creating a world of institutional privilege enclosing a range of powerful interests, among both providers and third-party payers. The critical question for corporatist arrangements is always how they can manage the consequences of 'closure' when the systems they attempt to enclose are embedded in societies that promote economic and social change through market competition and political competition: in short, how corporatism can survive the dynamism of capitalist democracy, with its continuous process of creative destruction, reshaping old interests and bringing new forces into existence. The history of reform in the German system between the middle of the 1970s and the early 1990s is a story of repeated attempts to adapt to change, and repeated failure to adapt successfully. But those experiences were not futile. They amounted to a long process of institution rebuilding and institutional learning, culminating in the breakthrough of the Seehofer reforms in 1993. That breakthrough decisively destabilised the consumption regime: greatly increased the role of the central state in controlling the financing of consumption; destroyed some of the cardinal principles of the insurance system; opened up the system to competition; and, for the first time, raised fundamental questions about the appropriate range of consumption entitlements in the German system.

The United States: from supply state to regulatory state

As we saw in Chapter 2, the historical legacy of American health care amounted to a supply state where an oligarchy of professionals and technology producers dominated. We left the American system in 1965 poised at a moment of great change. But change did not itself occur at the moment of reform in the mid-1960s. The battle for Medicare itself reflected the tension between the old and the new: as Marmor says, it was 'fought in public, but settled in private'.[75] The old government of consumption – a world dominated by the medical profession – was not initially disturbed by the new measures. In the legislation, neither the federal government, nor the governments of individual states, were endowed with any significant role in the government of consumption. The Medicare and Medicaid programmes, true, turned the federal government into a major third-party payer (by 1970 Medicare and Medicaid between them amounted to 19 per cent of all expenditures on personal health care); but it was a largely passive one.[76] The state had become a major funder of the current cost of the care, just as it already funded the infrastructure. The reforms did not displace the central role played by private finance in the consumption process. The largest part of the consumption process was not yet even collectivised: in 1970, fully five years after the reforms were signed into law, the portion of personal health care spending coming directly out of the pockets of consumers (not covered by third-party payment) was still 39 per cent.[77] There was, at the inauguration of the Medicare and Medicaid reforms, a truly mixed economy of consumption: much was paid without the direct intervention of third-party payers; the state was emerging as a significant third-party payer; and third-party payers in the private sector were a mixed bunch of institutions, both commercial insurers and non-profit insurance schemes.

We now know, with the benefit of hindsight, that this impression of continuity was misleading. The very arrangements needed to get the reforms past the old interests contained the seeds of transformation. In Jacobs' words:

> To protect against the charge that the government itself would regulate health care, policymakers decided to pay health providers on a 'reasonable cost basis'. Instead of imposing control over the expenditure of massive new sums of government money, they adopted permissive reimbursement arrangements that allowed providers to charge what they deemed reasonable.[78]

That arrangement turned out to have destructive inflationary consequences that would eventually force large-scale changes in the government of consumption. The reforms of the mid-1960s were not to produce a stable political settlement in health care. On the contrary: they started a generation of turmoil in health care politics. If we had to choose one phrase to summarise what that turmoil did to consumption, it would be to characterise it as the creation of a regulated regime of consumption.

The rise of regulation had several aspects. A consumption regime in which the single biggest block of transactions took the form of direct purchases 'out of pocket' by individual consumers was displaced by a regime where third-party payers dominated. In short, the process of collectivisation of consumption, already apparent by 1970, continued apace. The snapshot of 1970 offered above (when nearly two-fifths of all care was paid for out of pocket) conceals a remorseless trend: as I noted earlier, the figure in 1960 had been 56 per cent, and by the early 1990s was down to 20 per cent;[79] by 1996 it had fallen to 16.5 per cent.[80] Viewed over the long term, the process is unceasing: the individual as purchaser of health care is being replaced by institutional (third-party) purchasers. What is more, the changing character of third-party payment reinforced this process of collectivisation. Part consisted in the continuing growth in the role of the federal government as a financer of the cost of care: Medicare alone (the programme for the elderly), which accounted for 11.1 per cent of personal health expenditure in 1970, was by 1990 accounting for 18.6 per cent.[81] Meanwhile, private insurance coverage was mostly the product not of commercial contracts made between individual consumers and insurers, but of collective bargaining: in 1996, 75.9 per cent of all workers were covered by employment-based health insurance (only 2.9 per cent had an independent private insurance cover).[82] The private health insurance system is thus substantially shaped by the division of labour. The financing of consumption, in other words, is now dominated by big organisations, in either the private or the public sector.

Collectivisation helped produce another feature of the new regulated system: bureaucratisation. The world into which Medicare and Medicaid were born was for the most part a relatively simple world of cash disbursement: providers perfomed a service and delivered their bills for payment to individual patients or to insurers. These simple relationships were transformed by bureaucratisation over the next thirty years. The change has been aptly summarised by Morone:

> The emerging American health politics increasingly operates with the language, methodology, and mind-set of bureaucratic actors. Even highly politicized judgments are coded in dense, complex, technical constructions ... Examples include formula-driven rate-setting programs such as diagnosis-related groups ... New government agencies (in both the executive branch and Congress), the growth in private sector bureacrats (operating managed care plans), and federal sponsorship of medical outcomes research all extend the realm of bureaucratic politics.[83]

This passage also uncovers some other important signs of the shift to a regulatory regime. Whereas third-party payers had originally adopted a passive stance in meeting consumption costs, there has been a decisive shift to rate setting – a standard regulatory tool – in meeting the costs of consumption. The rise of managed care – the development by third-party payers of institutions such as health maintenance organisations – allows payers directly to control service delivery: by the mid-1990s nearly three-quarters of American workers with health insurance received coverage through some system of managed care.[84] While originally promoted to the Nixon administration as an alternative to regulation, managed care actually represents a shift to a more regulated, controlled world – a critical point for the traditional organisation of American medicine, as will become clear in our next chapter. Sparer summarises things well in his study of spread of managed care in the Medicaid programme:

although touted as privatization, Medicaid managed care actually increases the state's regulatory role. State Medicaid officials need to select health plans, determine capitation rates (and struggle with risk adjustment), supervise the marketing and erollment process, ensure quality of care, consider whether to adopt special programs to protect safety net providers during the transition to managed care, and so on.[85]

But perhaps the single biggest change in the consumption regime hinted at in the passage from Morone concerns the changing role of the American state. That alteration does not even primarily concern the state's rising importance as a third-party payer, significant though that is. From its role in the original 1965 reforms as a kind of cash cow for doctors to milk, the state has been transformed into a major force shaping the new regulated regime. The passage by Congress of measures of utilisation review and of capital investment regulation in the early 1970s (1972 and 1974) culminated in the Reagan administration-inspired introduction of a national Prospective Payment system for Medicare in 1983. The introduction of prospective payments did a number of things: it shifted the state from implementing *post hoc* reimbursement of the costs of consumption to one where it laid down in advance what it was prepared to pay for particular services; by expressing the payment rules in terms of diagnosis-related groups (DRGs) it committed the Health Care Financing Administration (HCFA), the federal agency responsible for Medicare, to an immensely detailed scheme of control involving the identification of over 400 categories of treatment in the DRG system; and it marked an end to local diversity by prescribing nationwide what the state would pay for health care. The state crossed a regulatory watershed, opening up new frontiers of control over consumption in the 1980s and 1990s. Brandon catches the epochal significance of the 1983 reforms:

> Despite the rhetoric of 'competition' then, the upshot of the Reagan administration's most important health policy initiative has been a massive increase in federal intervention that has tied the financial fate of hospitals across the country to decisions reached by [the HCFA] and Congress.[86]

Part of the significance of this decisive shift to a more regulated regime lies in its progenitors. Even the most avowedly 'deregulatory' president of modern times could not stem the rising tide of regulation; to the contrary, he was responsible for the single most interventionist reform of the health care system.

These 'high-policy' initiatives were themselves only a part of a profound change in the institutional world of the government of consumption. They signalled a great alteration in the regulatory capacities and inclinations of the American state. The transformation is connected to the original reforms, since when it instituted Medicare as, in effect, a large-scale scheme of health care insurance, the state also had to establish some means of administering that scheme. It is a sign of how relucantly governing elites recognised the momentousness of the 1965 reforms that it took over a decade before regulatory responsibility was consolidated into one institution, the HCFA, founded in 1977. The HCFA, which now oversees Medicare and Medicaid, has been at the heart of the transformation of state capacity in the government of consumption, partly through its direct regulation of the Medicare system, partly through the 'spillover'/demonstration effect on the wider government of consumption. Some sense of the growth of regulatory capacity can be gained from the history of the regulation of the two programmes originally established in 1965. Until 1977 Medicare and Medicaid were separately administered, the former by the Social Security Administration, the latter at federal level by the Social and Rehabilitation Services Administration. In 1977 the formation of the HCFA coordinated the two systems of control. Now, HCFA is a major federal agency, with 4,000 employees engaged in policy development, health care research, budget preparation and analysis, enforcement of health care quality standards and legislative analysis and liaison. In other words, there has now developed a substantial regulatory capacity within the federal government.[87] Peterson summarises the transformation thus:

> Prior to Medicare, the government had essentially no indigenous expertise on health care financing (nor did much exist outside of government) ... By the 1980s, however, program management and evaluation became the province of a sophisticated army of government specialists, many trained in health services and policy research, and their innumerable counterparts throughout the health policy community ... The institutional epiphenomena of the Medicare program's enactment served to expand the administrative experience and analytic capacity of the federal government.[88]

A more surprising, and if anything more profound, change in state capacities in the government of consumption has taken place, not at the federal level, but at the level of individual states. The Medicaid programme, it will be recalled, is a federally funded programme to finance care for some of the poor, and is administered at state level. From the beginning it was obvious – for instance from the very different entitlement regimes adopted by individual states – that states had a great deal of discretion in the administration of Medicaid. But as the crisis of coverage for large sections of the population has intensified, and as it has intersected with the fiscal crisis of public health care financing, the states have emerged as 'laboratories of reform'. Some of the most significant reforms have been in the government of consumption. Perhaps the most striking innovation in health care policy in recent years has occurred at the level of one individual state in the form of the Oregon experiment, the single most ambitious attempt to evolve a rationing and access regime for the government of health care consumption. It responds to the constrained finances of the Medicaid programme, and the existence of large numbers of uninsured Americans, by creating a basic benefits package. The plan attempts to: extend medical eligibility to all those below the defined federal poverty level; establish a policy process for defining a basic health care package; mandate all employers to provide health care coverage at levels equal to the Medicaid coverage; and establish an insurance pool for those medically uninsurable.[89] For our purposes the significance of the Oregon experiment lies less in the content of the package, important though that is, than in the policy creativity it shows now to exist at the level of individual states – a policy creativity demonstrated by the diversity of consumption regimes being experimented with across a wide range of state jurisdictions.[90]

In summary, characterising developments since the great reforms of the mid-1960s as the growth of a regime of regulation for consumption is shorthand for a range of (linked) developments: the decline of consumption paid for by direct exchanges between individual consumers and providers, and its displacement by systems of collective consumption where third-party payers are central; the bureaucratisation of consumption regimes, both in the sense of the elaboration of a dense thicket of rules and the development of bureaucracies, both public and private, for the implementation of those rules; and the emergence of the state, both at federal and sub-federal level, as a regulatory actor armed with considerable resources and an inclination to try to steer the system.

Why did these changes happen and what were their consequences for the government of health care consumption?

The proximate causes of this regulatory revolution are not difficult to understand. They lie at the heart of the crisis of the American health care system, and might be summed up in two policy problems: the inability of the system to deliver *either* effective cost containment *or* adequate health care coverage for the population. The former is encapsulated in the well-known trends of health care spending discussed earlier in this book. The settlement reached in passing the Medicare and Medicaid reforms was particularly disastrous for cost control. The combination of a historically established 'supply state', where the bias of policy was in favour of accommodating providers, with an open-ended commitment to pay providers on a 'reasonable cost basis', was a recipe for disastrous inflation. The fact that private health insurance was dominated by schemes negotiated as part of collective bargaining gave a particular shape to the interests at stake. Health care inflation damaged corporate America, including some of the biggest industrial corporations struggling to compete in world markets: between 1970 and 1989 employer spending (in real terms) rose 1 per cent for wages and salaries, 32 per cent for retirement benefits and 163 per cent for health care benefits.[91] The link with work was also the key to the inability of the system to provide coverage for a substantial part of the population: the uninsured were primarily those who, for one reason or another, were not covered by work-based schemes. By the 1990s about 37 million Americans were at any one time not covered by health insurance. What is more, the numbers of uninsured Americans had begun to rise, partly as a result of the way the link with the division of labour made the insurance system sensitive to occupational change: the decline of employment in well-unionised traditional heavy industries, and the growth of employment in poorly unionised sections (service firms, sectors with high levels of part-time employment) all contributed to the rise in numbers of uninsured Americans.[92] A 1994 national survey of access to care found that 16 per cent of Americans reported that they were unable to obtain at least one important health care service.[93]

The proximate problems *inside* the health care system are thus not difficult to understand. Nor is it hard to fathom the wider systemic context of these problems. In the federal budget, Medicare and Medicaid costs assumed an increasing proportion of spending at the very moment of growing stress in federal finances. The fact that both were entitlement regimes made control particularly difficult: after social security the cost of Medicare and Medicaid is the most costly of the entitlement programmes.[94] For employers – who as we have seen bore the brunt of the escalating costs of private health insurance – the burden of health insurance came at a period of intense international competition, and the penetration of domestic markets by foreign, notably Japanese, firms. The problem was particularly salient in the large automobile industry, a leader in occupationally based health insurance schemes, and a highly visible piece of evidence that American industry had problems in coping with foreign competition.

We thus need not labour long over why, for more than twenty years, there has been a perception of a crisis in the system: large numbers of Americans were left without health care, while the cost of providing cover for the lucky insured was an immense problem both for the state and employers. The more puzzling problem is to understand why the consumption regime developed as described here – why it was transformed into a complex regulatory model. Why have we seen the rise of a distinctively regulatory regime in consumption? To explain this we have to understand the range of the policy repertoire available in the US, and the best way to do this is to reflect for a moment on what was available in the two other countries examined in this book. There too, we have seen, there were problems in regulating consumption as a result of economic and social change. But the institutional structures in both Germany and the UK allowed the production of a range of policy responses from government – successive structural reforms of the health care system in Germany, for instance, and the radical British response of the 1990s. As the numerous analyses of the history of attempts at comprehensive reform of the American system show, however, the institutional structures of American federalism, coupled with the structure of decision making in Congress, have been powerful obstacles to reform. The biggest single obstruction to comprehensive health care reform has been the political system, notably the way the power structure of Congress advantages established interests resisting attacks on their established positions. The story of policy immobility in the case of health is part of the story of policy immobility over a wide range of policy arenas. The history of the Medicare and Medicaid reforms is a parable illustrating this state of affairs: it took the trauma of a presidential assassination, an unprecedented presidential election victory, and a president (Johnson) uniquely skilled in managing Congress, even to get through those reforms in 1965.[95]

Part of the story, therefore, is a story about what was not available in the American policy repertoire; and part is about what was available. In social and economic affairs the American state has an established tradition of extensive intervention, but this intervention has taken the form of regulation – the imposition of controls, usually backed by statute, on market transactions – rather than the form of direct state provision or public ownership. That tradition has, especially since the New Deal reforms, endowed the federal government with a battery of regulatory instruments and, across the range of markets, a large fund of experience in regulatory practice. The specialised personnel – notably lawyers and economists, the two professions at the centre of regulatory analysis – have for over a generation been pouring out of good graduate schools. The law-driven character of American policy making, and the premium put on a discourse in which rational arguments are mounted against each other in the legitimisation of policy outcomes, put at a premium the skills of professionals like lawyers and economists – and, in particular, put the economics of law at the centre of the regulatory process. By the time the consumption crisis in the American health care system became plain – during the decade of cost inflation after the passage of the Medicare and the Medicaid reforms – the regulatory tradition, and the resources needed to maintain that tradition, had been established for over a whole generation. In short, there was available both a policy response, and the resources needed for that response, to produce a distinctively American solution to the problems of governing health care consumption in an era of cost inflation.[96]

The American response to the problem of how to govern health care consumption has thus been to construct a highly complex regulatory regime. That response can be explained by the way the institutional structures of American politics blocked off some solutions and opened the way to others. But to explain is not to justify. The resulting regulatory regime is a distinctively American solution, but it is a highly unsatisfactory one. Four problems are obvious. First, despite two decades of regulatory innovation, one of the most serious original problems, the failure to provide health insurance coverage for all, is greater than ever: the numbers of uninsured, or incompletely insured, Americans are rising. The most important reason for this state of affairs is the decline in insurance coverage provided by employers, and the cause of this in turn is the changing occupational structure. Among workers in firms employing under a hundred workers, only 40 per cent have health insurance through their employer; the corresponding figure for workers in firms with a thousand or more employees is 83 per cent; yet of the 22 million new jobs created in the American economy from 1988 to 1995, 21 million were in firms employing less than a hundred workers, or were self-employed.[97] Second, again despite all this regulatory innovation, consumer dissatisfaction has been recorded at uniquely high levels by international standards: in Blendon's surveys comparing satisfaction levels among citizens with health care across ten nations this is the most distinctive feature of the US.[98] If one measure of the success of a consumption regime is the satisfaction of citizens, the US is a failure. Third, the system has produced rules of great complexity which citizens find immensely difficult to understand: surveys show that Americans have a very poor idea of their health care entitlements, while even rudimentary knowledge about the most highly publicised federal programmes, like Medicare, is very low. If one measure of the success of an entitlement regime is its transparency to citizens, the American system is a failure here too.[99] Finally, the growth of a complex regulatory system has had a standard regulatory consequence. It has imposed considerable compliance costs, adding to the expense of the system: a comparison of administrative costs in US hospitals, for instance, showed strikingly higher levels than in Canada.[100] It is much harder in the US for citizens to know what their entitlements are; and sorting out that complexity is itself an expensive business.

The features summarised above relate to some of the substantive consequences of the rise of a regulatory regime. But since new policies produce new politics[101] we should also expect changes in the way the politics of consumption struggles were carried on. Morone – in a passage quoted above – has already identified some of these: the substantive complexity of the regulatory regime means that policy discourse has been conducted in a dense, esoteric language, erecting high barriers to entry. Yet if the growth of regulatory complexity erected barriers to entry to policy discourse, it also created powerful incentives to interests to organise, for regulatory intervention has the capacity to affect group interests in a most dramatic way, often by quite small changes in rules. One of the most obvious consequences, because Medicare was targeted at the elderly, was to encourage the mobilisation of the aged into health care politics. The way apparently small (and probably unintended) regulatory consequences can affect mobilisation is well illustrated by the short, explosive history of the Medicare Catastrophic Coverage Act of 1988.[102] The Act tried to shift some of the burden of care onto those elderly Americans who, in addition to Medicare entitlements, also received benefits from a former employer. The effect was to turn the Act into a matter of burdens, not benefits, for the 30 per cent of retired Americans – mostly prosperous pensioners –

receiving benefits from former employers. The Act produced an unprecedented level of 'grey' mobilisation. So intense was the pressure on Congress that the measure was repealed at the end of the 1989 legislative session.

The rise of regulation has thus had a contradictory effect: it has simultaneously limited, and widened, the range of those with a voice in the government of consumption. The narrowing is associated with the growing complexity of the consumption regime, and the way issues are argued out in what for the lay person is an often incomprehensible language of regulatory expertise. Yet the precise fact that only organisation allows some possibility of influence over outcomes has helped produce an increasingly densely populated world of consumption politics. This is part of what is behind the shift in the character of the health representation system in the US identified by Peterson. He characterises the shift in health care as one that mirrors a change in the wider political environment noted some years ago by Heclo: a shift from enclosed 'iron triangles' to more open 'issue networks'.[103] Drawing on the work of Walker, and partly reanalysing his findings, Peterson shows that the representational world, at both state and federal level, has become more densely populated in recent decades.[104] There has been a particularly striking growth in the numbers and importance of not-for-profit and citizen groups. The latter are particularly distinctive:

> Citizen groups make up another essential element of the transformation of the representational community. No matter when they came into existence, the vast majority of them favor much more federal spending on health and human services and support increases in federal regulation ... They polarize the representational community. Two additional attributes of citizen groups contribute to their importance. First, the groups formed prior to 1946 include various associations promoting disease prevention and cures who traditionally have not been confrontational, unlike the organisations spawned in the 1960s and 1970s. Groups founded since 1970 are about twice as likely as their pre-1945 counterparts to be enmeshed in intense and regular conflict in their policy domain and to view the distinctions between the Democratic and the Republican parties as being relevant to their concerns. Second, because of the the emergence of supportive patrons of political action and new communications technologies, these later, cause-oriented organizations found it much easier to overcome collective action problems and grew dramatically in number compared to other types of groups.[105]

This account of the changing consumption regime in the US emphasises once again an observation made in Chapter 2: that the landmark reforms of the mid-1960s that produced Medicare and Medicaid were simultaneously the product of old politics and, in part, the originator of a new politics. The extent to which they were the product of old politics is shown, most obviously, by the very light rein placed on providers in the original measures – a light rein that was necessary to secure a legislative majority for the reforms. But the new measures stimulated developments that irrevocably changed the consumption regime: the very fact of the light rein proved disastrous for cost containment, and within less than a decade was leading to regulatory trans-formation; the institutions charged with administering the measures emerged over the decades as formidable regulatory institutions in their own right; and the immense resources at stake in regulatory decision making were a powerful incentive for the mobilisation of new groups into consumption struggles.

But the change was only partly due to conditions internal to the consump-tion regime. The economic and political systems within which health care institutions were embedded were also crucial influences. The failure to contain costs was disastrous because of what it did – or at least was perceived to do – to the competitiveness of key American industries in a world of increasingly sharp global competition, and because of the strains it imposed on the federal finances. Both the propensity to organise, and the means to organise, were partly created by wider changes in the American pressure group universe – particularly the sort of opportunities identified by analysts like Peterson and by Walker arising from the development of new technologies of mobilisation and the support of patrons for group mobilisation. These development have also had important implications for government of the medical profession – something which is the subject of our next chapter.

The converging government of consumption

At first glance the politics of consumption in health care looks like a study in national contrasts. Few areas of health care policy seem so shaped by the indi-vidual institutional features of separate nations. The origins of the consump-tion regimes in the three countries examined here are closely connected to their separate national histories, both the histories of their social policies and their wider political histories. The historically dominant consumption modes look almost like ideal types of different models: command and control (the UK), corporatist (Germany) and market (the US).

This story of national uniqueness in some respects continues in the accounts offered in the pages of this chapter. For instance, the government of consumption in the three countries has been heavily influenced by contingent circumstances which are best considered products of the unique historical or geographical location of the individual nations. Thus the story of the British case in recent years is inseparable from the long struggle with British economic decline, and in particular with the highly distinctive policy response to the problem of decline which dominated British politics after 1979 – a response which for shorthand is conventionally called Thatcherism. It is obvious that the shock to the German system administered by the quite unexpected reunification with the former German Democratic Republic has penetrated the health care system itself and is at least in part responsible for the equally unexpected history of policy innovation in the 1990s. And in the American case, the long search for some solution to the twin problems of cost inflation and incomplete insurance coverage are linked to the key problem that emerged from the middle of the 1970s – the challenge on the wider international stage to American hegemony in both the economic and political spheres.

These differences are important. But what is most striking about the preceding pages is the extent of *convergence* that is taking place in the modern government of health care consumption. In part this is a function of the common decay of traditionally established mechanisms for controlling the consumers – notably the patients – in health care; in part it is the product of the response to this decay, which is producing outcomes which are similar in the three systems.

Three elements of the decay of traditional controls that are commonly experienced should be highlighted. First, in none of these health care systems is what might be called the supply environment stable. Health care institutions are constantly innovating, and these innovations are in turn destabilising levels of demand for health care consumption. The most obvious example of this concerns innovation in the 'hard' technologies of medical care, notably pharmaceuticals and medical devices. The historical link between modern science and medical innovation produces a stream of innovations that constantly widen the potential range of health care consumption.

A second area where controls have decayed concerns the relationship between individual patients and doctors. Although longitudinal data sets concerning what are essentially individual relations are not easy to assemble, all the evidence for the three countries points in the same direction: the development of more assertive, less deferential and more demanding patient-consumers.

A third area concerns the organisational world of the government of consumption. Here a remarkably similar story can be told for all three cases: a generation ago, the political world was a highly enclosed one, typified in Peterson's characterisation of American arrangements as an 'iron triangle'. The displacement of those closed institutional patterns by more open and unstable issue networks, with larger numbers of institutional actors, marks a further decay in established mechanisms of control.

These developments have produced a number of common responses: they might be summed up as more market, more state, more regulation and more bureaucracy. As this summary shows, the responses are by no means consistent. The rise of the market is seen in attempts increasingly to use the price mechanism to govern consumption. In the language used at the start of this chapter, we are seeing an attempt to reverse the historical process of de-commodification of health care consumption. This might seem to imply a diminished role for states, were it not that in all three cases states have emerged as key actors in the reorganisation of health care consumption – *the* institution attempting to act strategically in the reorganisation of the governing regime. One way in which states have attempted to perform this strategic role is by strengthening their regulatory capacity: the emergence of public regulation in steering is, in particular, a feature of both German and American arrangements in the last couple of decades. The consumption arena is, as a result, much more overtly politicised than in the recent past. These developments are linked to, but are not the same as, growing bureaucratization, for the development of more institutional complexity, and of more complex rules governing consumption is not simply something that has taken place in the public sector: it has affected all consumption arenas, regardless of the identity of the third-party payer.

Behind all these developments lies a momentous change in the structure of power in the health care state. At the centre of traditional modes of control sat powerful and prestigious medical professions. Much of what has happened in recent years has been about the challenge to their central, powerful role. These are issues examined in the next chapter.

Notes

1   This is only a minimalist case for collectivisation: the collectivisation of payment serves to provide insurance cover against uncertain exposure to catastrophic health care expense. Beyond that, collectivisation might arise because, for instance, it is considered appropriate to treat health care as a public good, or because of the desire to disconnect access to care from ability to pay. These different motivations can be used to distinguish whole health care systems. For further discussion see S. Harrison and M. Moran, 'Resources and rationing: managing supply and demand in health care', in G. Albrecht, R. Fitzpatrick and S. Scrimshaw (eds), *The handbook of social studies in medicine* (New York, Sage, 1999, forthcoming).

2   In 1996, 47.6 per cent actually came from public sources: K. Levit, H. Lazenby and B. Braden, 'National health spending trends in 1996', *Health Affairs*, 17:1 (1998) 35–51, at p. 42.

3   K. Levit, C. Cowan, H. Lazenby, P. McDonnell, A. Sensenig, J. Stiller, and D. Won, 'National health spending trends, 1960–93', *Health Affairs*, 13:5 (1994) 14–31, at p. 22.

4   The figures are from L. Blumberg and L. Nichols, 'First, do no harm: developing health insurance market reform packages', *Health Affairs*, 15:3 (1996) 35–53, at p. 36.

5   My use of the language of collective consumption is indebted to Dunleavy's path-breaking work; however, as I read his account, collectivisation through the private insurance market would not be counted as collective consumption. My distinction between collectivisation and decommodification is intended to allow precisely this. See P. Dunleavy, *Urban political analysis* (London, Macmillan, 1980), esp. p. 53.

6   G. Esping-Andersen, *The three worlds of welfare capitalism* (Cambridge, Polity press, 1990), pp. 21–2.

7   For a good introduction to this movement see A. Blenkinsopp and C. Bradley, 'Patients, society, and the increase in self-medication', *British Medical Journal*, 312 (1996) 29–32 (9 March).

8   J. Holahan, C. Winterbottom and S. Rajan, 'A shifting picture of health insurance coverage', *Health Affairs*, 14:4 (1995) 253–74, reporting on trends to 1993, at p. 259, exhibit 4.

9   R. Klein, *The politics of the National Health Service* (London, Longman, 1989, 2nd edn), p. 1.

10   T. H. Marshall, 'Citizenship and social class', in Marshall, *Class, citizenship and social development* (Westport CT, Greenwood Press, 1973), pp. 67–122; the phrase occurs on p.101. The essay originally formed part of the Marshall Lectures given at Cambridge in 1949.

11   One of the earliest authoritative comparative studies discerned a pattern which has since become well established in successive releases of the OECD data on spending discussed in chapter one of this book: see R. Maxwell, *Health and wealth: an international study of health care spending* (Lexington, Lexington Books, 1981).

12   J. White, *Competing solutions: American health care proposals and international experience* (Washington DC, Brookings Institution, 1995), pp. 121–2.

13   The years actually span 1949/50 to 1957/8: the figures are given in C. Webster, *The health services since the war, volume II, government and health care, the National Health Service 1958–1979* (London, HMSO, 1996), p. 6.

14   The authoritative account is in C. Webster, *The health services since the war, volume I, problems of health care: the National Health Service before 1957* (London, HMSO, 1988), pp. 157–83.

15   This from Webster, *Health services since the war*, vol. I, pp. 187–92.

16   A. Earl-Slater and C. Bradley, 'The inexorable rise in the UK NHS drugs bill: recent policies, future prospects', *Public Administration*, 74:3 (1996) 393–411, at p. 405.

17   The central role of the UK general practitioner in gatekeeping is made explicit in *The European study of referrals: report to the concerted action committee of health services research for the European Community* (London, Royal College of General Practitioners, 1992), pp. 1–2; and see also B. Abel-Smith's 'Foreword' to F. Honigsbaum, *The division in British medicine: a history of the separation of general practice from hospital care 1911–1968* (London, Kogan Page, 1979).

18   The whole issue of the character and role of post–war general practice is succinctly summarised in M. Calnan and J. Gabe, 'Recent developments in general practice: a sociological analysis', in J. Gabe, M. Calnan and M. Bury (eds), *The sociology of the health service* (London, Routledge, 1991), pp. 140–61; and in D. Taylor and K. Bloor, *Care, health promotion and the future of general practice* (London, Royal Society of Medicine Press, 1994), pp. 132–5.

19   H. Aaron and W. Schwartz, *The painful prescription: rationing hospital care* (Washington DC, Brookings Institution, 1984), p. 101.

20   S. Harrison, *Managing the NHS: shifting the frontier* (London, Chapman and Hall, 1988), pp. 24–6 seems to be the originator of this observation.

21 B. Salter, *The politics of change in the health service* (Basingstoke, Macmillan, 1998), p. 53.

22 Bruce Wood (personal communication) also points out to me an important additional mechanism: the way the internal hierarchies of medicine relegated some specialisms – geriatric care is an obvious example – to a low place in professional status and thus to a low place in funding priority.

23 R. Saltman and C. von Otter, *Planned markets and public competition: strategic reform in northern European health systems* (Buckingham, Open University Press, 1992), esp. pp. 3–11.

24 This intersected with a debate about the extent to which general practice should follow a 'medical' model. embracing technological medicine, or a more 'social' model emphasising the links between general practice and the wider welfare delivery system: for a discussion see Calnan and Gabe, 'Recent developments in general practice', esp. at pp. 147–8.

25 For some material illustating these well known changes in educational and labour force participation see J. Pullinger (ed.), *Social trends 28* (London, The Stationery Office, 1998), pp. 61, 73–5.

26 Unsurprisingly, childbirth has been important in these developments. For a brief account of the significance of the Savage case in the UK – a conflict between a woman physician and male professional authority in the management of childbirth – see J. Williams, 'The controlling power of childbirth in Britain', in H. Marland and A. Rafferty (eds), *Midwives, society and childbirth: debates and controversies in the modern period* (London, Routledge, 1997), pp. 232–47, at pp. 242–3. An emerging area of tension concerns control of the decision about performance of elective caesarian sections in childbirth. Witness the debate in the pages of the *British Medical Journal*, 'Should doctors perform elective caesarian section on request?' *British Medical Journal*, 317 (1998) 462–5 (15 August).

27 B. Wood, *Patient power? Patients' associations and health care in Britain and America* (Buckingham, Open University Press, forthcoming), Chapter 3. I am grateful to Bruce Wood for allowing me to see the manuscript of this study.

28 It should be said, though, that there are remarkable national variations in treatment practices, in conceptions of illness, and in tolerance of illness, and here we may be picking up British peculiarity. The classic comparative study is L. Payer, *Medicine and culture: notions of sickness in Britain, the US, France and West Germany* (London, Gollancz, 1989).

29 R. Klein, 'The state and the profession: the politics of the double bed', *British Medical Journal*, 301 (1990) 700–2, at p. 700 (3 October).

30 There is a good discussion of this in S. Harrison, D. Hunter and C. Pollitt, *The dynamics of British health policy* (London, Routledge, 1990), pp. 75–87.

31 National Health Services Management Inquiry: *Report* (London, Department of Health and Social Security, 1983 – the 'Griffiths Report').

32 Harrison *et al.*, *Dynamics of British health policy*, p. 86.

33 *Working for patients*, Cm 555 (1989).

34 R. Baggott, *Health and health care in Britain* (Basingstoke, Macmillan, 1998, 2nd edn), pp. 215–16 and p. 238 discuss this.

35 J. Mohan, *A national health service? The restructuring of health care in Britain since 1979* (Basingstoke, Macmillan, 1995), p. 160. The growth, though, was from a

fairly low base: by 1987, 23 per cent of managers/employers had private health insurance; but contrast that with the 1 per cent recorded by Mohan for unskilled manual workers.

36   Mohan, *A national health service?*, p. 161.

37   For an account which sets the decline of the traditional gatekeeping function into the context of the reforms: S. Iliffe, 'Towards a primary care-led NHS', in S. Iliffe and J. Munro (eds), *Healthy choices: future options for the NHS* (London, Lawrence and Wishart, 1997), pp. 75–93.

38   *The new NHS: modern, dependable*, Cm 3807 (1997).

39   I rely here on B. Wood, 'Health policy', in D. Coates and P. Lawler (eds), *Labour into power* (Manchester, Manchester University Press, forthcoming).

40   See the evidence summarised in J. Lenaghan, 'Central government should have a greater role in rationing decisons', *British Medical Journal*, 314 (1997) 967–70 (29 March.)

41   A key finding of, for instance, R. Klein, P. Day and S. Redmayne, *Priority setting and rationing in the National Health Service* (Buckingham, Open University Press, 1996).

42   For a very good case study see N. Freemantle and S. Harrison, 'Interleukin-2: the public and professional face of rationing in the NHS', *Critical Social Policy*, 13:2 (1994) 94–117.

43   My source is Wood, 'Health policy'.

44   I discuss later in this chapter the recent sharp fall in the number of funds.

45   On the importance of 'security over equality' across the whole social security system, including health care, see W. Zapf, 'Development, structure, and prospects of the German Social State', in R. Rose (ed.), *The welfare state east and west* (Oxford, Oxford University Press, 1986), pp. 126–55.

46   On the complete redundancy of formal democratic procedures see A. Murswieck, 'Health policy-making', in K. von Beyme and M. Schmidt (eds), *Policy and politics in the Federal Republic of Germany* (Aldershot, Gower, 1985), pp. 82–106, at pp. 86–7.

47   Notably in the hospital sphere: see J. Alber, 'Bundesrepublik Deutschland', in Alber and B. Bernardi-Schenkluhn, *Westeuropäische Gesundheitssysteme im Vergleich: Bundesrepublik Deutschland, Schweiz, Frankreich, Italien, Großbritannien* (Frankfurt, Campus Verlag, 1992), pp. 31–176, at p. 76.

48   Alber, 'Bundesrepublik Deutschland', pp. 76–7.

49   The figure for 1949 is in Murswieck, 'Health policy-making', p. 85; that for 1993 in C. Altenstetter, 'Health policy-making in Germany: stability and dynamics', in Altenstetter and J. Björkman (eds), *Health policy reform, national variations and globalization* (London, Macmillan, 1997), pp. 136–60, at p. 152; for consolidations between Ortskrankenkassen see S. Giaimo and P. Manow, 'Institutions and ideas in politics: health care reform in Britain and Germany', in ibid., pp. 175–202, at p. 186, citing figures to 1995.

50   This was a key principle of the reforms that began in 1993: see K. Hinrichs, 'The impact of German health insurance reforms on redistribution and the culture of solidarity', *Journal of Health Politics, Policy and Law*, 20:3 (1995) 653–87, at p. 672.

51   The growth in (public) bureaucratic capacity is a major theme of M. Döhler,

'The state as architect of political order: policy dynamics in German health care', *Governance*, 8:3, (1995) 380–404.

52 This relies on: Alber, 'Bundesrepublik Deutschland', p. 74; B. Braun, 'Health reform in Germany – the discovery of managed and solidaristic competition', in S. Iliffe and H.-U. Deppe (eds), *Health care in Europe: competition or solidarity?* (Frankfurt, Verlag für Akademische Schriften, 1995), pp. 41–6, at p.43; and (on co-payments in the 1993 reforms) H. Lieverdink and J. van der Made, 'The reform of health insurance systems in the Netherlands and Germany: Dutch gold and German silver', in Altenstetter and Björkman (eds), *Health policy reform*, pp. 109–35, at p. 128.

53 There is a table in Alber, 'Bundesrepublik Deutschland', p. 42. Changes in the contribution system introduced in the later 1960s, however, make comparison before and after 1970 difficult, and the figures should therefore be taken only as broad indicators of change.

54 G. Eberle, 'Die Entwicklung der GKV zum heutigen Stand', *Sozialer Fortschritt*, 47:3 (1998) 53–8.

55 The standard demonstration of the statistical relationship is *Financing and delivering health care: a comparative analysis of OECD nations* (Paris, OECD, 1987), pp. 79ff.

56 The most important systematic comparative analysis making this point is J. Alber, 'Die Gesundheitssysteme der OECD-Länder im Vergleich', in M. Schmidt (ed.), *Politische Vierteljahrsschrift 1988* (Opladen, Wesdeutscher Verlag, 1988), pp. 116–50.

57 J. Alber, 'Der deutsche Sozialstaat im Licht international vergleichender Daten', *Leviathan*, 26:2 (1998) 199–227.

58 The figures are from 'The reform of health care in Germany', in OECD, *The reform of health care: a comparative analysis of seven OECD countries* (Paris, OECD, 1992), pp. 57–72, at p. 67. This volume was prepared by Jeremy Hurst, and the German chapter contributed by Hurst.

59 A good illustration of the way this headline figure is represented in political debate can be seen in the way time series analyses of contribution rates using simple graphical illustration routinely accompany journalistic discussions of the rising level of costs: for an illustration from one of many German high-quality papers see, for instance *Die Zeit*, 29 March 1991, p. 28.

60 The surveys are reported in Hinrichs, 'Impact of German health insurance reforms', p. 679, reporting his own findings. He also draws on J. Alber and A. Ryall, 'Die Krankenversicherung im Bewußtsein der Bevölkerung: Welt hinter den Bergen oder objekt rationalen Kalküls?', *Sozialer Fortschritt*, 39:7 (1990) 165–72. Alber and Ryall used a national sample to contrast the rational actor model which informs much policy debate with the very different model suggested by evidence about popular views of social insurance.

61 The study is reported in D. Göpffarth and B. Milbrandt, 'Das Gesundheitswesen als Beschäftigungs und Wachstumsfaktor', *Zeitschrift für Gesundheitswissenschaften*, 6:3 (1998) 233–47, at p. 242. The measures of total employment also come from this paper.

62 The academic and policy debates about the 'burden' of health insurance premiums is summarised in O. Winkelhake and J. John, 'Kostendämpfung im

Gesundheitswesen, Beitragsstabilität und Lohnnenebenkosten', *Sozialer Fortschritt*, 47:6 (1998) 144–50.

63 J. Leaman, *The political economy of West Germany 1945–85* (London, Macmillan, 1988), p. 209.

64 The argument of this paragraph relies heavily on the data in J. A. Wysong and T. Abel, 'Universal health insurance insurance and high risk groups in West Germany: implications for US health policy', *The Milbank Quarterly*, 68:4 (1990), 527–60.

65 'GKV-Beitragssatzentwicklung ungembremst', *Die Ortskrankenkasse*, 5/1988, p. 162.

66 There is a discussion of the risk selection process involving, especially, the successful parts of the auto industry in P. Pick and J. Plein, 'Betriebskrankenkassen: Risikoselektion versus Solidarprinzip', *Die Ortskrankasse*, 10–11/1989, pp. 297–303.

67 This account of the financing of the system in the immediate aftermath of reunification relies on three sources: K.-D. Henke, 'Fiscal problems of German unity – the case of health care', *Staatswissenschaft und Staatspraxis*, 2 (1991) 170–8; 'Recent trends in the finances of the statutory health insurance institutions', *Deutsche Bundesbank Monthly Report*, January 1991, 25–36, at p. 33; J. Wasem, 'Health care reform in the Federal Republic of Germany: the new and the old Länder', in Altenstetter and Björkman, *Health policy reform*, pp. 162–74.

68 This relies on J. Müller and W. Schneider, ' Entwicklung der Mitgliederzahlen, Beitragssätze, Versichertenstrukturen und RSA-Transfers in Zeiten des Kassenwettbewerbs', *Arbeit und Sozialpolitik*, 52:3/4 (1998) 10–32. The disparities are in the short term in part masked by the state enforced transfers of resources referred to below.

69 These passages rely on: J. Wasem, 'Im Schatten des GSG: Gesundheitspolitik in der 13. Wahlperiode des Deutschen Bundestages – eine (verläufige) Bilanz', *Arbeit und Sozialpolitik*, 52:7/8 (1998) 18–30.

70 This relies on F. Schwartz and R. Busse, 'Germany', in C. Ham (ed.), *Health care reform: learning from international experience* (Buckingham, Open University Press, 1997), pp. 104–18.

71 Hinrichs, 'Impact of German health insurance reforms', pp. 671–2.

72 This is the central theme of Döhler, 'The state as architect of political order'.

73 This draws on Hinrichs, 'Impact of German health insurance reforms', p. 674. *Health Insurance 2000* was a forward look at the financing of health care produced at official request.

74 The issues are discussed in R. Busse, C. Howorth and F. Schwartz, 'The future development of the rights based approach to health care in Germany: more rights or fewer?', in J. Lenaghan (ed.), *Hard choices in health care: rights and rationing in Europe* (London, BMJ Publishing Group, 1996), pp. 21–47, at pp. 43–5.

75 T. Marmor, *The politics of Medicare* (London, Routledge, 1970), p. 111.

76 The figures are calculated from C. Helbing,'Medicare program expenditures', *Health Care Financing Review*, Annual Supplement, 1992 (Washington, Health Care Financing Administration, 1993) p. 24, Table 3.1.

77 The figure for 1970 is from Helbing, 'Medicare program expenditures', p. 24.

78　L. Jacobs, *The health of nations: public opinion and the making of American and British health policy* (Ithaca NY, Cornell University Press, 1993), p. 209.

79　Levit *et al.*, 'National health spending trends, 1960–1993', p. 22.

80　Levit *et al.*, 'National health spending trends in 1996', p. 48.

81　Helbing, 'Medicare program expenditures', p. 24.

82　P. Cooper and B. Schone, 'More offers, fewer takers for employment-based health insurance: 1987 and 1996', *Health Affairs*, 16:6 (1997) 142–9, at p. 147. It should be noted, however, that this represented a retreat from the figures for the late 1980s, as workers began to reject insurance cover in the light of increasing cost shifting by employers, who were themselves responding to the huge rises in premiums caused by failures of cost containment.

83　J. Morone, 'The bureaucracy empowered', in J. Morone and G. Belkin (eds), *The politics of health care reform: lessons from the past, prospects for the future* (Durham NC, Duke University Press, 1994), pp. 148–64, at pp. 149–50.

84　G. Jensen, M. Morrisey, S. Gaffney and D. Liston, 'The new dominance of managed care: insurance trends in the 1990s', *Health Affairs*, 16:1 (1997) 125–36, at p. 125. The figure cited dates to 1995.

85　M. Sparer, 'Devolution of power: an interim report card', *Health Affairs*, 17:3 (1998) 7–16, at p. 10.

86　W. Brandon, 'Two kinds of conservatism in US health policy: the Reagan record', in C. Altenstetter and S. Haywood (eds), *Comparative health policy and the new right: from rhetoric to reality* (London, Macmillan, 1991), pp. 165–206, at p. 187. The preceding paragraph also draws on Brandon.

87　The figures are taken from *Health Care Financing Administration: Fact Sheet*, Washington, HCFA, February 1997: http://www.hcfa.gov.facts.

88　M. Peterson, 'The limits of social learning: translating analysis into action', *Journal of Health Politics, Policy and Law*, 22:4 (1997) 1077–114 (at p. 1086).

89　There is a very large literature on the Oregon experience. An accessible summary (on which my account draws) is in C. Paton, *Health policy and management: the health-care agenda in a British political context* (London, Chapman and Hall, 1996), p. 41. A more extended, but still very accessible, account is: T. Bodenheimer, 'The Oregon health plan', in two parts: *New England Journal of Medicine*, 337:9 (1997) 651–5 and 337:10 (1997), 720–3.

90　There is a summary in C. Weissert and W. Weissert, *Governing health: the politics of health policy* (Baltimore MD, Johns Hopkins University Press, 1996), pp. 211–17. For a study of state variation in one particularly important policy area (regulating the conversion of non-profit health plans to for-profit status) D. Shriber, 'State experience in regulating a changing health care system', *Health Affairs*, 16:2 (1997) 48–68.

91　The figures are quoted in L. Brown, 'Dogmatic slumbers: American business and health policy', in Morone and Belkin (eds), *The politics of health care reform*, pp. 205–23, at p. 206.

92　Cooper and Schone, 'Employment–based health insurance'.

93　M. Berk, C. Schur, and J. Cantor, 'Ability to obtain health care: recent estimates from the Robert Wood Johnson Foundation national access to care survey', *Health Affairs*, 14: 3 (1995) 139–46.

94　Weissert and Weissert, *Governing health*, p. 34.

95   Marmor, *The politics of Medicare*, is the standard political science study.

96   A good overview of the rise of the regulatory state is J. Wilson (ed.), *The politics of regulation* (New York, Basic Books, 1980.)

97   J. Gabel, P. Ginsburg and K. Hunt, 'Small employers and their health benefits, 1988–1996: an awkward adolescence', *Health Affairs*, 16: 5 (1997) 103–10, at p. 103.

98   R. J. Blendon, R. Leitman, I. Morrison and K. Donelan, 'Satisfaction with health systems in ten nations', *Health Affairs*, 9:2 (1990) 185–2.

99   R. Blendon, J. Benson, M. Brodie, M. Brossard, D. Altman and R. Morin, 'What do Americans know about entitlements?, *Health Affairs*, 16:5 (1997) 111–16.

100   S. Woolhandler, D. Himmstein and J. P. Lewontin, 'Administrative costs in U.S. hospitals', *New England Journal of Medicine*, 5 August 1993, pp. 400–3.

101   The phrase echoes a famous argument of Lowi's: T. Lowi, 'Four systems of policy, politics and choice', *Public Administration Review*, 30:3 (1970)314–25.

102   Relies on M. Morrisey, G. Jensen and S. Henderlite, 'Employer-sponsored health insurance for retired Americans', *Health Affairs*, 9:1 (1990) 57–75.

103   H. Heclo, 'Issue networks and the Executive establishment', in A. King (ed.), *The new American political system* (Washington DC, American Enterprise Institute, 1978), pp. 87–124.

104   The reference is to J. Walker, *Mobilizing interest groups in America: patrons, professionals, and social movements* (Ann Arbor MI, University of Michigan Press, 1991).

105   M. Peterson, 'Political influence in the 1990s: from iron triangles to policy networks', *Journal of Health Politics, Policy and Law*, 18: 2 (1993) 395–438, at pp. 416–17. This paper is substantially reprinted in Morone and Belkin, *The politics of health care reform*, pp. 103–47, under the slighly amended title 'Congress in the 1990s: from iron triangles to policy networks.' Peterson's argument is further elaborated in his 'Institutional change and the health politics of the 1990s', *American Behavioral Scientist*, 36:6 (1993) 782–801.

4

Governing doctors

Professions, states and markets

The government of the medical profession in the modern health care state is a study in regulation. That is because professionalism is a regulatory strategy – a distinctive mode of governing attempted by many organised private interests in capitalist democracies. Professionalism tries simultaneously to solve problems posed for those interests by capitalist competition and democratic government. Competition in market economies is both creative and destructive: creative as a source of innovation and, when new competitors are successful, as a source of new interests and new markets; destructive, because the success of the new threatens established interests – in many cases, as the decline of firms and industries shows, it can actually cause their extinction. Regulation characteristically involves 'closure': restricting entry to markets, and limiting competition between those already in the market, in order to limit the destructive effects of competition on established interests.[1]

But since competition offers great potential rewards to the enterprising and creative, the ambitious and innovative have powerful incentives to breach the rules of closure. They can only be restrained by the exercise of power. This need to exercise power creates the nexus between regulation and the modern state, since the authority of the modern democratic state, and the legitimate coercion which that underwrites, is a particularly important source of power for regulatory institutions. That explains Wilding's remark which we encountered in Chapter 1: 'What produces the privileges of professional status is a profession-state alliance.'[2] Yet the modern state is both interventionist and, where democratic, is governed by constitutional ideologies which demand public accountability over the exercise of state power. When professions borrow the authority of the democratic state, therefore, they have somehow to manage the relationship with the state so as simultaneously to appropriate public authority without surrendering to public control.

This is a problem faced by many private interests under market capitalism, notably in the business community, where the regulation of market competition has to be reconciled with preserving the rights of private property.[3] For business the task is eased both by the prevailing ideologies of market capitalism, and by the way ownership and control are institutionalised in the legal forms of private property.[4] Professions, by contrast, organise markets in labour, not property, and need to develop distinctive ideologies to protect the autonomy of their regulatory sphere. In this the medical profession has had important advantages, principally stemming from its historical connection with science and technology. Starr has put the point eloquently:

> The medical profession has had an especially persuasive claim to authority. Unlike the law and the clergy, it enjoys close bonds with modern science, and at least for most of the last century, scientific knowledge has held a privileged status in the hierarchy of belief. Even among the sciences, medicine occupies a special position. Its practitioners come into direct and intimate contact with people in their daily lives; they are present at the critical transitional moments of existence. They serve as intermediaries between science and private experience, interpreting personal troubles in the abstract language of scientific knowledge.[5]

In short, medicine is special. In the words of Freidson's classic study of the profession as a system of knowledge: 'Among the traditional professions established in the European universities of the Middle Ages it alone has developed a systematic connection with science and technology.'[6]

It is this very historical success which makes the government of doctors central to our understanding of the health care state. A key feature of the health care state, we know, is the way the institutions of the health care system and those of the state are wound around each other. The historical regulatory strategies of medical professions, relying as they have done on a special relationship with both the state and the market, exemplify these entanglements. That is why their regulatory strategies make doctors so important to health care government. Since entanglement is the essence of the health care state, any important changes in the entanglements created by the regulation of doctors tells us about something beyond doctors: it reveals something important about how far the wider character of health care government is changing.

The point is made more significant still because the regulatory strategies pursued by doctors are creations of the fairly distant past. In the case of the UK and of Germany they largely pre-date the rise of democratic politics. In the case of the US they pre-date both the rise of the giant health care industries and the creation of large and complex health care policy networks. In much of the existing modern literature on the politics of the profession the impact of change on the character of these historically established strategies is expressed in the language of decline – as a story of the passing of the political and the cultural supremacy of the profession.[7] But this straightforward characterisation obscures important differences in the way the regulatory strategy of medicine was created in different national circumstances – and the circumstances of original creation critically affect the way the regulatory strategy has fared in the modern world. The sections that follow try to take account of this fact of national diversity. In the case of the UK, the overwhelmingly important fact about the regulatory strategy was that it was worked out before the rise of a democratic, interventionist state, and the key problem facing the profession has been how to respond to the changed democratic environment. In the case of the US, by contrast, the regulatory strategy was in part a response to the existence of challenges from a populist, democratic political culture, but one where both the health care industries and government were small in scale. The key problems facing modern medicine have been what to do about the transformation in health care markets, and how to respond to the changed role thrust on the state by market change. The German case is also distinguished by the problem of accommodating change in the face of alteration in the state and in the market. As we saw in Chapter 2, after the Second World War health care government was rebuilt along corporatist lines. In the case of doctors many of the central institutions were the product of the Nazi period. The critical German problem has been how to fit these arrangements into the capitalist democracy that developed after the foundation of the *Bundesrepublik* in 1949.

The United Kingdom: doctors, the state and democracy

The origins of the modern regulation of the medical profession can be dated to the Medical Act of 1858, which established what was then known as the General Council of Medical Education and Registration (shortened to the General Medical Council (GMC) in 1951).[8] The Act established a relationship between the medical profession, the state and the market that was, unsurprisingly, a product of its time – a time when the state's regulatory capacities were small, its governing principles oligarchic and its domestic economic and social responsibilities few. The profession's historic problem has been how to stabilise that relationship in the face of political and economic change. Politically, in the intervening period the state has been transformed in obvious and well-known ways: from an imperial state with few responsibilities or capacities in the sphere of health care to a democratic, interventionist state running a command and control health care economy. Economically, the UK descended from a position as the world's industrial pioneer to a place as an international economy of the second rank plagued by chronic problems of industrial decline. Understanding the modern government of the profession is, at heart, a matter of understanding how the profession has tried to come to terms with these changes.

The GMC is by no means the whole of medical government in the UK[9] but the pressures to which it has been subject provide a measure of the tensions arising from the gap between the historical conditions that shaped the regulatory system and the modern government of health care. In these pages I use the case of the GMC to explore these tensions. The original title of the GMC (the General Council of *Medical Education* and *Registration*) encapsulates both the ambitions and the limitations of its historical regulatory strategy. That strategy had three features, all of which were to do with protecting doctors from state control and capitalist competition: the creation of institutions of private interest government; the elaboration of a regulatory ideology which defined professional misconduct so as simultaneously to restrict market competition and maximise the clinical autonomy of doctors; and the development of a system of medical education controlled by the profession itself. They are here considered in turn.

The system of private interest government was heavily skewed in favour of the profession. Formally the GMC was, as the Merrison Committee put it in 1975, an agent in a regulatory contract: 'the GMC is merely the instrument for the proper supervision of this contract ... it derives its authority, and indeed its being from legislation. The legislature – that is, Parliament – acts in this context for the public, and it is for Parliament to decide the nature of the contract and the way it is to be executed.'[10] In fact the prevailing ideology of self-regulation – an ideology faithfully reflected even in the report of the Merrison Committee itself[11] – meant that Parliament in practice hardly ever 'decided': Merrison, established in 1972, was the first general review of regulation of the profession for a century.[12] The regulatory contract gave the state few opportunities to intervene in the government of the profession. Until reforms introduced at the end of the 1970s most of the membership of the GMC was chosen by various constituencies in the profession itself. Even the small minority nominated by the central state (formally by the Privy Council) were doctors; not until the 1950 Medical Act was there any statutory provision for the nomination of lay members of the council.[13] The composition of the GMC was symptomatic of something more profound still – the insulation of the council from the institutions of the state. The successive acts governing regulation from 1858 onwards typically only sketched the procedures governing its operations, the details being filled in by Orders in Council. In other words, Parliament's say was in practice severely restricted: even the 1978 Medical Act, though it was passed in part as a result of a constitutional crisis in the GMC, did not prescribe the numbers in the various categories on the council, leaving that to a (subsequent) Order of (Privy) Council. The mechanism of working through Orders in Council marginalised parliamentary scrutiny of medical regulation.[14] The historical understanding marginalised central government, because the contents of the orders were in reality proposed by the GMC. The extent to which this was a settled understanding is shown by the constitutional shock administered by the refusal of the Privy Council (which in reality meant the Department of Health) in 1984 to 'nod through' GMC proposals which marginally changed the rules governing fitness of doctors to practice (on the grounds, precisely, that they were marginal when more radical reforms were required).[15] In short, for most of its history the GMC was able to insulate itself from the democratic, interventionist state that developed in the UK in the twentieth century.

The second historically established feature of the GMC was its distinctive ideology of professional regulation. The 1858 Act had a very precise, comparatively narrow object, which was to control the title of doctor (more precisely, registered medical practitioner) and the prestige and market advantage which flowed from the appropriation of that title. As the preamble to the Act said: it was 'expedient that persons requiring medical aid should be enabled to distinguish qualified from disqualified practitioners'.[16] (In some other countries the object was more ambitious: to outlaw the practice of medicine other than the medicine of which the profession officially approved; in Britain only the title was controlled.) Maintaining the register was the GMC's most important job, and exclusion from the register was the principal weapon it used to exercise control over professional practice. Its conception of professional and unprofessional conduct in turn reflected this simultaneously expansive and narrow conception of its role: on the one hand expansive, because it was used to impose a conception of medical practice which displaced a wide range of 'alternative' therapies and banned a wide range of competitive practices, like advertising for business; on the other hand narrow, because the grounds on which doctors could be struck off for individual misconduct were very restricted and had little to do with clinical incompetence. The staple diet of the GMC's disciplinary hearings concerned individual misconduct, often involving sexual relations with patients – an important issue given the combination of a male-dominated profession with clinical practice that involved physically intimate examination, but striking in its avoidance of any but the most extreme cases of clinical incompetence. As a set of cases in the 1980s showed, it was possible to treat patients in a grossly negligent way and not be found guilty of serious professional misconduct. It sometimes seemed that the GMC's conception of misconduct was concerned more with how doctors treated each other than with how they treated their patients. The biggest section of the Blue Book, the Council's disciplinary code, was even at the beginning of 1990s still concerned with the advertising of doctors' services.[17] At the heart of this notion lay a restrictive regulatory ideology. Its function was to ensure not only that doctors were not interfered with by the state, but also that they were protected against the competitive forces of a market economy, and were free in their daily clinical practice from the regulatory oversight of their own governing institution.

This very narrow conception of professional regulation was connected to the third key component of the profession's regulatory strategy – the regulation of education and training. The relevance of education and training to the creation and maintenance of professional authority in medicine is obvious: much of the authority of modern medicine derives in large part from the popular belief that it rests on the intellectual foundations of modern science, which doctors are presumed to use to guide their clinical decisions. That connection was emphasised by the reference to medical education in the GMC's original title: the General Council of *Medical Education* and *Registration*. Yet historically the GMC played a largely passive part in shaping the medical curriculum. It was responsible for the base of medical education – the undergraduate curriculum – and for inspecting and visiting medical faculties; but, in the restrained official language of the Merrison committee, 'direct supervisory powers have been used sparingly in recent years'. In fact, when Merrison enquired there had not been a single inspection or visitation of UK medical schools for fifteen years.[18] The GMC stressed guidance and advice, not prescription. Merrison, again faithfully replicating the dominant ideology, remarked: 'There seems little doubt that the chief influence of the GMC on undergraduate medical education is to be found in this work of discussion, advice, and encouragement rather than in the exercise of its formal powers.'[19]

In practice, medical education was controlled by the elite of the profession, especially in the leading universities. The universities had the right to nominate significant numbers of members of the GMC, and these university members controlled its education policy. The leading medical schools were virtually autonomous, despite the council's formal obligation to inspect them. The regulation of postgraduate education – which affected access to consultancy posts, the most prestigious in the profession – was in turn scattered in an uncoordinated fashion across a range of professional bodies, including the Royal Colleges.

The constitution of the GMC, its dominant regulatory ideology and its conception of education and training were therefore all of a piece, with the profession's historical project of 'closing' the occupation off from the twin influences of a competitive market economy and from the state. The modern fate of these three elements of the regulatory system shows the problems of pursuing that project in democratic, capitalist Britain.

The constitution of the GMC not only insulated the profession from the state; a system that allowed powerful interests to nominate members institutionalised domination by professional and social elites. Political and social change altered the demography of the profession in the post-war years; the government of the profession showed little ability to respond to these changes. Two striking instances – documented by Stacey – are the way the rising status and significance of the GP, and the growing numbers of women in the profession, failed to be reflected in the make-up of the council: before the reforms in the 1978 Act the Royal College of General Practitioners (the newest of the

Royal Colleges) was not allocated a seat on the council; and while between 1951 and 1971 the numbers of women registered as doctors rose from just over 7,500 to just over 12,500, the number of women on the council remained unchanged (at one).[20] The 1970s and 1980s were decades of periodic uproar about the government of the council, and this uproar, as far as the historic regulatory strategy was concerned, had a most undesired outcome: it drew the central state – including parliament – into arguments about professional government.

The initial occasion of this uproar, at the start of the 1970s, involved two of the most delicate elements in private interest government: money and authority. The two were connected. The GMC was a self-funded body levying its own 'tax', a registration fee imposed on newly qualified doctors. Finance independent of the state was critical to preserving the council's independence. This arrangement is typical of the practice of 'self-regulation' in Britain, for to rely on public finance is to incur the risk of public control. But how was the Council to acquire the authority to extend or raise its 'taxes' if financial circumstances dictated this necessity? The answer to the question, the events of the early 1970s suggested, was that it could not summon up that authority. Faced with financial problems in the late 1960s the GMC announced the introduction of a 'retention fee' for all those on the register – the replacement, in other words, of a single levy at the moment of registration by an annual tax on every doctor on the register. As the history of tax revolts against governments shows – witness the story of the poll tax in the UK[21] – the attempt to impose new taxes is often beyond even the authority of the state, and opposition to a tax is often bound up with deeper opposition to the taxing authority. That was exactly the story of the retention fee: attempts to impose it showed both the limits of GMC authority and brought to the surface deep dissatisfaction with its whole structure. The attempt to impose the annual retention fee in the face of bitter opposition from established doctors proved beyond the authority of the council primarily because, faced with opposition, its only sanction was deregistration. This was draconian and effective if imposed on a single isolated doctor; it was more problematic in effectiveness if it meant cancelling the registration of thousands of doctors, including some of the brightest and most articulate junior members of the profession. That is soon what the council found itself faced with: refusal of several thousand doctors to pay the fee; mass opposition organised, among other places, through the British Medical Association; and finally the election of rebels to the council itself, including some who faced being struck from the register. The leadership responded, in the manner of embattled oligarchies, with a mixture of threats and concessions: threats to impose the sanction of deregistration mixed with council-sponsored enquiries and working parties.[22]

The crisis over the retention fee is important for many reasons. It exposed the authority deficit faced by a council trying to operate a nineteenth-century regulatory ideology in twentieth-century conditions. It brought into the open intense competition within the profession for access to the resources and prestige enjoyed by those occupying positions at the head of the profession; since competition in the marketplace for these resources was suppressed, it could only take place via political struggle within the profession itself. (The fact that successful professions suppress market competition as a means of struggle for resources helps explain why professions are so commonly marked by internal political struggles between different generations of professionals; in the absence of market competition this is how ambitious juniors try to displace those who command the most lucrative positions in the market.[23]) Finally, the crisis over the retention fee showed that in a society where the state was the most important funder of health care the profession's constitutional autonomy could not be tolerated if it threatened the state's capacity to discharge its responsibilities. In 1972 the Secretary of State announced the establishment of a committee of inquiry into the regulation of the profession (the Merrison Committee). That was a defining moment: a nineteenth-century regulatory ideology had encountered a twentieth-century interventionist state. The state was forced to intervene because mass deregistration by the GMC would have caused chaos in the NHS. The subsequent history of regulation shows the profession struggling to defend three traditional aspects of regulation: the structure of the institutions themselves, the traditional conceptions of professional standards, and the GMC's traditional approach to education and training. Again I look at each of these in turn.

The crisis over the retention fees illustrates the problems faced by the GMC in trying to operate inside a democratic, interventionist state. But at least in the short term the elite that led the profession still had considerable resources to protect professional independence. The elite captured the Merrison Committee from the very start of the enquiry. Half the Committee were from the profession itself, and the Merrison Report faithfully supported the ideology of self-regulation, intoning: 'the most effective safeguard of the public is the self-respect of the profession itself.'[24] The elite of the profession used its lobbying power, notably the position of leading doctors in the Upper House of Lords, to shape the Medical Act which was eventually produced in 1978 as a result of the enquiry. The profession was forced to concede a larger council, with wider constituencies, more opportunities for doctors at large to elect members, more nominated lay members, and a more formally organised internal committee structure. But the legislation was, in Stacey's words, 'the profession's Act'.[25] Its most signal accomplishment was to stabilise a potentially disruptive issue – the appropriate constitution for a professional regulatory body operating under a licence from a democratic state.

But the history of the second part of the GMC's regulatory strategy – its approach to regulating professional conduct – shows the problem of keeping out the wider democratic state once its attention was drawn to the regulatory system. It will be recalled that the established ideology was designed to minimise incursion into the domain of clinical practice; it stressed instead personal misconduct (such as sexual misconduct) towards patients and misconduct towards fellow professionals (by banning advertising or the casting of aspersions on the competence of colleagues).

In the 1980s the pressures of democratic politics forced changes in this narrow conception of how to regulate medical conduct. The GMC was faced with a number of cases of particularly scandalous mistreatment of patients, but was forced to admit that, while not contesting the gravity of the cases, they were too central to issues of clinical competence to be covered by its established notions of 'serious professional misconduct'. The gap between the notion of what the regulatory ideology specified as misconduct, and what popular – indeed common sense – notions would suggest was highlighted by widespread parliamentary and media criticism of the council's approach to such cases. A notion of misconduct which marginalised the issue of the clinical treatment of patients was just not sustainable in a democracy, especially in a democracy where patients were becoming daily more informed, better educated and more self-confident.[26] Nor, it became plain in the 1980s, was a notion of misconduct which paid little attention to clinical competence sustainable in the face of a state which was attempting to reconstruct a wide range of British institutions, including the health service, to cope with the problems of British economic decline. This is the significance of the episode already referred to in passing, the unprecedented refusal of the Privy Council (which in reality meant the Department of Health) to nod through some marginal reforms which the GMC proposed in its government of clinical competence. The rejection was followed by a rapid widening of the range of debate about the competence and functioning of doctors. A reference to the Office of Fair Trading, and then to the Monopolies and Mergers Commission, resulted in a report which was highly critical of some competitive restrictions within the profession, obliging the council to relax its prohibitions on advertising.[27] There now occurred an incremental expansion of the range of the council's disciplinary scope, to encompass increasingly wide review of the clinical competence of members of the profession.[28] It is possible to argue that this process of widening has been, precisely, incremental, and does not address the gravity of the problems of regulating incompetent doctors. The key point from the view of the government of the profession, however, is that it has permanently destabilised the regulatory understanding which for so long allowed the GMC to operate a restrictive regulatory ideology that protected doctors from scrutiny of their clinical judgements. One potentially fatal consequence from the point of view of the council's control of medical professionalism is the long-term tendency for disciplinary matters to be dealt with by the mechanisms of the NHS rather than by the GMC itself, a trend that was already well established by the late 1980s.[29]

The issue of control of education shows, if anything, even longer-run instability. Even before the upheavals of the 1970s and the 1980s the GMC's control of medical education was being undermined by the state. As long ago as the establishment of the NHS in the 1940s, central state control of medical manpower planning, and the control of the teaching hospitals by governors acting as agents of the Minister, meant that it was the state, not the GMC, which controlled the numbers entering the profession: from then on the council was simply accepting onto the home register the numbers produced from the university medical schools as a result of national manpower decisions about the numbers of medical graduates to be produced.[30] (Some argue, however, that in a more subtle way the elite of the profession continued to influence these decisions through its domination of the committee which advised central government on manpower planning for the profession.[31]) The profession was likewise losing long-term control over the composition of entrants to medicine. Although selection of applicants to medical schools continues to be decentralised to the individual faculties, after the criticisms of selection methods made in the Todd Report on medical education in 1968 it became unacceptable openly to impose quotas, such as those governing numbers of women students.[32]

Nevertheless, until the 1990s the profession's autonomy remained substantial, guaranteed less by any overt instruments of control than by the way responsibility for medical education was scattered piecemeal across a range of institutions – the GMC itself, the universities, the Royal Colleges. Although there is still room as the century closes for argument about just how much in substance the profession has surrendered its autonomy to the wider democratic state, viewed over the two decades since the passage of the Medical Act in 1978 a number of long-term trends are identifiable, suggesting that control of education is passing outside the sphere of private interest government. The medical schools have surrendered some autonomy, partly to the central state, partly to the GMC itself. Reforms of the structure of medical education by the Department of Health in the 1990s created a regional framework in which university medical education was more closely integrated into the structure of the NHS.[33] (From another direction the growing significance of research assessment exercises for the allocation of state resources to medical faculties in universities has also diminished the autonomy of medical faculties.) The GMC itself has also begun to develop a more activist attitude both towards the content of the undergraduate medical curriculum and the inspection of the licensed schools. It has replaced the almost total lack of inspection that was the norm until the early 1980s with periodic, systematic inspections (though the thoroughness and effectiveness of these is contested[34]). That more activist stance is a product of many forces, but it partly results from the institutional changes introduced by the 1978 Medical Act which for the first time gave the council responsibility for coordinating all stages of medical education. That general responsibility was only slowly turned into GMC policy, but by the end of the 1980s the council was already receiving recommendations for the reorganisation of its responsibilities for the education of specialists. Stacey, however, nicely illustrates the great delicacy created for the council's position by the existence of the wider democratic environment and by a public opinion increasingly sceptical of medical authority. She notes that significant change would have required institutional reforms to the GMC involving legislation, and 'the Council was nervous throughout the 1980s of proposing legislation; the political atmosphere was unfavourable to professionals in general and to medicine in particular, suggesting that there might be above-average hazards in requesting legislation – better to hope the dogs would snooze if not disturbed'.[35] A system of private government which simultaneously tries to create a consensus between all incorporated interests, and to avoid invoking state authority for fear of state control, obviously runs the risk of changing policy so slowly that the state, faced with pressure to change, will simply move ahead of its own accord. With the creation by the Department of Health in the early 1990s of a single new *Advisory Group on Medical Education, Training and Staffing* (chaired by the Chief Medical Officer of the DOH), given responsibility for overseeing all medical workforce issues, there are signs that the GMC is indeed in danger of losing control of the agenda of medical education.[36]

In examining the government of the medical profession in Britain we have concentrated on the GMC, both because it is substantively important in the government of the profession, and because an exploration of its changing fate highlights the difficulties of preserving into a democratic age regulatory arrangements created in undemocratic times. Although in some respects the profession proved remarkably successful in maintaining the institutions of self-government, it is also obvious that the years since the passage of the 1978 Medical Act have seen great changes in how 'self-regulation' is actually practised. The changes might be summarised as: much more intrusion in the sphere of clinical judgement both by the council and by state agencies; employment relations which are much more tightly prescribed than was the case a couple of decades ago; and a council itself whose constitution and composition are subject to much closer scrutiny than was the case hitherto. The two decades after the passage of the Medical Act in 1978 saw an acceleration in the pace at which the enclosed regulatory world of medical government was invaded by agencies of the state. Although in the 1970s there were tensions between a system of regulation dating from the nineteenth century and modern political and economic conditions, those tensions were fairly successfully contained. The same can not be said about the experience of the last two decades. The development of a democratic political system in Britain in the twentieth century, coupled with the domination of that political system by ideologies which legitimised a highly interventionist state, meant that in constitutional terms there were powerfully anachronistic elements in the system of medical government. Nevertheless, the traditional ideologies of regulation proved strikingly resilient, buttressed as they were by powerful ideologies of self-regulation in the surrounding culture. Two developments exposed the weakness of the medical profession's constitutional position. One was the wider, more long-term weakening of the general ideology of self-regulation in the surrounding society. A more immediate force was the great national economic crisis of the mid-1970s which led to major changes in the economic statecraft of governing elites. The biggest change is usually, if inadequately, summed up in terms of the rise of Thatcherism as a force in British government: a force which combined hostility to many traditional elites, a determination to use the power of the central state machine to produce change, and a rhetoric of free-market economics which produced a natural scepticism about one of the major features of professionalism – the protection of whole occupations from the wider competitive forces of a capitalist economy.

It will be immediately apparent that some of the forces at work in Britain must also be present in other capitalist economies, but that some of the experience – especially of intense economic crisis in the 1970s – is not shared. How our two other countries fared is the subject of the succeeding sections.

Germany: doctors, the state and corporatism

The system of private interest government for doctors that was established historically in the UK was designed simultaneously to protect the clinical autonomy of doctors, to keep the state at a distance and to suppress market competition. It did this through what might be called a minimalist design: while the governing institutions borrowed authority from the state, they tried to keep the state out of the governing process; and their definition of regulatory responsibilities kept the substance of regulation – and thus of intervention in the working lives of doctors – to a minimum. When we turn to Germany we also see a system of professional self-government, but one with very different characteristics: one involving a historically close partnership with the state; extensive exercise of authority by self-governing associations over the working lives of doctors; an elaborately coded system of rules, many incorporated into the statute book; and extensive participation by the institutions of the medical profession in the wider government of the health care system. The historical British strategy might be summed up as the creation of a private governing world enclosed from the wider world of the state and the market; the German as a strategy involving the use of powerful self-governing institutions to intervene in that wider world. Not surprisingly, the German system of medical government has reacted differently from the British system to the pressures created by rise of democracy and the expansion of the health care state.

The contrast between the minimalist British institutional design and the German system is immediately evident when we bear in mind the character of the GMC – its marginal position in the world of health care delivery and payment, its scarce resources and its very narrow conception of its own institutional mission – and then look at German arrangements. The first obvious difference is the much greater complexity of the German institutional system. Two sets of institutions are at the heart of German arrangements: the institutions of the chamber system (*Ärztekammern*), and the associations of insurance doctors (*Kassenärtzliche Vereinigungen* (KVs)).

The most important chambers are organised at the level of individual *Länder*, and carry out functions delegated to them by the governments of the individual states. Thus the responsibility for licensing doctors, nominally the responsibility of the *Land* government, is in practice done by the physicians' chambers. From this power of licensing follow responsibilities related to the internal government of the profession: the control of medical ethics, the organisation of disciplinary processes, and the organisation of continuing education and training for the profession.[37] As we saw in Chapter 2, the associations of insurance doctors were created right at the end of Weimar era, but owe their continuing prominence to a structure consolidated in the Nazi period; the chambers, although enjoying a longer lineage, likewise owe much of their importance to decisions taken under the Nazi dictatorship.

By contrast with the historical GMC strategy of 'enclosing' a regulatory space away from the state, the chambers in Germany reflect a distinctive constitutional tradition, in which professions are 'sponsored' by the state. Three important consequences follow from this. First, the *public* character of the chambers is much more unambiguous than is the public character of the GMC: the rules of the state chambers, reflecting their public law status, are typically incorporated as state law. Second, the historical character of the 'contract' between the state and the profession has been both more explicit and more juridified than is the case in Britain. As we saw in our examination of the development of the system, a key part of the historical project of the medical profession was to ensure state-sanctioned protection from the competitive processes of a market economy: that was finally achieved under the Nazi dictatorship in 1935 with the proclamation that medicine was a profession not a trade.[38] From this judgment, and the protection against capitalist economics which it brought, flows a third feature of the chamber system: the, by British standards, comprehensive and detailed rules which it enforces. A simple measure of this is physical: to compare the even now short and skeletal rule book of the GMC (the Blue Book) with the German *Medical Profession Law* (at federal level) and the *Professional Medical Codes* of each individual *Land*.[39] This simple physical contrast goes with a substantive difference, in the extent to which the chambers impose on doctors substantive obligations – for instance, the obligations on office doctors to keep regular consulting hours, which are prescribed as appropriate by different state chambers.[40]

The comparatively substantively elaborate nature of the professional regulatory system becomes even more marked when we turn to the role of the second of the institutions that are central to the regulatory system, the associations of insurance doctors. It will be recalled that the historical origins of the associations (right at the death knell of the Weimar regime) had to do with the realisation of a key aim of the medical profession – to wrest control of pay and conditions from the third-party payers, the insurance funds. That victory created a network of associations, the most important of which are organised at the *Länder* level.[41] The conventional English rendering (associations of insurance doctors) fails to convey the significance of these bodies, implying as it does that they are voluntaristic in character. While formally not compulsory for all doctors, in practice membership of the relevant association is obligatory for all office doctors, because only members of KVs are eligible to claim payment for treatment of insured patients – the overwhelming majority of the population and the source of income for doctors in office practice.[42] The Associations too, in turn, have a public law status: they enjoy a range of privileges (see below) and in turn are contracted with the statutory insurance funds to ensure the delivery of a prescribed range of health care services. The associations have extensive obligations which are embodied in federal and *Land* law: 'The physicians' associations have to provide health services as defined by the legislature and they have to guarantee the sickness funds that this provision meets the legal and contracted requirements.'[43] In turn, the associations and their members have a monopoly over the market in ambulatory care in the community – the most lucrative and the most prestigious part of the German health care system.

But the institutional importance of the associations does not stop there. The heart of their role lies in the part they play in the payment system. The associations are the key actors on the doctors' side in negotiations to establish, in effect, the rates of pay for the clinical services provided by their members – principally by negotiating the details of an elaborate set of fee schedules that are central to the 'fee for service' system that is in turn central to payment arrangements. But their role in negotiation is only part of the story – arguably even the less important part. For the associations are also responsible for the implementation of payment arrangements. The way they have done this precisely has varied over the history of the post-war Federal Republic – and the range of this variation is itself an index, as we shall see, of the changing institutional structure of medical government. But the heart of this role lies in the function of the Associations in distributing payments to doctors in office practice. The medical profession's great triumph in establishing the Associations in the early 1930s was to free individual doctors from the need to deal directly with the insurance funds – and thus to remove the great threat to doctors' ambitions to remain a liberal profession.[44] Payments for services rendered are disbursed by the associations, who receive for this purpose a lump sum based on collective negotiations between them and the funds. This fact makes the associations vital to the working lives of their doctors – involving a high, and increasing, level of intrusion into everyday clinical decision making. Schwartz and Busse give a hint of the control potential in the system: 'The physicians' associations have to distribute these total payments according to the unified value scale and their regulations on the distribution of payments. The physicians' associations have to check, record and sum up the data that form the basis of these calculations.'[45]

This bare institutional detail, impressive though it is by comparison with the skeletal UK system, still fails to convey the full importance of the institutions of medical government in the German system, for what it fails to communicate is the central role occupied by the leading figures in medical government, by virtue of their institutional position, in the wider world of health care policy making. The historic GMC strategy was to try to enclose the government of doctors in a world separate from the state; one price of this was to separate the world of the government of doctors from the wider world of health care policy – with the sort of strains and stresses outlined in the last section. But the public law character of the chambers and the associations, the central role of the latter in the payment system, and the relatively marginal role of the core state machine in the shaping and implementation of policy, have made the governing associations central, not just to the government of doctors, but to the wider government of the health care system. The flavour of this has been well caught by Döhler in an important comparative study of health policy networks:

> the German health policy network is characterized by a strong vertical integration of single associations which is complemented by an additional horizontal interdependence between peak associations at the regional and federal level which is a result of corporatist concertation. This latter trait distinguishes the German case from Britain and the US where there is almost no horizontal linkage in health care and no indicator for corporatist policy processing.[46]

This system, as we saw in Chapter 2, is in essence the product of the culmination of a particular historical project, and was successfully reconstructed in the years immediately following the Second World War. But of course the system has not been static since the 1950s, and the evolution of the system of medical government can be thought of as exemplifying the problem of maintaining a world of corporatist government within the framework of a market economy and a democratic polity. The end point of these changes – at least at the time of writing – is, as we shall see, to leave the corporatist system of government in a destabilised and fragile state as the century closes.

Three interlinked features illustrate what has been going on: structural change in the profession itself; the problem of controlling entry to the profession using the established mechanisms of corporatist regulation; and the way pressures for cost containment – pressures which in the last chapter we saw affecting the government of consumption – have helped reshape the institutions of medical government.

The historical world into which the institutions described here were born was one where office-based doctors dominated the profession – and indeed the health care system. One simple index of that domination is provided by numbers: in 1956, just about the moment when by our arbitrary cut-off in Chapter 2 'history' ended, there were just over 45,000 doctors in office practice (compared with 30,000 employed in hospitals).[47] But office doctors were not just more numerous; they were also the most prestigious group in the profession. The Weimar reforms and the Nazi aftermath had transformed the nature of office practice in Germany. Politically, they were the dominant medical actors in the health care system (indeed, probably the single dominant group of actors overall in the system). That domination was reinforced by their monopoly of ambulatory care. Coupled with the fee for service system it encouraged developments unknown in the UK: the appearance of specialists in particular branches of medicine in office practice; and, partly as a consequence of this, the proliferation of high technology medicine in office practice.[48] These developments in turn only magnified the prestige of office practice further by associating it with the most desirable (from the point of view of medical professionals) form of medicine. This dominant part of the profession has, however, been unable to insulate itself from the three developments associated with competition and structural change: alterations in the character and composition of the medical profession; problems of controlling the wider labour market in medicine; and problems in stabilising the relationship between the profession and the state.

The changing character of medicine can partly be illustrated by some bare trends in figures. There has been a long-term rise in the proportion of the profession employed in hospital rather than in office practice: in 1975 numbers of hospital doctors for the first time exceeded those in office practice; by the end of the 1980s there were about 15,000 more doctors working in hospitals than in office practice.[49] (The early 1990s saw a surge of doctors into office practice, but this was only a short-term opportunistic development, as doctors sought to anticipate the introduction of restrictions on numbers who would be admitted to practice as a result of the Seehofer reforms.[50]) These figures do not in themselves indicate a decline in the prestige of office-based medicine, but they do have implications for the balance of interests in the wider health care system. The sharp separation of ambulatory from institutional care is paralleled by an equally clear separation of their associational worlds: there are separate representative associations for office doctors and hospital doctors (*Hartmannbund* and *Marburger Bund*), while the negotiations for payment for care are also conducted separately.[51] Hospital doctors are for the most part salaried professionals employed in institutional hierarchies – a very different model of professional practice from the liberal professionalism of office practice.

The rise in numbers of hospital doctors, however, is also symptomatic of powerful internal tensions in the profession. In part, hospital doctors are 'doctors in waiting': in other words, a large proportion are in hospitals while they seek a place in the lucrative and prestigious world of office practice. The changing social composition of the profession means that hospital doctors are therefore not only more poorly paid and less prestigious; they are also younger and, because of changes in the gender balance of medicine, they include a higher proportion of women. The changing balance between hospital practice and office practice is thus a symptom of a struggle for position in the wider medical labour market.[52]

That struggle has been intensified by the inability of the profession to control the supply of doctors entering either the profession at large, or office practice. The problems in both cases reflect a failure of the profession (among others) to control the wider political environment – notably the environment resulting from the creation of a post-war state governed by the norms of a written constitution interpreted by an independent judiciary.

The problems of control over initial entry are well illustrated by what happened to medical education. In Germany, as in the UK, medical qualification begins with an undergraduate curriculum. But whereas in the British system the central state exerted the most minute and detailed control over numbers entering undergraduate medicine, medical schools in Germany, like the rest of the German university system, experienced great growth from the late 1960s: in 1960 there were 26,000 students studying medicine in Germany; within a quarter of a century the figure had risen to 84,000. In broad terms the expansion followed the contours of expansion of the wider university system.[53] These control problems were the product in part of the nature of the German university system and in part a product of the nature of the German political system. The historical character of German universities is very different from their British counterparts. The traditional British university was dominated by a teaching mission – to train an elite through the undergraduate curriculum and immersion in the closed world of a college. German universities were research driven. As far as teaching was concerned, they have been places where all those qualified – not just those selected by an individual institution – could attend to learn from the most distinguished researchers. That presumption of open entry was reinforced in the *Bundesrepublik* by the dominant understanding of the Basic Law (the Constitution) formulated after the war to try to safeguard the individual and institutional freedoms violated in the Nazi dictatorship. As far as medical education is concerned the most important result has been the way the constitution, in entrenching Land control over education as a way of dispersing power in the federal system, has made immensely difficult the development of precisely the sort of centralised control of student numbers which has characterised the UK. The difficulties in controlling entry to medical education are an illustration of the sort of wider steering deficits pointed to by observers of the German political system.[54]

The way to think about this kind of experience is to recollect the phenomenon of *embeddedness* identified in our opening chapter: the way what happens in health care institutions is contrained by the wider political and economic setting in which they lie. Democratic politics is obviously a key part of that phenomenon of embeddedness. The historical construction of the profession was a pre-democratic anachronism – the result of a regulatory contract between the old Prussian state and an emergent *Bildungsbürgertum*.[55] In the *Bundesrepubublik* it had to live in a world of democratic politics where there were powerful constitutional restraints on the exercise of power. These constitutional understandings have been even more important in efforts to regulate a second key point of entry – to office practice, the top of the occupational ladder. At the root of the problem lay the institutional arrangements designed to safeguard post-war democracy, and the fact that the old structures of doctor power were rebuilt in the decade after the Second World War. The institutional arrangements quite consciously weakened the capacity of the central state to steer public policy. As we have seen, it was particularly weak in the sphere of health care. The Insurance Doctors' Law of 1957 was an attempt by the federal state to exert some control. It prescribed a fixed ratio of doctors to population. This was struck down in 1960 by the Constitutional Court, after a challenge by representatives of hospital doctors, who naturally saw the law as a threat to their members' ability to progress into office practice. The court's reasoning was that the law was an infringement of the constitutional right freely to practise a profession – a provision that was an obvious attempt to safeguard the autonomy of the liberal professions against the controls to which they had been subject under the Nazi dictatorship.[56] Thus, distinctively German constitutional ideologies of democratic government have been important in struggles for position in the professional labour market.

Although one purpose of the clause on which the court drew was to safeguard the autonomy of liberal professionalism from public power, it would be wrong to picture these developments as the straightforward exercise of medical power against the state. The profession was itself divided, because those doctors already established in office practice had a powerful interest in controlling the rate of entry into the market. Despite all the impressive resources of the corporatist institutions that regulated the medical labour market, the history of medical education shows a serious authority deficit in the policy-making system, and that deficit is the product of a combination of factors: a weak central state, a powerful written constitution, and the attribution of authority to corporatist bodies. The decision of the Constitutional Court in 1960 put a powerful hobble on to the making of authoritative decisions. In the 1980s only marginal controls were imposed: some limits on entry to medical education were set by universities on grounds of sheer physical capacity; and there were some very limited restrictions on entry to practice as an insurance doctor in areas where there was judged to be overcapacity (for the problem has been not only the number of doctors but the way they concentrate in areas where practice is most lucrative and pleasant).[57]

The true significance of the hesitant attempts to regulate entry to practice as an insurance doctor was that they represented an effort by the federal state to regulate a key part of the medical labour market which had previously been an area of autonomous corporatist regulation. The years since then are marked by two linked tendencies in the government of doctors: more state intervention; and more detailed, hierarchical controls over doctors by the corporatist institutions themselves, notably by the associations of insurance doctors. The first of these tendencies is illustrated by developments in controls over labour market entry; the second by the spread of various kinds of utilisation review. These I examine in turn.

The power of doctors and their political allies ensured that the 1989 health care reform law evaded the problem of how to control entry to the medical labour market.[58] Partly in response to the experience of 1989 the Seehofer structural reforms (passed into law in 1992, effective 1993) were prepared and driven through in a very different way, in the teeth of fierce opposition from the organisations representing doctors. For the first time a retirement age (68) has been prescribed for doctors in office practice. Most significant of all, the 1992 law gave power to the assocations of insurance doctors in individual *Länder* to refuse to accept new entrants to office practice if they judged their region to be oversupplied with doctors – a sharp breach with the entrenched constitutional right freely to practice a liberal profession.[59] Although hemmed in with numerous qualifications, delayed until the end of the century in the implementation of its measures, and containing some clauses of dubious constitutional legitimacy, the 1993 law represented a decisive shift to state – indeed central state – steering of the corporatist system.

The shift to more detailed utilisation review shows how the control potential implicit in a highly institutionalised system of corporatism is beginning to be realised. The system of payment for office doctors – in which a collective sum, negotiated with the insurance funds, is then disbursed by the associations to their members in response to *ex post* claims for payment based on a 'fee for service' schedule – is the key to the development of utilisation review. Historically the associations acquired some inspection functions, if only to try to ensure that the claims made by doctors were not fraudulent. Under the pressure to contain costs – and because the system of paying from a fixed global sum means that any excess payments to one doctor or group of doctors reduces the sum available to the rest – there has been a steady increase both in the intensity of the surveillance of the inspection system and a steady widening beyond the purely financial matter of ensuring that payments claimed correspond properly to services performed, into the broader area of the range and frequency of services performed by doctors. The 1993 reforms increased further the extent to which the corporatist institutions and the state engage in surveillance over, and control of, the clinical practices of doctors. There has been a further decisive shift away from surveillance for purposes of combating financial irregularity, to a concern with influencing the actual treatment practices of clinicians. These involve the introduction of annual budgets regulating the increases allowable to individual doctors; the introduction of flat-rate payment systems; and the creation of a fixed budget for drug prescription with doctors collectively held liable for overspending (this last providing the associations with a powerful incentive to regulate).[60]

But perhaps the greatest significance of the 1993 reforms as far as the medical profession is concerned is the way they fit into the wider institutional landscape of health care. When we combine what has happened – even given that much of it is delayed, and some may still be challenged in the Constitutional Court – with the sort of changes that were described in our last chapter on the government of consumption, we get a picture of a system where regulation is increasing, the power of corporatist institutions over members is becoming greater and the state – notably the central state – is becoming an increasingly significant actor. Giaimo, in her study of the 1993 law, has nicely expressed the significance of the change. It represents not the abandonment of corporatism, but a recasting of the political bargain which it embodies:

> the Seehofer reforms entail only a limited breach of corporatism. By and large, the reforms work through the corporatist mode, with the aim of rescuing it from its own self-destruction. But this rescue attempt requires that doctors accept limits on the exercise of their collective power and new authority for the sickness funds ... if fully implemented, [the reforms] have profound ramifications for physician power and influence in health policy.[61]

Change in the regulation of the profession in Germany is hemmed in by powerful forces: by the entrenched institutional interests of key parts of the medical profession, by the legal framework within which health care policy has to be made, and by the institutional fragmentation of public authority which is a characteristic feature of the *Bundesrepublik* as a polity. Perhaps the most important long-term contribution of the Seehofer reforms to the regulation of the medical profession has been to destabilise the corporatist structure which governed relationships for most of the post-war years. Since the passage of the original reforms, there have been a series of crises of control. For instance, the imposed global budget for drugs on all insurance doctors had by

1996 been so grossly exceeded that doctors in some *Länder* faced huge bills for reimbursement of cost over-runs. The short-term financial problem has been settled by *ad hoc* arbitration, but the long-term control problem remains. There is constant pressure, from the insurance funds and from health care economists who occupy an increasingly important role in public debate, for a reduction in the autonomy of doctors, either by a more active management of care by the funds or by the imposition of more market forces.[62] The increasing competition between funds for members, described in the last chapter, adds to the pressures. As funds are forced to compete, so they are also forced, as third-party payers, to scrutinise ever more closely the economic implications of the clinical practices of doctors. This is the economic background to the growing interest in recent years on the part of the funds in evidence-based medicine.[63] In short, doctors are coming under pressure from both the state and from the institutions of corporatism.

The United States: doctors, states and markets

As we saw in Chapter 2, the British, German and American medical professions shared a common historical strategy: to create and defend a model of liberal professionalism which protected doctors simultaneously from the controls of the market and of the state. But they each adopted different means of realising that strategy, and these different means were dictated by the particularities of national setting. The history of state building in the US left the medical profession with its own highly distinctive regulatory history. In Germany and Britain, medicine established itself as a secure professional interest before the rise of democracy. In America, professionalised medicine had to struggle to free itself from Jacksonianism and populism: to repel those forces that endowed individuals and movements beyond the boundaries of scientific medicine with medical authority, an authority that was often founded on some form of charisma, religiously derived or otherwise. The American model of liberal professionalism had both a political and an economic face. Politically, it both marginalised and fragmented the state: the federal government was only a peripheral actor in professional government; authority – for instance over licensure – was fragmented between individual states; and the actual governing process was controlled in large measure by members of the profession. Economically, the market was organised to give hegemony to the solo practitioner charging discretionary fees for services.[64]

The pivotal role played by the medical profession, and the hegemony of its ideology of liberal professionalism, were powerful influences on the reforms passed in the mid-1960s.[65] In the intervening generation this governing model based on liberal professionalism has been revolutionised; our first task here is to sketch the character of the revolution. The key to understanding lies in making sense of what competitive markets have been doing to the place of doctors, since these markets – and especially those in insurance – have been powerful driving forces. Market-driven changes have in turn altered the character of the political arena in which the profession has been governed; the most important result has been to widen the range of institutional actors – notably at the level of the federal government – prepared to intervene in governing issues. In short, the recent regulatory history of the profession in the US exemplifies one of the starting points of this study: the importance of the wider economic and political systems into which health care institutions are embedded.

These market-driven changes have involved a transformation of two key elements of liberal professionalism: the structure of practice and the terms of payment. Changes in the structure of practice amount to a fundamental alteration in the bedrock of the liberal system – the solo practitioner who traditionally dominated American medicine both economically and politically. At the root of this have been market-enforced changes in delivery systems – enforced by the power of third-party payers responding to the crisis of cost containment in the American system. These changes accelerated in the 1980s and 1990s as the crisis became more severe. They amount, in an often-used phrase, to the managed-care revolution.

The phrase 'managed care' covers a complex range of organisational forms. The conventional definition, which manages to encompass the main forms, is 'health plans that contract selectively with providers on a discounted basis and provide utilization management and quality assurance'.[66] What all these different organisational forms share is an arrangement in which third-party payers contract with doctors on the terms of service delivery, thus replacing the traditional system where usage and charging were the outcome of an individual encounter between the patient and the physician. Gabel economically summarises the dimensions of the change in recent years and the economic forces that helped bring it about:

> When the 1990s began, indemnity insurers, nonprofit community hospitals, and solo fee-for-service physicians had a commanding role in the financing and delivery of care. Health insurance premiums had increased by nearly 20 percent per year in the previous two years. By 1995, managed care plans had established their dominant role, while indemnity insurance covered fewer than one of three Americans with private health insurance. The growth of managed care plans stimulated a wave of hospital mergers and the formation of many large physician group practices ... Between 1990 and the end of 1995, the number of Americans enrolled in a health maintenance organization (HMO) grew from 36.5 million to 58.2 million.[67]

These changes are dealing a death blow to the key *institutional* basis of liberal professionalism in American medicine – the solo practitioner. The speed of structural change is dizzying: in 1988 the percentage of workers in private

Table 4.1 *How health maintenance organisations paid primary care physicians,
1989 and 1994*

Method of payment	1989[a] (%)	1994 (%)
Fee for service	36%	24%
Salary	23%	26%
Capitation	35%	50%

Source: J. Gabel, 'Ten ways HMOs have changed in the 1990s', *Health Affairs*, 16:3 (1997) 134–45,
at p. 140.

Note: [a]Figures for 1989 do not sum to 100% in original.

firms enrolled in some form of managed care was 29 per cent; by 1995 the
figure was 70 per cent.[68] Similarly, rapid change is coming over publicly
financed systems: for instance, in 1991 9.5 per cent of Medicaid beneficiaries
enrolled in managed care, while in 1996 the figure was 40.1 per cent.[69] In the
case of Medicare the structural revolution has taken longer but is gathering
pace: in 1990, only just over 3 per cent of enrollees were in managed care; by
1996, a figure of 10 per cent was reached, with the HCFA, the regulatory
authority for Medicare, predicting a figure of more than 30 per cent in the
succeeding decade.[70] These changes are associated with a critical change in
the industrial structure of the medical profession: in 1985, 43 per cent of all
physicians were in solo practice; by 1994 the figure was 28 per cent.[71] The
industrial bedrock of the liberal professional model is decaying.

But the rise of managed care is also dealing a death blow to a key financial
practice associated with the liberal professional model, the fee for service
system. As recently as the introduction of the Medicare and Medicaid reforms
the fee for service system was seen as part of the cornerstone of medical
autonomy in the American system, at least in the form it was understood in
the payment arrangements established at the inauguration of Medicare and
Medicaid. It is this economic pattern which is in steep decline as a result of the
rise of managed care. Table 4.1 summarises some recently surveyed changes.

The governing consequences for the medical profession of these structural
changes have been profound. The growing corporatisation of medicine
involves not just a change in market arrangements; it also involves changes in
governing structures. Arnold has traced some of these features in the case of
the hospital industry. She writes:

Whereas the majority of hospitals remain nonprofit institutions, most have
undergone corporate reorganizations, spun off for-profit subsidiaries, integrated
vertically through affiliations and joint ventures with physician groups or health
maintenance organizations, or diversified into new markets and services to
increase market share, obtain access to capital, and improve their competitive

position in an increasingly market-oriented industry ... the reorganization of the hospital industry reflects a change from multilateral forms of governance (monitoring, promotional networks and associations) dominated by the medical profession to bilateral forms of governance (markets, obligational networks, and hierarchies).[72]

The rise of the corporate form, and the way it is integrating the medical profession into corporate America, is even more marked in the shifting character of managed care systems. Take the case of health maintenance organisations (HMOs), perhaps the most important institutional form taken by the new system of managed care. Since the early 1980s HMOs have been transformed from primarily not-for-profit organisations into institutions controlled by investors: between 1981 and 1997 for-profit HMOs grew from representing 12 per cent to 62 per cent of total HMO enrollees, and from 18 per cent to 75 per cent of health plans.[73]

Health care institutions in the US are embedded in a dynamic competitive economy; but the dynamism of this economy is not simply spontaneously generated. It is produced in part by interaction between market competition and the processes of democratic politics. That exactly summarises the story of the structural change described above. The momentous changes in the hospital industry, with all their consequences for the medical profession, were the direct product of the Medicare reforms of the mid-1960s. Stevens summarises the sequence of events in the hospital industry set in motion by the introduction of Medicare:

> Its great expansion made possible by the dollars available for reimbursement was to lead, first, to a rapid expansion of services and expenditures but along pre-existing lines; and second, in sequence, to a focus on capital expansion, an overtly profit-making nexus, huge industrial growth, and federal regulation.[74]

The examples of the UK and Germany show that models of liberal professionalism which allow doctors large amounts of autonomy are compatible with many different ways of organising a health care system. We cannot therefore jump to the conclusion that a change in the structural context within which the American model of liberal professionalism is practised means that the government of the profession has altered in some fundamental way. What has nevertheless in reality induced great change is the way the rise of the corporate form has happened: in the context, of a huge injection of public money following the mid-1960s reforms, the existence of a cost-containment crisis which now spans more than two decades and the wider structural dynamics of the American economy. The results take us back to one of the opening themes of the book: the way the embedded character of health care systems – embedded in democratic politics and market economics – shapes the character of the key parts of those systems. The Medicare and

Medicaid proposals were negotiated through the established structures of American pluralist politics. As we saw in Chapter 2 one consequence was that a particularly powerful group – the medical profession – extracted a payment system that proved both highly advantageous to the profession and highly inflationary. It also, as we have just seen, gave a considerable impetus to the corporatisation of the health care system by injecting a large stream of resources into a dynamic market economy where well-organised financial markets were available to capitalise on the opportunities presented by this stream of resources.

The core of the profession's historical regulatory strategy had involved separating professional government from the wider political system, and in the process strengthening the capacity of the profession to control the market in the labour of its members. The financial consequences of the mid-1960s settlement helped destroy that strategy. Democratic politics and market economics became locked in a mutually destabilising relationship. By the early 1970s there was a widespread consensus – correctly based, as the figures showed – that the mid-1960s settlement was creating serious problems of cost containment in the health care system – and, as we saw above, was also producing profound structural change in the system. The realisation that there was a policy problem – chronic health care price inflation caused by defects in the reimbursement system – helped produce interventions that in turn contributed to some of the structural changes sketched in the opening passages of this section. But they also changed the government of the profession by embedding it in precisely the system that historically doctors had tried to avoid – the wider regulatory system, and thus the wider regulatory politics that have come to characterise American government in the last half-century.

Part of this story is a story of *substantive* policy change, and part is a story about the way substantive change has been linked to procedural change – to altered expectations on the part of numerous institutional actors. The policy history since the early 1970s is a complex one, full of twists and turns, but the serpentine shape nevertheless contains a clear continuing thread – the growth of a regulatory world of medical government. Doctors have fought, often successfully, to control the new regulatory world; but the terrain over which they have to fight has been profoundly altered in the last generation. Two examples show the sort of change that has been taking place: utilisation review and reimbursement rules.

As the federal government has struggled to control costs, utilisation review has emerged as one of the key areas of struggle, since it is through utilisation review that some control might be exercised over the clinical practices of doctors. The most ambitious early attempt to implement utilisation review came in the form of the Professional Standards Review Organisation (PSRO) enacted in the Social Security Amendments Act of 1972. The general consensus is that the medical profession managed to colonise the review process.

Nevertheless, as Björkman says, 'technical autonomy was indeed decreased under PSROs ... Previously physicians had enjoyed the professional prerogatives of individual self-regulation within formal and informal constraints. Formal constraints included legal and professionally promulgated ethical rules; informal constraints included the exclusion of "bad physicians" from peer referral. PSRO activities transgressed all these boundaries.'[75] The PSRO did not survive the early deregulation phase of the first Reagan presidency,[76] but as managed care has spread through the health care economy, utilisation review has followed it. Utilisation review is at the heart of the practice of managed care, since it is the instrument by which the institutions of managed care try to exercise control over clinical decison making. Arguments about the significance of utilisation review have focused, almost to the point of obsession, on how it affects the power of the medical community. Yet it must be obvious that this is a contingent matter. It depends on how far the profession in any particular circumstance is able to control the review process. As the phrase 'utilisation review' itself suggests, it could range from 'light touch' monitoring of what physicians are actually doing, to the imposition of the most detailed demands that physicians not commit resources without authorisation. As Schlesinger and his colleagues show in their study of firms specialising in utilisation review, the process has the potential to limit or to protect professional autonomy: it can limit it by restricting the clinical freedom of physicians, or it can protect it by reinforcing the legitimacy of those decisions by conferring on them the *imprimatur* of external regulation.[77] But the very contingent character of the outcome of utilisation review for the power of physicians shows the significance of the change which has come over the government of the medical profession. The institutional terrain has been irrevocably altered by the rise of managed care and the new control mechanisms associated with managed care. The profession's historic strategy was to close off professional decisions from outsiders in the market and the state; now it is obliged to contest decisions.

If the resort to utilization review altered the terrain over which the profession had to fight for control of professional governance, the struggle over reimbursement marked a profound shift in institutional capacities and inclinations. The details of the landmark changes introduced in the early 1980s by the Reagan administration in its Social Security Amendments have already been summarised in Chapter 3 in our account of what they did to the regulation of consumption, but it is necessary to emphasise here what they did to the regulation of doctors. The 1983 measures, which were focused on the control of hospital charges, were succeeded later in the decade by an attempt to develop a federal scheme to control Medicare Part B payments to physicians. The new system was based on an elaborately researched attempt to create (in the form of the so-called *resource-based relative value scale* (RB-RVS)) a comprehensive, synoptic system of physician payment. A 'ten-year study of

7000 medical procedures had sought to measure four major dimensions of physician input: time; mental effort and judgement; technical skills and physical effort; psychological stress'.[78] The substantive significance of the requirement (passed by Congress in 1989) that the new scale be used by Medicare has been summarised by Brandon: 'the adoption of a national RB-RVS for paying physicians' bills constitutes the first attempt to institute a uniform national payment system for physicians.'[79] Symbolically, this episode represents another stage in the demystification of professional judgement. It is Taylor-like in its dissection of the professional task into discrete work segments.

Utilisation review, we saw, offered the possibility of either enhancing or diminishing medical control. The same is true of new payment systems. Episodes like the development of RB-RVS in part represent continuity: the continuing search, in a manner identified by Morone, for technocratic, 'non-political' solutions to policy problems.[80] The elaboration and technical complexity of solutions like RB-RVS bury policy debates beneath a mountain of esoteric language; the technical complexity of the procedures mean that the endowments of professional elites – such as doctors – put them at a distinct advantage in shaping policy outcomes, since those outcomes are highly sensitive to the way technical detail is shaped in the first place and to the way that technical detail is worked upon in the process of implementation. To take the immediate example: payment outcomes become the result of elaborate games played between providers and payers. This elaborate games playing, or the complex manoeuvring associated with utilisation review, is a world away from the realm of democratic politics, where citizens, or their elected lay representatives, try to intervene so as to shape the decisions of government. Indeed, this new world of professional government is in some respects less penetrable by the agents of democratic politics than the old 'private' world of professional government in the US, precisely due to the extraordinary technical complexity of the policy language. That is one of the most obvious differences, for instance, from the debates about reform in the 1960s, where the issues were discussed in terms of broad brush principles and where technical details could be sketched out (indeed were literally sketched out) on a scratch pad.[81]

It is therefore too much to say that the changes summarised here have negated the profession's historic strategy – which was to achieve autonomy from democratic politics through the creation of a world of private government. But just as the market setting of clinical decision making is being revolutionised by the rise of managed care, the political setting has been revolutionised in the last generation. In essence, the medical profession has been incorporated into the world of American regulatory government. The success with which it achieves its objectives is a function of its ability to operate within that world, not a function of how well it insulates itself within its own private governmental sphere. Thus one of the key defining characteristics of the health care state – the intertwining of state institutions and organised private interests – has become more marked in the last generation.

The development of this new, intertwined regulatory world can only be illustrated, not fully described, in the space available here. Three instances should make the point: the growing influence of individual states in the regulatory process; the growing importance of regulatory law – which means also the influence of economists and lawyers – in the government of the profession; and the growth, more generally, of a juridified regime where clinical decision making is constrained by the courts.

Since the mid-1960s the role of individual states has been transformed. This transformation originates in part in the central role of the states in delivering one key component of the mid-1960s reforms – Medicaid – and in part in the wider transformation in the resources and capacities of institutions at the state level.[82] The range of intervention by states in delivery systems, using their Medicaid responsibilities, is nicely summarised by Weissert and Weissert:

> In the early 1980s California replaced its fee-for-service system with one relying on negotiation, and Arizona set up a system for competitively bid fixed-price arrangements for Medicaid. Four states – Maryland, New York, Massachusetts, and New Jersey – adopted all-payer hospital reimbursement systems under which the cost of uncompensated care is distributed proportionally across all payers ... Beginning in the 1980s states began to utilize managed care in Medicaid. Under this system, states set a predetermined fee for a health facility, often a health maintenance organization, to provide care for each patient. Other managed-care programs include prepaid health plans, preferred provider arrangements, and selective contracts. More than thirty states had experimented with managed care in the Medicaid program by 1992.[83]

The role of regulatory politics in the control of competitive conditions in medicine is a striking instance of the growing influence of regulatory agencies and regulatory law. The political impact of the features summarised earlier – the cost-containment crisis, the huge scale of federal spending on health care – has been to widen the range of participants in debates about the organisation of American medicine. In the 1970s and 1980s that debate took place in a particular historical setting: the relative decline of the American economy in the face of foreign competitors. That prompted debates among policy elites about the best way to respond to problems of decline. Many of the debates were conducted within the agencies of the American regulatory state, for the regulatory agencies are among the most important concentrations of policy expertise in the American system. But other actors were also able to intervene as a result of the opportunities created by the new issue networks described so memorably by Heclo: intellectuals, policy entrepreneurs, career politicians and bureaucrats, all forming shifting coalitons advocating a range of policy solutions.[84]

By the late 1970s there emerged from these debates a powerful 'liberal market' analysis of the problems of the economy, and a set of prescriptions to solve those problems. In essence they involved using the power of the regulatory state to enforce greater competitition in regulated industries. These ideas proved particularly influential over federal regulatory policy under the Carter and the Reagan presidencies.[85] Liberal arguments to promote more competition were particularly dangerous to the medical profession for an obvious reason: one of the key parts of its historical regulatory strategy was to control the market in its own labour. The anti-trust lawyer Clark Havighurst elaborated arguments originally voiced by Friedman in 1962 that professional organisations like the American Medical Association were operating a cartel in the labour market.[86] The wider significance of Havighurst's critique is twofold: it came at a moment when structural change was undermining the old economic foundations of the model of liberal professionalism; and it came from someone who had spent time as an adviser to a federal regulatory agency, the Federal Trade Commission (FTC), whose historical mission and culture has given it a special role as the guardian of free trade in the American economy.[87] In the 1980s the FTC used the courts to force the AMA to change a wide range of rules governing competitive practices: restrictions on advertising (traditionally a cornerstone of professional suppression of competition), price fixing, educational accreditation and boycotts of 'unorthodox' medical practitioners like chiropractors.[88] The rise of managed care has hastened the rise of regulatory politics in health care, for the transformation of the market has created precisely the kind of market structures, involving concentration in markets hitherto dominated by large numbers of independent entrepreneurs, which has historically triggered regulatory intervention in the American economy.[89]

The rising importance of the federal regulatory system in the regulation of the profession has, as the last instance suggests, also been accompanied by a more general trend: the growing intervention of the courts in the clinical domain. Historically, the medical profession's success in keeping the courts out of clinical practice was achieved because doctors managed to command very high levels of authority in the mind of the public. In the 1960s and 1970s that authority drained away: for instance between 1966 and 1982 the percentage of polled Americans expressing 'a great deal of confidence' in medicine fell from 73 per cent to 32 per cent.[90] This collapse of confidence in medical authority is one reason why the US has led the way in medical malpractice suits. These suits have a number of important effects on the way doctors behave in clinical domains previously autonomous from the state. They allow the courts not only to intervene after the event in particular clinical episodes, but they also, in the judgments of courts, set boundaries governing acceptable and unacceptable clinical practice in the future. The numbers of suits, when coupled with the wider litigiousness of American culture, make the courts a pervasive presence in everyday relations between doctors and their patients.

In part as a result of this, there has been a rise in the incidence of defensive medicine – carrying out therapeutic procedures primarily in order to demonstrate to an institution of the state, the courts, that the individual physician has behaved in a legally defensible manner. Nor has the impact of these developments been confined even to the domain of clinical care. It has also fed back into the economics of medical practice: one force driving up the cost of some primary health care has been the growing expense of indemnity insurance for doctors against the risk of medical malpractice suits.[91]

The American medical profession has had a distinctive regulatory history when compared with other great interests in American society. That distinctiveness is now disappearing. Historically, it managed to separate its regulatory structures from the state, especially from the federal state. It is striking that the critical period in this act of separation – the later decades of the nineteenth century and the early years of the twentieth century – were also those that saw the genesis of the American regulatory state. The expansion of the regulatory state in the 1930s – an expansion that began to subject previously autonomous actors in spheres like financial markets to regulatory control – passed the medical profession by. It took the new era of regulatory activism in the late 1960s and early 1970s to impinge on the profession. That renewal was sparked by a mix of changes in democratic politics and market economics: by secular changes in the political culture which resulted in challenges to traditionally powerful elites (reflected, for instance, in the problems experienced by powerful sections of the business community[92]). The economic changes were in part specific to health care, and amount to some of the structural consequences of the the Medicare and Medicaid reforms noted earlier. The wider economic forces amounted to the decline of American economic hegemony and the attempt to use state institutions to do something about that decline. Since the regulatory agencies were the most potentially important means of intervention, they were in the front line of attempts to combat decline. The manifestations included the burst of 'new social regulation', and the powerful deregulatory movements that affected a wide range of agencies from the 1970s.[93] This explains why the recent regulatory history of the profession exhibits a seeming paradox shared by the regulatory history of other important private interests: the fact of an active, interventionist regulatory policy done in the name of deregulation. The paradox is more apparent than real, for in medicine as in other spheres the state has increasingly begun to use the interventionist instruments at its disposal to try to refashion competitive practices to counter decline. Doctors are not necessarily becoming less powerful, but they are being incorporated into the American regulatory state.

States, doctors and private interest government

This examination of the changing government of the medical profession shows the complexities that lie behind the images of 'embeddedness' with which we began this book. In all three countries examined here the medical profession operates through a regulatory 'contract' with a capitalist democratic state. The fact that the states are both democratic, and try to govern a capitalist economy, are crucial influences on the character of this contract. There are striking similarities between the regulatory aims of the three national medical professions: notably, they have all tried to preserve some model of liberal professionalism where doctors operate with a high degree of autonomy from state control and with a high degree of protection from market competition. There are also some striking similarities in the modern fate of professions in pursuing these aims. In particular, the impact of democratic politics and structural change in markets has undermined both the political and the economic foundations of liberal professionalism. Doctors, to recall Abel's metaphor, are finding it increasingly hard to walk the tightrope between the market and the state.[94] But the order of difficulty varies between nations, and these variations hint at the complexities of embeddedness. The three accounts offered here show how different historical origins endowed both the profession and the state with different institutional forms and resources, and presented the profession with different problems: the most obvious distinction is between professions (Germany and the UK) where the institutional framework was settled before the advent of democratic politics, and the US, where it was settled, in some degree, to cope with the problems of democracy. It is also obvious, however, that medical government in the UK and Germany displays very different legacies, notably in distinctive endowments of the powerful German corporatist institutions.

Many of the changes discussed here have been examined exhaustively in the large literature on the 'decline' (or otherwise) of the medical profession. But from the point of view of a study of the health care state, what is important is less the debate about power – a highly contingent matter – than what these changes suggest about the central feature of the health care state identified in Chapter 1 – the way the institutions of the state and of the health care system are intertwined round each other. Nothing could illustrate better how misleading are images of state retreat and deregulation than what has happened to the government of doctors. As the American case reveals most graphically, the project of liberalising markets – of breaking down the protection enjoyed by doctors from market competition – has been accompanied by a wholesale integration of medical government into the world of regulatory politics, at both the state and federal level. And across our three nations, states are more important than ever before, either in the direct surveillance of the profession or in supervising the institutions of surveillance. This has not necessarily diminished the power of doctors; but it has profoundly changed the institutional landscape upon which they have to operate. In the government of doctors we see one of the defining features of the health care state – the intertwining of health care institutions and the wider institutions of the state – becoming more pronounced. In all three countries governing doctors was historically a matter for private interest government. Those historical models of private interest government are no longer viable. The profession can still control its own governing process, but only by contesting control continuously within the wider arena of the state. The states, in all three cases, are very different from those where the original historical models of private interest government were created. One transformed quality which all three states share is that they now have to operate within a competitive global economy. We have seen in this chapter that this consideration has been important in shaping the relations between states and doctors; in the next chapter we shall see these global forces even more prominently at work.

Notes

1 Once again my debt will be evident to R. Murphy, *Social closure* (Oxford, Oxford University Press, 1988), pp. 186–8 and 246–8.

2 P. Wilding, *Professional power and social welfare* (London, Routledge, 1982), p. 12.

3 For an extended comparative treatment of this theme in the regulation of financial markets see, for instance, M. Moran, *The politics of the financial services revolution* (London, Macmillan, 1991).

4 The argument echoes my use of Lindblom from Chapter 1: see C. Lindblom, *Politics and markets: the world's political-economic systems* (New York, Basic Books, 1977), p. 172.

5 P. Starr, *The social transformation of American medicine* (New York, Basic Books, 1982), p. 4.

6 E. Freidson, *Profession of medicine: a study of the sociology of applied knowledge* (New York, Dodd Mead, 1970), p. xviii.

7 The debate is examined critically in, for instance, M. Moran and B. Wood, *States, regulation and the medical profession* (Buckingham, Open University Press, 1993), pp. 124–39.

8 The two standard historical sources on which this draws are J. Berlant, *Profession and monopoly: a study of medicine in the United States and Great Britain* (Berkeley CA, University of California Press, 1975) and I. Waddington, *The medical profession in the industrial revolution* (Dublin, Gill and Macmillan, 1984).

9 Though it was for much of its history more than the UK: until 1979 representatives of universities in the Irish Republic sat on the GMC: M. Stacey, *Regulating British medicine* (Chichester, John Wiley, 1992), p. 77.

10 *Report of the committee of inquiry into the regulation of the medical profession*, Cmnd. 6018, 1975, p. 5. (Chairman: A. W. Merrison.)

11 See Merrison, *Report*, p. 5, for instance.

12 So Merrison, *Report*, p. 2, says; I can find nothing since the original legislation of 1858.

13   Though by convention since the 1920s one of the Privy Council nominees had been a lay person: Stacey, *Regulating British medicine*, p. 23.

14   The important substantive point here is that Orders in Council are not the subject of any parliamentary debate or scrutiny; they represent a field of executive decision making free of parliamentary control.

15   Stacey, *Regulating British medicine*, p. 185.

16   Quoted in Merrison, *Report*, p. 3.

17   *Professional conduct and discipline: fitness to practice* (London, General Medical Council, 1991). The measure of size is by paragraph number: advertising gets twenty paragraphs.

18   Merrison, *Report*, p. 13.

19   Merrison, *Report*, pp. 13–14.

20   Stacey, *Regulating British medicine*, p. 22; Merrison, *Report*, p. 141 recommended adding the Royal College of General Practitioners, among others, to bodies able to nominate a member.

21   The authoritative study of this infamous episode is D. Butler, A. Adonis and T. Travers, *Failure in British government: the politics of the poll tax* (Oxford, Oxford University Press, 1994).

22   This account relies on: M. Stacey, 'The General Medical Council and professional accountability', *Public Policy and Administration*, 4:1 (1989) 12–27; and 'A sociologist looks at the GMC', *The Lancet*, 1 April (1989) 713–14. For an account using the same material to develop an argument about professions more generally see M. Brazier, J. Lovecy, M. Moran and M. Potton, 'Falling from a tightrope: doctors and lawyers between the market and the state', *Political Studies*, 41:2 (1993) 197–213.

23   It also helps explain why able junior lecturers in universities so often hate elderly professors.

24   Merrison, *Report*, p. 5.

25   Stacey, *Regulating British medicine*, p. 65, on which this account of the legislative aftermath of Merrison relies.

26   There is a very good account in R. Smith, 'Discipline 1: the hordes at the gates', *British Medical Journal*, 298 (1989) 1502–5 (3 June); and for debates within the Council itself, *Report of the working party on the Council's disciplinary procedures in response to allegations of failure to provide a good standard of medical care* (London, General Medical Council, 1989, mimeo).

27   Monopolies and Mergers Commission, *Services of general practitioners*, Cm 582 (1989).

28   The episode is discussed in Brazier *et al.*, 'Falling from a tightrope', p. 202; the problems of widening the Council's jurisdiction, notably to encompass clinical competence, is a central theme of Stacey, *Regulating British medicine*, esp. pp. 181–99.

29   See the figures in R. Smith, 'Discipline III: the final stages', *British Medical Journal*, 298 (1989) 1632–4 (17 June).

30   For the teaching hospitals and the reorganisation at the foundation of the NHS see C. Webster, *The health services since the war, volume 1, problems of health care: the National Health Service before 1957* (London, HMSO, 1988), pp. 271–82, from where the phrase 'agents of the Minister' is borrowed, at p. 271.

31 A. Maynard, 'The case of Britain', *Health Policy*, 15 (1990), 93–104 (special issue on medical manpower planning).

32 Royal Commission on Medical Education 1965–68, *Report*, Cmnd. 3569, 1968, pp. 121–3. (Chairman: Lord Todd.)

33 See for instance National Association of Health Authorities and Trusts, *Partners in learning: developing postgraduate training and continuing education in general practice* (Birmingham, NAHAT, 1994).

34 Stacey, *Regulating British medicine*, pp. 111–12.

35 Stacey, *Regulating British medicine*, p. 121.

36 NHS Personnel Directorate, *Human resources in the NHS*, issue 2, June 1995, is the source of these details.

37 This passage follows closely Moran and Wood, *States, regulation and the medical profession*, pp. 61–4.

38 The most accessible account of this in English is in D. Stone, *The limits of professional power: national health care in the Federal Republic of Germany* (Chicago IL, University of Chicago Press, 1980), p. 40.

39 There are good summaries of the contrasting legal regimes in the country chapters in E. Deutsch and H. Schreiber (eds), *Medical responsibility in western Europe* (Berlin, Springer Verlag, 1985): I. Kennedy, 'England', pp. 117–62; E. Deutsch, H. Schreiber and B. Lilie, 'Germany', pp. 217–84. My account of the German chambers relies heavily on R. Knox, *Germany: one nation with health care for all* (New York, Faulkner and Gray, 1993), pp. 81ff.

40 This passage relies on Knox, *Germany*, pp. 86–7.

41 There is a succinct, accessible account of structure in M. Schneider, 'Evaluation of cost-containment acts in Germany', in OECD, *Health: quality and choice* (Paris, OECD, 1994), pp. 63–81.

42 The language used to describe the occupation of a primary-care physician obviously varies between nations. For a British audience the description 'general practitioner' will immediately convey the identity of the most important category of primary-care physician. For the German case I have employed the American usage of 'office doctor' to signify a physician who practices from an office/surgery in the community, offering ambulatory care to patients, as distinct from the care offered in the institution of the hospital. In the UK almost all primary-care physicians are GPs – which is to say that their specialism lies not in a particular clinical field, but in the general care of patients. Normally, for instance, all members of a family living in the same household will be registered with a single GP. In Germany, by contrast, a wide range of clinical specialists practice as office doctors, thus offering to ambulatory patients access to specialised, often high technology, medicine.

43 F. Schwartz and R. Busse, 'Germany', in C. Ham (ed.), *Health care reform: learning from international experience* (Buckingham, Open University Press, 1997), pp. 104–18, at p. 111.

44 The negotiation of tariff rates is institutionally complex; to simplify, the complicated points schedule for a wide range of therapies is negotiated between nationwide associations of doctors and funds, and the amount of money available for distribution against billing using these points is decided by negotiations at *Land* level. There is a close institutional description of the arrangements in J. Alber,

'Bundesrepublik Deutschland', in Alber and B. Bernardi-Schenkluhn, *Westeuropäische Gesundheitssyteme im Vergleich: Bundesrepublik Deutschland, Schweiz, Frankreich, Italien, Großbritannien* (Frankfurt, Campus Verlag, 1992), at pp. 101–11; the impact of the Seehofer reforms, and the continuing innovation in payment practices, are summarised in T. Jost, 'German health care reform: the next steps', *Journal of Health Politics, Policy and Law*, 23:4 (1998) 697–711.

45 Schwartz and Busse, 'Germany', p. 112.

46 M. Döhler, 'Policy networks, opportunity structures and neo-Conservative reform strategies in health policy', in B. Marin and R. Mayntz (eds), *Policy networks: empirical evidence and theoretical considerations* (Frankfurt, Campus Verlag, 1991), pp. 235–96, at p. 246; this chapter is also reprinted in J. Björkman and C. Altenstetter (eds), *Health policy* (Cheltenham, Elgar, 1998), pp. 377–435.

47 Alber, 'Bundesrepublik Deutschland', p. 82.

48 Knox, *Germany*, pp. 95–6 has a particularly illuminating summary of an obsession with high technology.

49 Alber, 'Bundesrepublik Deutschland', p. 82.

50 Jost, 'German health care reform', at pp. 700–1. Another force expanding private practice in a single step was of course unification which allowed numerous doctors in the former GDR to transform themselves into private entrepreneurs: see H.-U. Deppe, 'Gesundheitspolitik im Kontext der deutschen Vereinigung und europäischen Integration', in Deppe, H. Friedrich and R. Müller (eds), *Gesundheitssystem im Umbruch: von der DDR zur BRD* (Frankfurt, Campus Verlag, 1993), pp. 9–37.

51 In the wake of the Seehofer reforms there was, however, a convergence in the form of control tools used to contain costs – principally amounting to the attempt to spread global budgets across the different sectors. For a summary of the system in the wake of Seehofer see R. Busse, C. Howorth, and F. Schwartz, 'The future development of the rights based approach to health care in Germany: more rights or fewer?', in J. Lenaghan (ed.), *Hard choices in health care: rights and rationing in Europe* (London, BMJ Publishing, 1996), pp. 21–47, at pp. 38–9.

52 This passage draws heavily on H.-U. Deppe, *Krankheit ist ohne Politik nicht heilbar* (Frankfurt, Suhrkamp Verlag, 1987), pp.46ff.

53 The figures are extracted from J. Frerich, *Sozialpolitik: das Sozialleistungssystem der Bundesrepublik Deutschland* (Munich, Oldenberg Verlag, 1987), p. 501.

54 P. Katzenstein, *Policy and Politics in West Germany: the growth of a semisovereign state* (Philadelphia, Temple University Press. 1987), is perhaps the most distinguished account in English.

55 This draws on H. Bollinger and J. Hohl, 'Auf dem Weg von der Profession zum Beruf: Zur Deprofessionalisierung des Ärzte-Standes', *Soziale Welt*, 32:4 (1981) 440–64.

56 The issue and judgments are summarised in Alber, 'Bundesrepublik Deutschland', pp. 103–5; and a very subtle exploration of the connection between constitutional ideologies and competing occupational interests is given in H.-U. Deppe, 'Zulassungssperre: Ärzte in den Fesseln der Standespolitik', in Deppe, H. Friedrich and R. Müller (eds), *Medizin und Gesesselschaft: Jahrbuch* (Frankfurt, Campus Verlag, 1987), pp. 37–67, at pp. 42–4.

57   This draws on Deppe, 'Zulassungssperre', pp. 59ff.

58   I rely on D. Webber, 'Zur Geschichte der Gesundheitsreformen in Deutschland –
      II Teil: Norbert Blüms Gesundheitsreform und die Lobby', *Leviathan*, 17:2
      (1989) 262–300.

59   This relies on Knox, *Germany*, p. 117.

60   This relies on Knox, *Germany*, p. 118, and on Jost, 'German health care reform',
      where some of the painful consequences of fixed budgets for the once lucrative
      system of private practice are discussed.

61   S. Giaimo, 'Health care reform in Britain and Germany: recasting the political
      bargain with the medical profession', *Governance*, 8:3 (1995) 354–79, at pp.
      366–7.

62   Jost, 'German health care reform', summarises the continuing debate and – at
      p. 701– describes the fiasco over drug budgets.

63   The rise of an interest in evidence-based medicine, and the link with competi-
      tion, is described in: F. Oldiges, 'GKV Leistungs-und Vertragswesen im Umbruch
      – wohin?', *Sozialer Fortschritt*, 47:9–10 (1998) 250–6.

64   The paragraph repeats the argument of Chapter 2; my debt in this passage to
      Starr, *Social transformation of American medicine*, will be obvious.

65   T. Marmor, *The politics of Medicare* (London, Routledge, 1970), pp. 79ff is defin-
      itive.

66   J. Gabel, 'Ten ways HMOs have changed during the 1990s', *Health Affairs*, 16:3
      (1997) 134–45, at p. 144, note 2.

67   Gabel, 'Ten ways HMOs have changed', p. 134.

68   L. Etheridge, S. Jones and L. Lewin, 'What is driving health system change?',
      Health Affairs, 15: 4 (1996) 93–104, at p. 94.

69   M. Sparer, 'Devolution of power: an interim report card', *Health Affairs*, 17:3
      (1998) 7–16, at p. 9.

70   J. Lamphere, P. Neuman, K. Langwell and D. Sherman, 'The surge in Medicare
      managed care: an update', *Health Affairs*, 16:3 (1997) 127–33, at p. 128.
      Strictly, the figures cited refer to risk contract HMOs, but these are 95 per cent of
      all contracted plans.

71   C. Simon and P. Born, 'Physician earnings in a changed managed care environ-
      ment', *Health Affairs*, 15:3 (1996) 124–33, at p. 131.

72   P. Arnold, 'The invisible hand in healthcare: the rise of financial markets in the
      U.S. hospital industry', in J. Campbell, J. R. Hollingsworth and L. Lindberg (eds),
      Governance of the American economy (Cambridge, Cambridge University Press,
      1991), pp. 293–316, at pp. 293–4.

73   S. Srinivasan, L. Levitt and J. Lundy, 'Wall Street's love affair with health care',
      Health Affairs, 17:4 (1998) 126–31, at p. 126.

74   R. Stevens, *In sickness and in wealth: American hospitals in the twentieth century*
      (New York, Basic Books, 1989), p. 283.

75   J. Björkman, 'Politicizing medicine and medicalizing politics: physician power in
      the United States', in G. Freddi and J. Björkman (eds), *Controlling medical profes-
      sionals: the comparative politics of health governance* (London, Sage, 1989),
      pp. 28–73, at p. 57.

76   Björkman, 'Politicizing medicine and medicalizing politics', p. 56.

77   M. Schlesinger, B. Gray and K. Perreira, 'Medical professionalism under

managed care: the pros and cons of Utilization Review', *Health Affairs*, 16:1 (1997) 106–24.

78 Moran and Wood, *States, regulation and the medical profession*, p. 81.
79 W. Brandon, 'Two kinds of Conservatism in US health policy: the Reagan record', in C. Altenstetter and S. Haywood (eds), *Comparative health policy and the New Right: from rhetoric to reality* (London, Macmillan, 1991), p. 165–206, at p. 195.
80 J. Morone, 'American political culture and the search for lessons from abroad', *Journal of Health Politics, Policy and Law*, 15:1 (1990) 129–43.
81 An anecdote reported in M. Peterson, 'The limits of social learning: translating analysis into action', *Journal of Health Politics, Policy and Law*, 22:4 (1997) 1077–114, at p. 1086.
82 The evidence on the latter is summarised in C. Weissert and W. Weissert, *Governing health: the politics of health policy* (Baltimore MD, Johns Hopkins University Press, 1996), pp. 182–5.
83 Weissert and Weissert, *Governing health*, pp. 216–17.
84 H. Heclo, 'Issue networks and the executive establishment', in A. King, (ed.), *The new American political system* (Washington DC, American Enterprise Institute, 1978), pp. 87–124.
85 For an account see M. Derthick and P. Quirk, *The politics of deregulation* (Washington DC, Brookings Institution, 1985).
86 My account of this historical episode relies heavily on Brandon, 'Two kinds of Conservatism', esp. pp. 178–80.
87 Havighurst himself has given a very good account of his anti-trust thinking, and has sketched the trade law background, in a piece intended to influence UK policymakers: C. Havighurst, 'Applying anti-monopoly law to doctors', in C. Havighurst, R. Helms, C. Bladen and M. Pauly, *American health care: what are the lessons for Britain?* (London, Institute of Economic Affairs, 1988), pp. 47–64.
88 Moran and Wood, *States, regulation and the medical profession*, p. 77.
89 For a discussion of this see D. Moran, 'Federal regulation of managed care: an impulse in search of a theory', *Health Affairs*, 16:6 (1997) 7–21, and the associated contributions to the forum on regulation in this issue of the journal.
90 D. Dutton, *Worse than the disease: pitfalls of medical progress* (Cambridge, Cambridge University Press, 1988), p. 21. See also R. Blendon *et al.*, 'Bridging the gap between expert and public views on health care reform', *Journal of the American Medical Association*, 269:19 (1993) 2573–8.
91 Medical malpractice issues are summarised in M. Roberts, *Your money or your life: the health care crisis explained* (New York, Doubleday, 1993), pp. 132–5. See also D. Giesen, 'Medical malpractice and the judicial function in comparative perspective', *Medical Law International*, 1:1 (1993) 3–16.
92 L. Silk and D. Vogel, *Ethics and profits: the crisis of confidence in American business* (New York, Simon and Schuster, 1976).
93 Good accounts of the new social regulation can be found in J. Wilson (ed.), *The politics of regulation* (New York, Basic Books, 1980), pp. 191–353.
94 R. Abel, 'Between market and state: the legal profession in turmoil', *Modern Law Review*, 52:3 (1989) 285–325, at p. 285.

5

Governing technology

Medical technology and capitalist democracy

Examining technology brings us directly to the connections between the health care state and capitalist democracy. Technology and the health care state are inextricably bound together, both historically and institutionally. The modern health care state – that arrangement by which the institutions of the state and the health care system wind round each other – has its roots in the emergence of curative, science-based medicine: in the moment when the artifacts of modern medicine began to be produced by organised industrial processes and were traded in the market economy.[1] Institutionally, the modern medical technology industries grew up in partnership with the state, often as the by-product of one of the state's key functions, fighting wars. Thus when we look at medical technology we look at the industrial economy of health care, and at how that industrial economy intersects with the democratic capitalist state.

The kind of industrial economy which has been created in health care imposes a structure on this chapter which differs from that created for its predecessors. *Consumption* and *professional organisation* are in the main still processes which are defined by national boundaries: describing consumption regimes and systems of professional government involves describing how the different national health care systems are organised. Transnational processes, true, impinge on the decisions that national institutions make: global economic conditions have been important constraints on the generosity or otherwise with which states organise consumption regimes; in professional organisation there is a well-developed international market in doctors, and in the European Union an emergent regulatory system. But it is national institutions and processes which lie at the heart of consumption regimes and professional government, and those institutions and processes have dominated the accounts given in the preceding chapters.[2]

The modern health care technology industries are different, and the differences are shown by three features. First, large parts of these industries are

Table 5.1 *OECD and non-OECD nations: % of world population, wealth, health care expenditures and selected medical technologies installed, 1990*

Countries	Pop/n	GDP[a]	HCE	CTs	MRIs	ESWLs	CUs	LAs	CUs +LAs
OECD	14.7	71.7	87.5	88.2	90.2	73.8	66.5	78.3	74.2
Non-OECD	85.3	28.3	12.5	11.8	9.8	26.2	33.5	21.7	25.8

Source: P. Lázaro and K. Fitch, 'The distribution of "big ticket" medical technologies in OECD countries', *International Journal of Technology Assessment in Health Care*, 11:3 (1995), 152–70, at p. 556.

Note: [a]GDP as proxy for share of world wealth.

Key: HCE: health care expenditure; CTs: computed tomography scanners; MRIs: magnetic resonance imaging scanners; ESWLs: extracorporeal shock wave lithotripters; CUs: cobalt units; LAs: linear accelerators.

integrated with the modern industrial economy which in turn operates on a global, or near global, scale. There are numerous indicators of that integration. The most obvious is the extent to which both the pharmaceutical and medical devices industries (essentially the span of the medical technology industries) are integrated, through ownership structures and industrial processes, with other parts of the modern industrial economy: in the case of pharmaceuticals there are close connections with the chemicals industries; in the case of the most sophisticated medical devices with the electronics industries.[3] A second distinctive feature separating medical technology systems from nationally bounded systems of consumption and professional government lies in the extent to which the products of these industries are traded internationally – and in the extent to which states are central to the management of that trade. But it is the third measure of distinctiveness which takes us to the heart of the connection between medical technology and the modern capitalist state. The global distribution of health care spending is highly skewed towards the most advanced capitalist states, and as an unsurprising consequence the distribution of technology, and the markets in which it is traded, are likewise skewed. Table 5.1 illustrates this point. It selects the set of countries acknowledged to be the core of the advanced capitalist world – the OECD nations – and compares them with the rest of the world for distribution of population, of global wealth (measured by share of GDP), share of global health care expenditure, and – the pertinent point for this chapter – share in the distribution of some of the most sophisticated medical technologies (often colloquially called 'big ticket' technologies).

These figures are in no way surprising: the disparity they show between population distribution, on the one hand, and wealth (measured by GDP) and total health care spend (HCE) on the other, reflects the unequal distribution of resources worldwide. It is equally unsurprising that the distribution of technology is similarly skewed. What the figures do make explicit, however, is the extent to which the world market in medical technology is predominantly a market in the world of the economically advanced capitalist democracies.[4] What the table does not reveal is something quite as significant: the way the figures are in turn skewed within the countries of the OECD. The single most remarkable fact about the world health care technology industries is the extent of American domination. That domination is striking by almost any measure. In pharmaceuticals, a key part of the medical technology industries, the US has just under 30 per cent of world production and consumption, with Japan next with about 17 cent. The only serious rival to the US in size is Europe, but only when considered, dubiously, as a single block (about 30 per cent).[5] In medical devices, the figures consistently show that the US is dominant: throughout the 1980s, for instance, the US produced just over 60 per cent, and bought just under 60 per cent, of the global production of medical devices and equipment.[6]

We should pause for a moment to reflect on this bald arithmetic of markets. The medical technology industries are technologically and institutionally locked into the most developed parts of modern industrial economies. The markets in medical technology belong overwhelmingly to the markets of the advanced capitalist world, and within that world exhibit an extraordinary domination by the leading capitalist nation. This gives us a hint of a key feature of the medical technology industries: they are shaped – and by virtue of their industrial weight in turn help shape – the wider political economy of the advanced capitalist world. The post-war boom in health care spending greatly expanded the markets in medical technology and contributed to the creation of world markets for the medical technology industries. After the mid-1970s, across much of the advanced capitalist world, cost-containment policies slowed down the rate of growth of health care spending – with the significant exception of the US. This had two important consequences: for markets beyond the US it increased the intensity of struggle, since manufacturers were no longer able to rely on the sort of buoyant domestic demand that had previously existed; and it made more intense still the competition for the immensely lucrative domestic American markets. Struggles for markets have in turn become central to the wider rise and fall of economic power in the advanced capitalist world, in particular the long drama of Japan's rise and challenge to American economic hegemony: part of that bigger drama is, we shall see, played out on the stage of medical technology.

In medical technology, therefore, the significance of individual countries varies greatly, and much of that significance resides in the place occupied by a nation in the international division of labour in the industries. The US dominates both by virtue of size and by the extent to which American conditions shape the markets of other countries. Germany and the UK, for all the absolute size of their medical technology industries and their medical technology markets, are *takers* rather than *makers* in the health technology arena. What is more, their efforts are disproportionately affected by the US: in medical devices, for example, in the mid-1990s over 16 per cent of non-EU exports from the UK went to the US; the next most important destination was Japan, with just over 4 per cent.[7]

The point has been put in more analytical terms by Weisbrod in a landmark survey of the literature on the economics of technical innovation in health care. The US is unusual, he remarks,

in the extent to which its actions as a producing and a consuming country influence the rate and direction of health care R&D [research and development]. No other country is so major an actor in both the R&D (producing) sector and the health care (consuming) sector. For most other countries, outputs of the R&D sector are essentially exogenous to their methods of financing health care, and their systems of health care finance are also essentially exogenous to their own R&D activities. Switzerland, for instance, is a substantial producer of health care R&D (especially pharmaceuticals), but it is a small consumer; the United Kingdom and Japan, although they are not trivial elements in the R&D sector, are larger consumers of the outputs of that sector. It is the enormous size and therefore impact of both the producing and consuming elements in the United States that make it such a fine subject for study.[8]

The very special circumstances of the US thus impose a structure on this chapter different from that used in previous chapters. The US drives world medical technology markets; hence it deserves separate, prior and lengthy examination. Germany and the UK, because they are *takers* of American created forces, are considered in the light of the American analysis. (In a wider sense American technological innovation is a driving force in diffusing knowledge of innovations among consumers: there is growing anecdotal evidence of the use of the Internet as a source of medical information.[9]) But in the case of Germany and the UK there is another consideration shaping the structure of the chapter. The production and trading of medical technologies in these two jurisdictions increasingly take place within a larger supranational jurisdiction, that provided by the European Union. Joining the German and UK cases together, as is done in this chapter, recognises the increasing importance of this wider supranational jurisdiction, and of the way it shapes state strategies in medical technology.

The United States: democracy, capitalism and technology[10]

The American state played a key part in creating the medical technology industries that now so dominate world markets. It funded the research base, shaped the markets and regulated those markets. The changing character of the American state – both the changing character of its internal democratic arrangements, and its changing role as a world power – are likewise exercising a great influence over change in those industries.

Before the Second World War the medical goods industries were technologically simple. In the intervening period they have been transformed. In pharmaceuticals, for instance, the 'therapeutic revolution' associated with the discovery of sulfanilamide penicillin initiated, in Temin's words, 'a revolution in the production and distribution of medical drugs'.[11] Before that revolution drug companies manufactured a limited range of products dictated by a fixed technology, and engaged in no large-scale research; after it, they became leaders in R&D, the range of products widened greatly, and success in product innovation became a key to success in markets.

The state's contribution was in part a by-product of one its traditional jobs – fighting other states. Although many of the intellectual advances that created the therapeutic revolution took place in the interwar years, war accelerated their exploitation.[12] The military commitments of the state also transformed parts of the medical devices industry. Sonar technology, which has made an important contribution to modern diagnostic imaging, was developed to hunt down the enemy in the Second World War. It is a harbinger of the global character of the post-war medical technology markets that the original innovations were not distinctively American, but were the product of a global military conflict from which the US emerged as an economic and military superpower.

Nor was the connection with defence a once-and-for-all affair confined to innovation in wartime.[13] The continuing post-war search for business by firms involved in the military equipment industry meant that some of the most significant innovations in diagnostic imaging have come from adaptations by these firms, seeking new business as traditional defence markets contracted. IBM, General Electric, McDonnell Douglas, all major defence contractors, are also leading health technology contractors.[14] The route originally opened by war cleared the way for a sustained link between medical innovation and high technology innovation. The most important connection is between the micro-electronic revolution and medical devices innovation. Micro-circuitry and advances in the storing and digitalisation of information have been at the root of many of the advances in 'big ticket' technology such as body scanners. Some sense of the historical break is communicated by Trajtenberg in his study of the adoption and diffusion of CT scanners (colloquially, body scanners): 'there is a key commonality to the great majority of items now figuring in the available menu of goods, namely the ever growing power of electronics. In fact, there is probably as much in common today between, say, a jet fighter and a CT scanner, as between either of them and its corresponding predecessor of a generation ago.'[15]

Much of the technologically dynamic part of the medical goods industries is thus a legacy of the great military conflicts between states in the middle decades of the twentieth century. As Foote summarily puts it in her study of the American medical devices industry: 'The [Second World] war affected innovation in dramatic ways. At the discovery stage, medical device innovation was stimulated and encouraged. Many technological innovations in materials science, radar, ultrasound, and other advancements had significant medical implications in the postwar period.'[16]

That technological dynamism has been maintained by the involvement of the state in the post-war years. In the US, in the first three decades of the century, the original connection between medicine and the technologies exploited by industrial capitalism was created with the help of some of the great foundations funded by the fortunes of successful capitalists, notably Rockefeller and Carnegie.[17] After the Second World War the state took over much of the responsibility of promoting basic research and development. The resistance to state involvement in the direct provision or financing of health care concentrated the state's role on funding the capital base of the industry, an involvement which fitted the interests of the medical profession. As we saw in Chapter 2, the Hill-Burton Hospital Construction Act poured money into hospital construction while leaving the disposition of that money to the medical professionals. Hill-Burton was designed with the 'explicit purpose of expansion in the name of hospital science'.[18] Support for the hospital – the factory of medicine – was complemented by support for R&D. That too was connected to war: in 1938 the Public Health Service's research budget was $2.8 million; by 1955 the budget of the National Institutes of Health (NIH), the main channel for federal funding of research, was $60 million.[19]

The state's role went beyond laying the knowledge base. It also shaped markets. Already in the inter-war years measures produced by the federal regulator, the Food and Drug Administration, in response to problems of product quality and drug safety, had resulted in a sharp decline in the proportion of pharmaceuticals sold over the counter. The power to purchase was transferred from the patient to medical professionals.[20] That shift in turn reshaped the marketing strategies of the pharmaceutical industry: it turned firms away from advertising in the mass media to one of the characteristic modern marketing strategies, the employment of large specialised sales forces targeting medical professionals, especially doctors, and to advertising in the professional trade press.[21]

The regulatory impact in the medical devices industry is even more striking: 'prior to World War II there was no device industry to speak of', though there were devices. The 'industry' – its boundaries, the classification of its products – is the result of the expansion of regulatory jurisdiction by the Food and Drug Administration (FDA).[22] 'Government helped to shape the industry by defining who was in or out for regulatory purposes.'[23] Government also created markets. The political settlement that created Medicare in 1965 – a settlement that traded professional acquiescence in return for professional control over hospital costs – provided powerful incentives for hospitals to invest in expensive technology.[24] The extent of the impact is well illustrated by Foote: 'The story of the artificial kidney shows how government spending literally created the market ... The introduction of the CT scanner ... illustrates the effect of government spending policy on the diffusion of high-cost capital equipment ... the rapid growth of the cardiac pacemaker market reveals how unrestrained payment can to lead to market abuse.'[25]

The medical goods industries prospered by the application of technologies originally created through state competition in arenas other than health care, like war. The chance to exploit these opportunities was created by the historical alliance of scientific medicine and industrial capitalism. That alliance in turn was supported by the cultural authority of science and technology – by its demonstrable claims to therapeutic effectiveness when applied to health care. But in the 1970s concerns about such effectiveness were joined, or even displaced, by others to do with cost. As we now know, the political settlement that created Medicare and Medicaid was disastrously inflationary, and since the early 1970s policy makers have struggled with the consequences.

The preoccupation with cost containment took a striking form in the US. The 1983 Social Security Amendments overturned a key element of the original Medicare settlement: they mandated the introduction of Prospective Payment systems, and introduced administered prices determined by a federal agency (the Health Care Financing Administration) in place of the professional autonomy in the original settlement.[26] Their most remarkable feature as far as the medical goods industries were concerned was the way they tackled the incentive system to try to cope with cost escalation: not by stemming the supply of technology but by constricting demand for technology, especially by narrowing the clinical autonomy of doctors. Faced with the choice of trying to curb technological innovation by tackling the suppliers of innovation, or the users of innovation, policy makers concentrated on the latter. Why?

One source of this bias was the lobbying power of the medical goods industries, a matter to which we turn shortly. But another was the changing structure of the world market in medical goods. The rise of the medical goods industries was helped by the state's support for research, prompted first by the great mid-century war, and then by the promise of therapeutic effectiveness. That sponsorship created major industries. When the era of cost containment arrived, policy makers could not attack technological innovation in medicine because successful innovation was vital to the wider American economy. The case of diagnostic imaging technologies is instructive. For much of the 1970s and 1980s the American diagnostic imaging market was growing at around 10 per cent per annum, a rate comparable to that achieved in high technology sectors like computing.[27] There were thus powerful forces encouraging the creation of a market for glamorous and expensive pieces of diagnostic imaging technology. Patient safety and therapeutic efficacy could not command dominant positions in policy decisions. Here is Banta in 1980 summarising the experience of the early diffusion of CT scanners: 'Despite more than five years of experience with CT scanning, its usefulness and ultimate place in medical care are largely unknown. The development and diffusion of CT scanners took place without formal and detailed proof of their safety and efficacy.'[28] The need to protect medical technology innovation was reinforced by the connection between American domination of the world medical devices market and the wider American economic hegemony – and by the way the problems of the medical technology industries in the 1980s mirrored the problems in maintaining that hegemony. In 1984, for the first time, the US had a trade deficit in medical devices with Japan. Trade in medical equipment and in pharmaceuticals was part of the market-oriented, sector-selective (MOSS) negotiations at the centre of American–Japanese trade diplomacy during the decade.[29]

In summary, by the 1980s the size and technological sophistication of the medical goods industries presented policy makers with a dilemma: they had simultaneously to try to curb the inflationary effects of technological innovation, and to promote technological innovation. But by this time the fate of the medical technology industries was also intersecting with changes in the character of democratic politics in the US. To understand the significance of this we must recall for a moment the political history of scientific medicine.

The historical origins of scientific medicine were anti-democratic. Scientific medicine reduced popular control over health care and made the practice of medicine more esoteric and socially exclusive. It did this partly by displacing therapies – like herbal medicine – that relied extensively on lay medication, and by marginalising therapies – like chiropractic – that were a populist challenge to the device-based character of scientific diagnosis.[30] The triumph of scientific medicine was not the product of mystification. It swept away rivals because it could do the job all therapies claimed to do – cure sickness – more effectively than any of the lay therapies. The new scientific rigour was also associated with the reform of medical education, a change signalled in the US by the publication of the Flexner Report in 1910. An increased emphasis on formal educational attainments, coupled with some conscious discrimination, ensured that in the aftermath of Flexner medicine became socially more elitist: the recruitment of women, Jews, and blacks all declined.[31] After the triumph of the scientific model medicine became a more esoteric and more socially exclusive profession. It is difficult to imagine anything further from the Thomsonian notion, 'every man his own physician'.[32]

The authority of scientific medicine in the political arena reached its high point in the thirty years after the Second World War. By then, that authority was more than cultural: the medical goods industries were concentrations of money, regulatory expertise, and of votes through their labour force and their connections with other great employers in universities and hospitals. (Even as early as 1960 more Americans were working in hospitals than in the automobile or the steel industries.[33]) Congress lavishly financed the industries and the research elite. This was the age of hugely ambitious research programmes often echoing, in their ambitions and rhetoric, the military quality of previous technological advances: some typical examples include the drive against cancer (a campaign compared by President Nixon with splitting the atom or landing a man on the moon) and the construction of an artificial heart.[34] Rettig summarises things thus:

> In the first twenty years after World War II, (the National Institutes of Health) developed into the powerhouse of American health. By the time Medicare and Medicaid were enacted in 1965, NIH had solidified its relations with Congress, routinely received more appropriations than the Budget Bureau (later the OMB) requested in the president's budget, exercised *de facto* autonomy from the secretary of health, education, and welfare ... secured the undying loyalty of academic medicine, and basically escaped the discipline of a close relation to health care financing.[35]

The pursuit of innovation was sometimes totally out of control. At one stage in the search to invent an artificial heart, for instance, there were three independent, competing programmes: one sponsored by the NIH; a second sponsored by the Atomic Energy Commission, which saw industrial possibilities in plutonium-driven hearts; and a third in Utah, developed independently of federal agencies, which actually succeeded both in implanting a heart in a patient and in attracting corporate finance.[36]

This powerful nexus – linking corporate interests, a Congressional oligarchy and the research elite – was weakened by several forces. Some were economic. The costs of health care became increasingly burdensome, especially after the political settlement that established Medicare pushed up spending. Maintaining American hegemony also created wider fiscal problems, illustrated by the drain on resources in the Vietnam War.[37] These substantive policy developments were accompanied by institutional changes. Two are worth highlighting: the changing character of authoritative knowledge in debates about medical technology, and the changing political setting within which the industries now have to operate. I consider each in turn.

The distribution of authoritative knowledge – or at least its perceived distribution – is plainly important in an intellectually complex domain like that of medical technology. Part of the authority of the medical goods industries and of the research elite stemmed from control of knowledge – both of scientific and of regulatory expertise. But within the federal bureaucracy there now developed concentrations of expertise, in particular about regulatory issues. The Food and Drug Administration provides a good example: beginning in 1906 with the opportunistic incorporation of some pharmaceutical regulation under its traditional mandate to regulate the purity of food, it expanded that mandate, first to wider pharmaceutical regulation and later to regulating the production and marketing of medical devices.[38] A more recent example is the rise of the Health Care Financing Administration (the agency charged with the administration of the Medicare programme) as a significant source of expertise about the whole health care system. The role of economists and lawyers within the HCFA reveals another strand in this changing institutional pattern: the increasing use of economists, lawyers and specialised health policy analysts alongside, and even in place of, professional scientists, in debates about policy.[39] The change parallels the growing influence (touched on in the last chapter) of ideologies of anti-trust in the regulation of the medical profession and the way this change in turn reflected the increasing prominence of regulatory lawyers as a professional group. It also reflects a cultural shift: the declining popular confidence in business institutions and business elites which can be traced in public opinion surveys from the 1960s.[40]

The connections between medical technology and democratic politics are inseparable from the wider connections between health care politics and the democratic political system. We saw in our account of the government of consumption how the work of Peterson has demonstrated a link between changes in the associational world of health care consumption and changes in the wider associational character of American democracy. Those findings are also relevant to understanding the changed associational character of medical technology policy. Peterson has shown how the American health care politics arena is changing: since the 1940s there has been a shift from domination by an iron triangle – linking an oligarchical Congress, corporate interests and professional elites – to more open, unstable policy networks. The shift is connected only in part to changes in the health care arena itself. It is also due to wider changes in the nature of political representation and lobbying of the kind explored in the work of Walker: the formation of increasing numbers of advocacy groups transcending the occupational and professional range of established pressure politics; the rise of political entrepreneurship and patronage in the creation of those groups; the spread of political skills and new technologies among the wider population, in turn helping the mobilisation of new interests.[41] Peterson has also shown how, in the health care arena, these forces have led to the proliferation of a wide range of advocacy groups. Of course these groups have concerns well beyond the sphere of medical technology. But what is striking is how far they integrate efforts to shape medical technology policy into their wider activities in the health care policy arena, and how far they have used innovative lobbying to break into the iron triangle linking the Congress, the industries and the research elite. Aids advocacy groups provide a striking case study:

> AIDS activism, led mainly by the gay community ... has successfully lobbied for earmarking substantial monies for AIDS-related medical research, for changing

the organization of clinical trials, and for an internal research czar within the NIH having autonomy from the Office of the Director. Within the FDA, this lobby has forced changes in the criteria for assessing the safety and effectiveness of new drugs for treating AIDS, and has forced the use of new outcome measures.[42]

This is probably an extreme case, because of the special cultural significance attributed to the disease. In a less spectacular way, however, breast cancer advocacy groups have had marked success, adding $200 million dollars to the Department of Defense budget for breast cancer research.[43]

It is tempting to picture the breakup of the iron triangle, and the spread of advocacy groups, as evidence of a democratisation of the policy arenas concerned with medical technology. Patient-focused groups, notably those uniting sufferers from chronic conditions, have sometimes been seen as reflecting a new scepticism about technological medicine and a desire to empower the patient at the expense of the medical professionals. As the Aids case shows, however, the new lobbies can actually help perpetuate the interest in crash programmes and the obsession with finding a technological fix that characterised medical politics at the height of the military style campaigns against diseases like cancer. The new world of advocacy groups, in other words, offers the traditionally powerful interests in medical technology, in the corporate sector and among the research elite, considerable lobbying opportunities. The rise of advocacy coalitions has not altered fundamental inequalities in the distribution of power resources. The firms in the industry have all the usual concentrations of power resources accruing to corporations in a capitalist democracy: property rights, technical and regulatory expertise, money. (Political Action Committees in the health sector have been among the most lavish contributors in recent election campaigns.[44]) Corporate capacity to suborn, corrupt, manipulate or simply outwit regulators remains. The link between the research elite and NIH remains powerful: the most telling index of that is the size of the NIH budget.

Perhaps the best sign of the continuing power of the traditional forces driving technological innovation in medicine, however, is provided by the fate of programmes of health technology assessment. Health technology assessment is a battery of techniques, some derivative of cost-benefit analysis, designed to produce measures of both the therapeutic effectiveness and the cost effectiveness of technologies. The international spread of interest in technology assessment is a sign, in the era of cost containment, that many different health care systems are trying to subject technological innovation in medicine to more systematic scrutiny and control than hitherto.[45] Effective assessment of course presents formidable intellectual and institutional problems, but solving great problems is nothing new in medical technology: the history of technological innovation in medicine is, after all, a history of dazzling scientific research and engineering ingenuity. That dazzling history is due in large part to the investment of huge resources. The history of the assessment of that technology is, by contrast, an affair of very modest investment and correspondingly modest intellectual advance.[46] The striking feature of the funding of medical research, even in the era of cost containment, is the great disparity between the resources allocated to technological innovation and the resources allocated to the assessment of that innovation. In the words of Durenberger and Foote: 'The history of government's role in technological assessment is characterised by tentative steps.'[47] Some of those steps have indeed been backward. The National Center for Health Care Technology, established by statute in 1978, ceased to exist four years later when the Reagan administration sought no appropriations for it in 1982.[48] It was not until 1990 that an Agency for Health Care Policy and Research (AHCPR) was finally established with a mandate to engage in evaluative research.[49] The history of the AHCPR in the 1990s shows some of the problems of governing the creation and use of the products of the medical technology industries. The AHCPR – whose mandate stretches across the field of outcomes research beyond technology assessment – soon became entangled in controversies over some of its clinical judgements and in the debates about the Clinton health reforms, where it was perceived by the then Republican majority in Congress as partisan on the side of the President's proposed reforms. It suffered a cut in funding and barely survived an attempt at abolition by some Republicans.[50] The episode highlights the precarious institutional position of those agencies that try to scrutinise the effectiveness of high technology medicine, by contrast with the entrenched institutional strengths of those – like the NIH – that promote it.

The industries, meanwhile, have responded to the development of health technology assessment by using their considerable resources to shape the assessment process itself: 'insurers, pharmaceutical companies, and medical device manufacturers also have assumed major roles in technology assessment.'[51] The medical devices industry has established a Health Care Technology Institute to promote the industry's view of technological innovation and to anticipate the tension between innovation and cost containment.[52] Pharmaceutical companies have responded to the threat of economic analysis by investing in their own pharmacoeconomics divisions.[53] The democratic politics of medical technology policy are changing, but change is not necessarily diminishing the power of corporate and professional interests. The break up of the iron triangle forced the development of more open, competitive lobbying; but the old elites are well equipped to compete.

The government of medical technology in the US is unique in all sorts of ways. In trying to govern medical technology the US state is also helping to govern the world market in medical technology, because American demand, American supply and American regulatory standards dominate globally. On the last, the obvious example is the impact of American regulatory standards in pharmaceuticals and in medical devices: the dominance of the American market means that products, to be really successful, must be marketable in the US and to be marketable must conform to US standards. In some degree, therefore, in medical technology, as in some other globalised industries like automobiles, American regulatory institutions set world standards.[54]

From a political point of view, however, what is most remarkable is the contrast in the role of the federal state in the government of the three spheres examined in this book: of consumption, of professions and of production. As we have seen, the American state was historically marginalised in the first two of these, and has only gradually, in the face of the cost-containment crisis, begun to assert itself as a regulatory presence. That is a remarkable contrast with conditions in the medical technology industries, where there has existed for over a generation a well-established partnership between the state and the industries. That partnership has its historical roots in two critical episodes: the first is the link forged early in the century between the elite of industrial capitalists that dominated American society and an emergent research elite in medicine; and the second was the link forged between the state, key defence industries and the medical technology industries in and after the Second World War. The war, and the emergence of the US as a military and economic superpower, put the defence industries at the centre of the American indus-trial state. It was in the defence industries that there existed the closest sponsorship and partnership between the federal state and corporate interests. The medical technology industries were in part integrated into this industrial state, especially after the emergence of the public sector as a major customer for their products following the health care reforms of the mid-1960s. That incorporation was helped by the original role of war in stimulating medical technology innovation; by the way many of the same firms were active in both the defence and the medical technology sectors; and by the way technological innovations – especially in electronics and computing – were common to the two sets of industries.

The medical technology industries, by virtue of their central position in the American industrial state, were also exposed to the pressures on that institu-tional configuration in the 1980s and 1990s. These pressures were partly economic, having to do with the challenge to American economic hegemony from rising industrial powers, notably Japan; and partly to do with the chang-ing character of American democracy. There is here something of a parallel between the experience of the medical technology industries and the experi-ence of the American medical profession: to wit, the gradual incorporation of what was once an enclosed political world into a more open, contested system of regulatory politics – but one in which the industries have very considerable resources to allow them to compete effectively.

The story is not only a story about democratic politics, however; it is also a story about industrial politics – about the way the way the sheer scale of the medical technology industries, and their central role in the dynamism of the

American economy, increasingly influence public policy towards the industries. Medical technology, historically conceived as the servant of health care,
has taken a marked industrial turn: technological innovation can, in Rettig's
words, 'be invoked as a talisman to ward off cost containment policy options
that threaten the competitive economic position of the United States in international health product markets'.[55] This industrial turn is, we shall see, also
observable in Europe.

The United Kingdom and Germany:
medical technology and industrial politics

Medical technology in both the UK and Germany is inseparable from the wider
management of the national industrial economy. In the last twenty-five years
the distinct national medical technology systems of the two countries have
increasingly been overlain by a common regulatory framework, deriving from
membership of the European Union. Making sense of the government of
medical technology is a matter of making sense of the complex interaction
between the pre-existing national systems, this emergent European regulatory
system and the role of both the European Union and national state agencies in
the wider global struggle for markets. The succeeding pages are designed to
illustrate these three features: they begin by sketching the regulatory history
at national level in the two countries; proceed to describe the impact of the rise
of the European Union as a regulatory actor; and finally, using the UK in
particular, show how the development of the idea of promoting national
industries in world markets has emerged as a key strategic notion.

These two pre-existing national systems are marked by important similarities but also by striking differences. The most important similarity – a
commonality shared with the US – is that in both the UK and Germany the
medical technology industries are viewed as significant parts of the industrial
economy, and thus as important not only to health care but to wider industrial
policy. Germany has claims, indeed, to be the most historically important intellectual originator of the modern medical technology industries. In the last
decade of the nineteenth century alone German scientific genius produced
discoveries as various as X-rays (1895) and the chemical agent that forms
the basis of aspirin (1899).[56] The research complexes fostered by the capitalist
foundations in the US in the decades around the turn of the present century
were inspired by the great historic centres of scientific research created by
the reforms of the Prussian university system early in the nineteenth century
– reforms which later in the century endowed the new German Reich with a
leading position in the research sciences.[57] That intellectual eminence
also helped lay the foundations of Germany's position in the latter part of
the nineteenth century as the dominant economic power in the chemicals
industries, and by extension in the new pharmaceutical industries.[58] The

process is exemplified in the career of the Nobel prize-winning immunologist, Paul Ehrlich, an originator of one of the most powerful families of modern immunising pharmaceuticals. Ehrlich's career as a research scientist was closely bound up with the chemical firm AG Hoechst, a connection that gave Hoechst a comparative advantage stretching into the interwar years.[59] His career was also linked to the emergence of an interest in *Kriegshygiene* (military hygiene) – a reminder that the connection between medical technology and war is not only an American phenomenon. The emergence of *Kriegshygiene* in Imperial Germany was itself a product, to use Liebenau's words, of 'the link between medical research and the growing military state'.[60]

The historical strength of the German chemical industry is reflected in the modern condition of the German pharmaceutical industry. Whereas American pharmaceutical companies in the main started out in the drugs business (with subsequent diversification into ancillary areas, like cosmetics and animal health products) the German industry is the result of diversification out of the production of heavy chemicals.[61] (A pattern of diversification into pharmaceuticals is also observable in the UK: Glaxo, latterly Glaxo-Wellcome, historically diversified out of foodstuffs.[62]) The German industry remains the third largest in the capitalist world, after the US and Japan, and the largest exporter of pharmaceutical products.[63] It is also a vital component of the domestic industrial economy: it provides an estimated employment in excess of 117,000; offers high value-added production; and has an export quotient well above the average for the economy as a whole.[64]

German strengths in engineering research and production are also reflected in the condition of the country's medical devices industries. Although comprehensive figures for such a diverse set of industries are impossible to locate, it is nevertheless clear that in terms of sales the German domestic market is the largest in Europe and is the third largest in the world, again after the US and Japan. Something of the scale of the German presence in world markets is indicated by data for diagnostics – 'reagents and instrumentation' – where German firms in the early 1990s accounted for about 25 per cent of world sales.[65] Domestically, the pattern for pharmaceuticals is repeated: high value-added and an export quotient well above the average for the whole economy.[66]

These crude indicators point an important lesson: the health care technology industries in Germany are integral to the sectors that led the post-war *Wirtschaftswunder*. What is more, the historical pattern of links with innovation in defence industries also continues: one of the most important recent German contributions to medical device innovation – the creation of the lithotripter, a device that dissolves kidney stones through ultrasonic waves, thus eliminating the need for invasive surgery – resulted from work on ultrasound commissioned by the German armed forces.[67]

Some similarities with Germany, but some differences, emerge when we examine the structure of the British medical technology industries. The most obvious difference concerns the gap between the performance of the medical devices and pharmaceutical industries. The poor performance of the British medical devices industries reflects the modern weaknesses of British engineering in world markets: the industries run a trade deficit, and their share of world markets is very small (despite that the fact that some of the innovations for the most lucrative 'big ticket' technologies, like CT scanners, originated in Britain).[68] By contrast, the British pharmaceuticals industry is one of the few important sectors of the British economy to have maintained a significant world presence in the face of British economic decline: two British firms remain in the top ten world pharmaceuticals companies, and in 1990 the industry generated a balance of trade surplus of around £1.2 billion, making it the nation's third largest contributor to the balance of trade (after power generating and the petroleum industry).[69] By one estimate, about 100,000 jobs are created in the UK by pharmaceuticals.[70]

Germany and the UK share a common structural feature: their medical technology industries, though of differing size and importance, are both central to the wider industrial economy, and thus to the management of the modern industrial state. But if they are similar in this wider industrial respect, they are very different in the role medical technology plays in their health care systems. The most important difference lies in the extent of diffusion of medical technology. Table 5.2 gives a measure of differences in diffusion of key 'big ticket' technologies allowing us to compare all three countries and (through the ranking column) to compare them against all other OECD countries. (Five technologies are examined, using units installed per million of population as a measure of diffusion, and as a means of providing a rank in the hierarchy of all OECD nations in the set. To make shorthand sense of the rankings recall that there are twenty-four nations in this particular set, and that the higher the ranking the more extensive, comparatively, is the degree of diffusion.)

The table shows some striking variation, much of it unsurprising. Thus, the US emerges as a world leader in the use of technology. The UK and Germany present some clear contrasts: big ticket technology is much more extensively diffused in the latter; and in the rankings, Germany emerges high among the population of OECD countries while the UK is consistently near the bottom. This contrast is apparently not confined to 'big ticket' items. It seems to be the case, for instance, that dentistry in the Federal Republic involves much more extensive use of technology, both for inspection and repair, than in the UK.[71]

Why do these differences exist? We can in short order dispose of one possibility – that the British have a more effective system of technology assessment in health care, leading to a more rational allocation of resources. The UK uses less technology, and less expensive technology, but it has not arrived at this position because its system of technology assessment is more developed.

Table 5.2 *'Big ticket' medical technologies installed in selected OECD countries: 1990, units per million population*

									Radiation therapy units		
Country	CT	Rank	MRIs	Rank	ESWLs	Rank		CUs	LAs	Total	Rank
Germany	11.89	7	2.27	9	1.73	4		2.85	2.96	5.82	7
UK	4.35	21	0.96	18	0.31	20		1.17	2.16	3.33	19
US	26.17	2	8.09	1	1.36	8		1.95	8.03	9.98	1
OECD mean	11.45		2.12		0.94			1.83	2.76	4.59	

Source: P. Lázaro and K. Fitch, 'The distribution of "big ticket" medical technologies in OECD countries', *International Journal of Technology Assessment in Health Care*, 11:3 (1995), 552–70, at p. 557.

Note: In the original table from which this is derived data are assembled for all OECD nations, national rankings are assigned for each technology, and measures of mean, of standard deviation and the coefficient of variation are calculated. The paper adapted here reports the rankings for the three nations and reports only the OECD mean.

Key: CTs: computed tomography scanners; MRIs: magnetic resonance imaging scanners; ESWLs: extracorporeal shock wave lithotripters; CUs: cobalt units; LAs: linerar accelerators. The last two are both used for radiation therapy, hence the grouping in the table.

Medical technology assessment is indeed weak and underdeveloped in both countries – more so even than in the US where, as we have seen, it is already unable to cope with the innovative activity of the industries. As Table 5.3 shows, at this undeveloped level, there has been almost no difference in activity levels between the two countries. The table uses data collected for the technology assessment unit of the German *Bundestag* to compare the national distribution of 815 medical technology assessment studies carried out over the fifteen-year period, 1980–95.

In fact, Aaron and Schwartz's comparative study of the way high technology medicine is rationed in the US and the UK, though dating from the early 1980s, provides an all-too-convincing picture of how the UK arrives at lower levels of usage: allocation is made through the dispersed decisions of numerous clinicians leading, not to efficient allocation, but to sharply uneven distributions: 'the most striking aspect of these [UK/US] comparisons is that the pattern of rationing evident in Britain is so uneven: Britain provides some services in negligible quantities and some at nearly the same levels as found in the much less constrained U.S. system.'[72] Their judgement of the efficiency of the British system is emphatic:

Efficiency in the use of medical resources means that the last dollar spent on any particular type of care purchases medical benefit worth no less than the last dollar spent for any other type of care. This is just another way of saying that if resource allocation were efficient, it would not be possible to increase total medical benefits by taking some money away from one service, for example cancer chemotherapy, and spending it on another, say x-ray. *Even superficial inspection in Britain indicates that this condition is not satisfied.*[73]

Table 5.3 *National distribution of medical technology assessment studies,*
1980–95 (number of studies reported)

Europe	387		N. America	314
Belgium	1		Canada	57
Denmark	13		USA	257
Germany	34			
EC/EU	3		Australia	99
Finland	2			
France	128		Japan	6
Great Britain	39		New Zealand	8
Italy	1		South Africa	1
Netherlands	106			
Nordic States	1			
Austria	5			
Sweden	24			
Switzerland	8			
Spain	22			

Source: Büro für Technikfolgen-Abschätzung beim Deutschen Bundestag, *Stand der Technikfolgen-Abschätzung im Bereich der Medizintechnik*, Arbeitsbericht Nr 39, Bonn, August 1996.

Differences in the diffusion of medical technology cannot be traced to differences in the extent to which the two national policy systems subject technology to processes of rational evaluation. They probably do reflect, in some degree, differences in national medical cultures of the sort identified in Payer's study.[74] In drug consumption, for instance, there is in Germany a much larger over-the-counter market in 'herbal' and homeopathic remedies than in the UK.[75] Likewise, the peculiarly mid-European cult of the spa produced a post-war surge in the technology of balneology – water and mud applications, massage – resulting in an extraordinary growth in the size of the paramedical professions that apply this technology: the number of masseurs and bath attendants rose from 556 in 1952 to over 16,600 thirty years later.[76]

Beyond these slightly elusive differences in medical culture, however, there are well-established contrasts in the wider government of health care which plainly do help explain the differences identified here. These differences in governing systems affect both the capacity to control the adoption of technology, and the incentive on the part of providers to do the adopting. Three should be highlighted: the very special position of office doctors in the German system; the corporatist structure of decision making in the German system; and the long-term effect of global budgets in the British National Health Service.

For German office doctors, their historical position, the historically established system and the connections between payers and providers have all provided incentives for investment in technology in the surgeries providing ambulatory care. At the root of this is the entrenched position of office doctors as private entrepreneurs endowed with the property rights conferred on entrepreneurs in a market economy. This is reinforced by some contingent features, notably the place of specialists in German medical practice. As we saw in our examination of the medical profession, one of the dominant structural features of the German profession is the extent to which specialists – the biggest users of advanced medical technology – are in office practice, something almost unknown in the UK. This structural feature is reinforced by the economic position of the office-based practitioner – in effect, a private entrepereneur competing with other office-based doctors (and with hospitals) for the business of patients. A strictly regulated fee for service system, coupled with prohibitions on some other ways of competing in markets (like advertising) meant that investment in technology became a powerful weapon in trying to attract patients, and in boosting income: that helps explain why the income of specialists like radiologists, who have been able to use the technology to exploit the fee for service system, has greatly exceeded that of physicians without similar opportunities to exploit a particular technology. This emphasis on paying for technology-based treatment through fee for service also explains the unusually lucrative rewards for dentistry as a profession in Germany.[77] More generally, the fact that the system is a fragmented form of corporatism means both that there is competition for patients between different sectors – notably between office doctors and hospitals – and that there has been no institution capable of taking a comprehensive strategic view about the allocation of resources to health care. A range of case studies of the adoption of technologies in the German hospital system confirms this picture of fragmented, weak control mechanisms.[78] Of course, these conditions may change as a result of the Seehofer reforms described in earlier chapters – notably the attempts to get a grip on spending by doctors and the more assertive role by the state in steering the corporatist system. But the diffusion and use of technology can only be expected to respond slowly to such changes. The contrasts between Germany and the UK are obviously the consequences of past governing arrangements.

These points become more obvious still when set alongside the UK command and control system which characterised the NHS for most of its history. GPs had no independent budgets for investment in technology, and even had such investment been possible the payment system gave no opportunities to recoup the cost. The global budgets set at the centre for health authorities meant that the claims of investment in hospital technology had to succeed against all other resource claims on the budget. In a nutshell, the comparison of Germany and the UK suggests that the slower rate of adoption of technological innovations in the UK was the product of two linked features of the system: the more centralised and hierarchical form of health care government in the UK; and the fact that this centralised and hierarchical structure suppressed much more comprehensively than did the fragmented German corporatist system the opportunities for competition, especially non-price competition in the form of offering patients new technologies.[79] The slower rate of diffusion of medical technology in the UK does not therefore reflect any superior system of technology assessment in the UK; it reflects the fact that the British system has until recently been better at suppressing technological diffusion. Thus the British system could only be described as superior to the German if the (huge) assumption were made that 'less means better' in modern medical technology.

At the core of the process by which medical technologies are produced and diffused in these two countries lies an elemental fact, one shared with the US: the process takes place in a market economy which assigns property rights – including intellectual property rights – to private institutions and persons. But these rights are also assigned in societies where the wider governing framework is provided by the institutions of liberal democracy. The process of production and diffusion in Germany and the UK can thus be understood as in part the interaction between the competitive processes of a market economy and the processes of democratic politics. These twin forces explain the evolution of the governing systems in the two countries, something to which we now turn. Both these countries share a common feature: the late development of any extensive system of public regulation of medical technology, and the preference, when regulation did develop, for 'light touch' control which allowed private interests a close grip over the process. But both countries also share the partial decay of networks of control that gave primacy to private actors, and the decay has a lot to do with the impact of both market competition and democratic politics.

Two examples, one British and **one** German, help make the point. The first concerns the evolution of the network for pharmaceutical regulation in the UK, in respect of product safety and of price. These are two key issues for the industry: the first affects the freedom to develop new products and bring them to market, a vital matter since competition via product innovation is a central feature of pharmaceuticals; the second obviously affects profitability. The establishment of the NHS in 1948 faced the industry with a potentially powerful regulator, since the state, and its dominant central agency, the Ministry of Health, had now emerged as a monopsonistic domestic purchaser of the industry's products. But the state chose not to exercise that power in any assertive way, preferring to work through voluntary agreements with the industry. The reasons for this choice encapsulate the structural advantage to the industry arising from the fact that pharmaceuticals were concentrations of private capital which democratic government had to manage. Wright calls these 'contextual' factors, and summarises them as follows:

> The (Ministry of Health) could enhance its legal authority to control prices
> without the co-operation of the industry. It did not do so, because of other

constraining contextual factors. Crucially, it lacked the information about costs, and about the costs of individual branded products. Secondly, it lacked the technical resources to assess costs and efficacy. Thirdly, the political salience of the issue of cost-control was low, although the Treasury and the House of Commons Public Accounts Committee (PAC) were concerned at the increasing costs and lack of control. Fourthly, the MOH was both the regulator and the sponsor of the pharmaceuticals industry. Its latter role was in tension with its regulatory functions. The economic position in domestic and international markets had to be protected and fostered: the industry provided employment and earned foreign currency on its exports. Finally the strength of other actors collectively was considerable – principally the medical profession (BMA), and the ABPI [Association of the British Pharmaceutical Industry]. Individually, other actors such as GPs had almost unassailable powers as prescribers of drugs; while foreign multinational suppliers could threaten to exit the domestic market.[80]

The delayed development of product safety controls in the UK is explicable by the same mixture of contextual factors – a felt need to promote innovation for reasons of industrial policy, coupled with an imbalance in regulatory resources. The contingent occasion for upsetting this state of affairs was the Thalidomide scandal in the 1960s, when a drug prescribed to expectant mothers resulted in disastrous physical harm to babies in the mother's womb. The Thalidomide affair was of regulatory significance, however, not because of the damage it caused to innocent infants but because, occurring within a wider society where there existed an open press and a presumption that the state's job was to protect citizens against abuse of corporate power, it proved highly damaging to the enclosed world of informal regulation operated by the industry. It was the existence of a free press and questioning politicians which transformed the abuse of the unborn into a public scandal, and therefore an appropriate subject of regulatory reform.[81] It forced a reform of safety controls and, in doing so, opened up the regulatory arena to new actors: a new Medicines Division was created inside the Ministry to process minor product applications; a Committee on the Safety of Medicines was instituted to deal with more serious registration and licensing issues; and an appeal system was designed to allow appeal against the decision of the Committee which involved a panel of outside experts and, in turn, appeal to an elected politician, the Minister.[82] Although Hancher (in her standard study of drug regulation) stresses the continuing ability of the industry to shape regulatory outcomes, the key point to notice is the change in the way that ability was now exercised: from conditions where the issue of product safety was simply not on the policy agenda to one where, being on the agenda, the industry has been obliged to mobilise its lobbying resources to influence what happens.[83]

A similar story can be told about the evolution of price regulation. For over thirty years after the foundation of the NHS prices were controlled through a voluntary agreement with the industry. That agreement set British drug prices at a high level internationally, and gave the industry a lucrative domestic market on which to base its operations in world markets.[84] Hancher's history of price regulation in the 1980s shows the mechanisms by which that arrangement was destabilised, and the (successful) efforts by the interests endowed with the greatest structural power (the big firms) to protect their position. The symbolically important moment was the unilateral imposition of price cuts by the Conservative government in 1983.[85] The origins of the breakdown in a voluntary and consensual regime were changes in market structures (giving governments access to drugs produced by firms other than British ones), technological developments that widened the range and availability of generic substitutes for patented drugs, and growing criticisms of the performance of the price control system from public agents beyond the pharmaceutical policy networks, like the Comptroller and Auditor General. In other words, we are looking at disturbances created by two familiar forces: an innovative and competitive economy and a political process which allowed agents of the democratic state (the Comptroller and Auditor General was a servant of parliament) to intervene.

The history of price regulation since the breakdown is essentially a history of a running battle between the state and the industry, involving growing formality and complexity but also, as the evidence of Maynard and Bloor shows, continuing success by the industry in defending a price regime favourable to its interests.[86] The industry continues to win the battle, but at the price of more formality and complexity. Wright summarises the upshot for the regulatory world:

> The most obvious difference in the re-constituted network negotiated at this time was its greater formalisation. What before had remained informal, tacit and unarticulated, now became institutionalised, explicit and written down. This applied to both the rules of policy regulating the agenda of issues, and the norms of behaviour of the members.[87]

A similar pattern is observable in the Federal Republic of Germany: late regulation, a shift to a more formally organised regulatory world, the continuing exercise of industrial influence in that new world. The legal regulation of drug production and marketing only dates from 1978. The introduction of measures then reflected the slow penetration of the policy-making world by democratic politics: the regulation reflected in part a delayed reaction to the Thalidomide scandal, and the muted, delayed response to the return of a Social Democratic/Liberal Democrat coalition in Bonn as long ago as 1969. Medical device regulation only appeared as a result of a series of radiotherapy accidents in the 1970s caused by instrumentation defects; the law did not come into force until 1985. These developments have been accompanied by features which should not at all surprise the reader. Drug product regulation has been closely controlled by the industry (which itself controls the trial process) and the public regulatory institutions have been plagued by weaknesses, particularly shortage of resources. The range of regulation is also highly circumscribed: medical device regulation, for instance, is designed solely to provide protection against safety hazards and has no concern with clinical efficacy.[88] In 1988, concluding his study of the diffusion of the lithotripter in Germany, Kirchberger offered the damning summary: 'The lithotripter is another example of the argument that medical technology justifies its application through its very existence.'[89] Writing nearly a decade later Graf von der Schulenberg found a similarly self-referential system: 'Most economic evaluation studies in medical care are paid for by pharmaceutical companies.'[90]

In the manner of the UK, however, we can observe a slow growth in the formality of the system, and a shift, under the pressures of cost containment, to more open attempts to exercise control. In the German case the signs include: the emergence of the group of experts who advise the institutions of Concerted Action as an increasingly significant source of expertise, information and independent advice; the creation, as a result of the 1993 health reform law, of an institute for the first time to develop a catalogue of the drugs eligible for reimbursement under the insurance system; and the growth, admittedly still fragmented and hesitant, of attempts at technology assessment.[91]

The medical technology industries in the UK and Germany, although they exhibit some important structural differences, not least in their industrial performance in world markets, show some remarkable similarities as far as the health care state is concerned. They exemplify its characteristic feature: the way the institutions of health care, and notably private sector institutions, are entwined with the institutions of the state. The *industrial* significance of the health care state has made this entwining especially close: consider the important historical connection between innovation and the pursuit of that traditional state objective, waging war. The medical profession managed to live in this entwined relationship with the state, and protect its autonomy, by developing a distinctive regulatory ideology. For the industries the task was more straightforward: the institution of private property, and the way this assigned legal entitlements and control of the production process to the firms in the industries, put the state at a clear disadvantage in regulating production and marketing. That is part of the story of the late emergence of legal regulation, and of the way regulation, once it emerged, has tended to be controlled by the industries themselves. Scandals like the Thalidomide disaster are essentially a symptom of the difficulty experienced by the industries in operating the old regulatory system in a democratic environment. The more open world of democratic politics has administered a series of shocks to the regulatory system.

Another shock, of a rather different kind, has come from the development of a regulatory system at the level of the European Union. Easily the most significant impact is observable in the pharmaceutical industry, where the Union (and especially the Commission) has assumed a threefold importance. First, in the drive to create a single market, and to manage the interests of that market in competition with other major capitalist blocs (notably North America and East Asia) the Commission has emerged as a key negotiator. Thus, one purpose of EU participation (with the US and Japan) in the International Conference on Harmonization of Technical Requirements for Registration of Pharmaceuticals for Human Use is to help harmonise the technical requirements for registering new medicine.[92] This initiative must be seen against the background of the use of safety requirements and licensing procedures as non-price barriers to trade: Japan, for instance, has consistently argued that the unique racial make-up of its population means that only products passing Japanese standards can safely be marketed domestically.[93]

The second area of impact concerns the EU-wide harmonisation of product licensing. EU directives go back as far as 1965, while the European Court of Justice has built up an extensive case law on the industry.[94] The process, which resulted in the incremental creation of a European regulatory system over a period of over two decades, was given a sharp impetus by the passage of the Single European Act and, from 1992, the project to accelerate the creation of a Single European Market. The process of incremental change has already produced agreements on directives on advertising, good manufacturing practice, and on provisions relating to labelling, package inserts, and the licensing of wholesalers.[95] In 1995 the EU established a central regulatory agency, the European Medicines Evaluation Agency (EMEA), in London. The establishment of the EMEA introduced three sets of registration procedures for pharmaceuticals across the Union:[96] a centralised procedure, administered by the new EMEA, for innovative products, leading to a single EU-wide autho-risation valid in all member states; a decentralised procedure, expected to apply to a substantial majority of products, based upon the principle of mutual recognition between member states; and a national procedure, for applications of local interest concerning a single member state.[97]

The growth of the EU as a regulatory actor helps explain its third area of impact, on interest representation. There now exists a well-organised system of EU-level interest representation, notably for the pharmaceutical industry, using peak associations centred on Brussels.[98] The process by which the EMEA came to be established in London shows how the governing system is evolving to create a complex series of relationships between industrial interests and state agencies at EU level. The siting of the EMEA in London (in the redevel-oped Docklands complex at Canary Wharf, perhaps the most important symbol of the British state's effort to use private and public sector partnerships to regenerate decaying urban industrial areas) was the result of a combined campaign by the Department of Health and the Association of the British Pharmaceutical Industry (ABPI). Two calculations were at work; they both emphasise the significance of the 'industrial' face of health care. The first has to do with a wider competition within the EU to influence the location of Union institutions because of the benefits to regional and city economies: agencies like EMEA bring jobs and demand for other goods, like property. The second calculation resembles that at work in the contest to determine the location of the other European regulatory agencies, like the European central bank: that the location of a regulatory agency will have long-term effects on where product development takes place. The calculation is particularly important in the case of pharmaceuticals, for the industry is an especially heavy investor in R&D: it usually ranks among the four or five top industries in international comparisons, alongside those like electronics, aerospace and computers. After marketing, expenditure on R&D is the most significant expenditure by pharmaceutical firms.[99] The explicit theory behind the campaign to locate the EMEA in London is hence that it will encourage a concentration of R&D activities in the vicinity of the Agency – and thus will reinforce British strength in the world pharmaceutical industry. What we are witnessing here is a particular model of internationalisation, of a kind identified by Mohan: one where the the the inward investment strategies of the state are used to try to strengthen the position of particularly favoured metropolitan locations.[100]

The EMEA episode acquires added significance when we set it alongside the wider development of investment strategy in the UK in the 1990s, and the growth of a national strategy in medical technology designed to promote British products. The government of medical technology took an increasingly industrial turn as it became integrated with one of the central features of state economic strategy – building networks between corporate actors and state agencies to promote British-made goods in world markets. The medical equipment industry has been an obvious target, because of the historic underperformance in international competition. The contrasting performances of pharmaceuticals and medical equipment were highlighted in a Cabinet Office report of 1986[101] and underlined in the report on medical research of the House of Lords Select Committee on Science and Technology two years later: 'the apparent inability of the British medical equipment industry to use the British domestic market as a base for developing internationally competitive equipment is deeply to be regretted.'[102] The problem is longstanding. There have been a series of reports into the procurement function in the NHS attempting to establish why a domestic market dominated by a monopsonistic purchaser does not provide a base for a competitive medical equipment industry. The report in 1978 of a (then) Department of Health and Social Security (DHSS) working group led to the establishment of a single NHS Supply Council, drawing members from the DHSS, the NHS and the supplying industry, with the object of 'encouraging a strong, home-based supplying industry, able to compete in export markets'.[103] Since then, public policy has increasingly stressed the industrial dimension of medical research and technology. The Report of the Lords' Select Committee, referred to above, led to the appointment in 1991 of Professor Michael Peckham as Director of Research and Development in the Department of Health,[104] and the formulation of a national R&D strategy for health. In Professor Peckham's words: 'A key objective of the R&D strategy is to strengthen the relationship between the NHS, the science base and the industry.'[105] Following the ACARD (Cabinet Office) report of 1986 there was established a British Health Care Trade and Industry Confederation, designed to give the industry a stronger voice in health care policy.[106] By the 1990s the Department of Health, the Department of Trade and Industry, and medical technology firms were linked in a series of working groups and promotional activities, with two purposes: to encourage inward investment by foreign capital (thus connecting to the key part of the wider economic strategy of the Conservative governments after 1979); and to promote medical technology exports.

The institutional centre of these developments has been the Health Care Sector Group of the Department of Trade and Industry's Overseas Projects Board. The Overseas Projects Board was originally established in 1977, as part of the British Overseas Trade Board, 'to provide advice to Ministers on major export projects and to give industry a voice in the development of Government export policy.'[107] The Health Care Sector Group was formed in 1996, under the chairmanship of the Chief Executive of Vickers, itself both a leading defence and medical technology contractor (a symbol of the enduring connection between the defence and the medical technology industries).[108] The core of the enterprise is the Association of British Health Care Industries (a successor to the British Health Care Trade and Industry Confederation) which is reckoned to cover about 80 per cent of the medical systems industry. The Association works in partnership with the Department of Trade and Industry (which has appointed its own Export Promoter for Health Care), receiving financial support for such projects as mapping the industry, identifying target markets and organising trade missions to those markets.[109] Although effort is focused on the export of medical devices, one of the emerging features of this promotional exercise is the wider commercialisation of the health care system, based upon the realisation that services and consultancy, as much as hardware, might be marketable abroad, especially as countries reform their health care systems under pressure from international financial institutions like the World Bank. (Part of the logic of identifying Argentina as a potential market, for instance, was that the Argentine system had been reformed in this fashion, partly under the influence of the British internal market reforms.[110]) The result is to increase the extent to which all aspects of the health care system are considered resources in the struggle for share in world markets. We have already seen something of this in the influence of health care industrial policy on the NHS R&D strategy. What is striking about the work of the Overseas Projects Board, however, is the way the total resources of the health service are considered potentially available for the struggle in export markets, with the UK health care system conceived as a single corporate entity organised to compete in world markets. Thus in November 1996 the Health Care Sector group created a 'UK PLC Exporting Sub-Group' chaired by Sir Duncan Nichol, a former Chief Executive of the NHS Management Executive. The group was designed to create an alliance of service professionals and industrial interests supported by a secretariat from the Departments of Health and of Trade and Industry. Its object was to:

> bring together representatives of the medical profession, private-sector care organisations, management training organisations, contractors, consultants and trade associations ... It was hoped that the Group's membership would ensure that an unprecedented level of health-care experience and expertise could be co-ordinated and focused onto target markets.[111]

This account is not intended to suggest that there has been some transformation in British strategic capacity intelligently to identify and target export markets. The result of the application of the 'unprecedented' expertise referred to above was, for instance, the conclusion that efforts should be concentrated on 'Indonesia, land of opportunity' – the single biggest casualty just a year later of the East Asian economic crisis.[112] It is not that the British are targeting markets with more strategic acumen than in the past, but that these efforts illustrate the extent to which, originating in the struggle for share in medical technology markets, the whole health care system is now considered an instrument of industrial policy. It also explains the attention given in these closing pages to the British efforts to develop an export strategy: health care, which a generation ago was pictured as belonging mostly to the domain of citizenship, is now conceived as an arm of national industrial policy.

Property rights, medical technology and democracy

Medical technology is the point at which health care systems most obviously intersect with the wider industrial economy of capitalism; the most obvious sphere, thus, where the constraints of a capitalist economic order impinge on democratic decision making; but the most obvious sphere, too, where the dynamism of a market economy constantly disrupts established interests and where the changing character and capacities of the institutions of democratic government in turn can constrain private actors, whether individuals or institutions. In short, nowhere is the embedded character of health care systems more in evidence: embdded in market economies and embedded in democratic political systems. Most of what consists of medical technology is private property and much is traded by exchange in markets. To label something as private property is obviously only to say that property rights embodied in law are assigned and protected by the power of the state. In spheres like medical technology, where technological innovation is a key way of securing competitive advantage, the state's role in validating rights in *intellectual* as much as in material property becomes critical. The protection of intellectual property rights – which means the protection of the right to their commercial exploitation – is central to the workings of the industries. Without that protection the incentives for innovation disappear. Indeed the significance of the state as a protector of such rights expands as the range and intellectual power of medical technology grows. Kenny's brilliant study of innovation in biotechnology, the discipline founded on the manipulation and commercial exploitation of the genetic world, shows how the state's role has grown to validating as private property new areas of the natural world, thus allowing the patenting of living organisms.[113]

This bald summary might make the state seem merely the validator of private property rights, but that view is contradicted by the evidence of the preceding pages. States and medical technology industries live, and have lived for a long time, in a condition that may fairly precisely be called one of symbiosis: they have developed together, intertwining in ways that sometimes produced support, sometimes stress and tension. Three forces are continuing to shape and reshape this symbiotic relationship: innovations by the industries themselves, both technological and institutional; innovations in regulatory arrangements, of which the most obvious is the impact of the growing importance of the European Union as a regulatory state;[114] and the changing character and capacities of democratic states. Since the first two of these are virtually commonplaces in the regulatory literature, it is worth taking a few words to emphasise the significance of the third.

Medical technology has created a range of very different problems for democratic states: how to contain the costs of technological innovation; how to ration the benefits of innovation; and how to regulate the risks of innovation. Problems of cost containment and of rationing are not the same, but they are related, and have cropped up in different forms in our examination of both the government of consumption and of the medical profession. Although all the problems just identified have shown themselves in an acute form in recent decades, there is not much convincing evidence that the problems themselves are new. What is new is the political environment in which they have to be confronted. The example of risk in medical technology is a good illustration. As we have seen, the damage caused by technology – especially in appalling cases like the Thalidomide tragedy – created public scandals that forced more state regulation, albeit regulation limited by the lobbying capacities and the structural power of the industries. It is tempting to picture this in the language of a 'risk society' – of a society where technology presents ever larger and more incalculable risks to citizens.[115] But this account hardly fits the history of medical technology, which is one of decreasing, not increasing, risk of damage to patients.

Like medicine generally, the dangers of encounters with medical technology declined greatly as a result of the scientific advances made in, roughly, the fifty years after 1870. Perhaps just around the turn of the century it became for the first time less risky for patients to use, than to avoid, medical technology. But the world into which modern, science-based medical technology was born was politically very different from the present. In Europe it was pre-democratic; in the US the new communities uniting research science and corporate power were used to create a protective wall against populist democracy. When technology damaged patients, scandal rarely resulted, or if it did the results could be securely contained. The golden age of scientific medicine in the thirty years after the end of the Second World War owed much to the spectacular therapeutic advances that medical technology offered, often as a result of innovation spurred by war. But it also owed much to the protection offered by the Schumpeterian system of democratic politics – one where policy was shaped by elites, where there existed a historical residue of deference, and where popular participation was closely constrained. The stresses on the Schumpeterian model – the erosion of confidence in established elites, including scientific elites, the breakup of cohesive policy communities – made the management of medical technology much more difficult, especially the management of those cases, like Thalidomide, where there was great damage to patients. Of course industries fight back, and states, as managers of industrial economies, are often highly receptive to the terms of that fightback: in the 1980s, for instance, the language of competition and industrial efficiency was used on both sides of the Atlantic to subvert the effectiveness of regulatory safeguards in the pharmaceutical industry.[116] But as a result of the altered character of democratic politics the management of medical technology became an increasingly contested affair. The rise of contestation is, of course, a theme which we have encountered already in other chapters. It is also part of the story of the government of doctors and of consumption: the transformation of decision arenas from enclosures where established elites operated on understood, often implicit norms, to more open, unstable environments where new actors and new interests had to be managed. That story is evidently central to the changing politics of the health care state – a story which in the next chapter we survey.

Notes

1   The historical roots are examined in Reiser's fine study: S. Reiser, *Medicine and the reign of technology* (Cambridge, Cambridge University Press, 1978).

2   For an elaboration of this argument see M. Brazier, J. Lovecy, M. Moran and M. Potton, 'Professional labour and the Single European Market: the case of doctors', *Journal of Area Studies*, 1:1 (1992) 115–24.

3   I provide some examples below of the role of important chemicals and electronics firms in the pharmaceuticals and the advanced medical devices markets.

4   But for a study examining how regulatory weaknesses in the third world are exploited to market drugs in a manner not allowed in more controlled jurisdictions see M. Silverman, P. Lee and M. Lydecker, 'Drug promotion: the third world revisited', *International Journal of Health Services*, 16:4 (1986) 659–67.

5   These figures are from: C. Tarabusi and G. Vickery, 'Globalization in the pharmaceutical industry: part 1', *International Journal of Health Services*, 28:1 (1998) 67–105, at p. 74.

6   S. Foote, *Managing the medical arms race: public policy and medical device innovation* (Berkeley CA, University of California Press, 1992), p. 179.

7   P. Butler, 'Trade marks', *Health Service Journal*, 12 September 1996.

8   B. Weisbrod, 'The health care quadrilemma: an essay on technological change, insurance, quality of care, and cost containment', *Journal of Economic Literature*, 29:1 (1991) 523–52, at p. 526.

9   I owe this point to Steve Harrison, personal communication. See also E. Coiera, 'The Internet's challenge to health care provision', *British Medical Journal*, 312 (1996) 3–4 (6 January).

10 This section draws on parts of M. Moran and E. Alexander, 'Technology, American democracy and health care', *British Journal of Political Science*, 27:4 (1997) 573–94.

11 P. Temin, *Taking your medicine: drug regulation in the United States* (Cambridge, Mass., Harvard University Press, 1980), p. 58.

12 Temin, *Taking your medicine*, pp. 64–6 on the wartime development of penicillin.

13 And neither was it solely an American or a mid–century phenomenon: for the interconnections between industrial strategy, science and a military state in Imperial Germany see J. Liebenau, 'Paul Ehrlich as a commercial scientist and research administrator', *Medical History*, 34 (1990) 65–78; and for the connection in the UK during and after the First World War between the need to treat victims of gas attacks and the technology of oxygen therapy, S. Sturdy, 'From the trenches to the hospitals at home: physiologists, clinicians and oxygen therapy, 1914–30', in J. Pickstone (ed.), *Medical innovations in historical perspective* (London, Macmillan, 1992), pp. 104–23.

14 See the table of firms in V. Navarro, *Dangerous to your health: capitalism in health care* (New York, Monthly Review Press, 1993), p. 26.

15 M. Trajtenberg, *Economic analysis of product innovation: the case of CT scanners* (Cambridge, Mass., Harvard University Press, 1990), p. 2.

16 Foote, *Managing the medical arms race*, p. 52.

17 This original history is told in E. Brown, *Rockefeller medicine men: medicine and capitalism in America* (Berkeley CA, University of California Press, 1979).

18 R. Stevens, *In sickness and in wealth: American hospitals in the twentieth century* (New York, Basic Books, 1989), p. 219.

19 Brown, *Rockefeller medicine men*, pp. 225–6.

20 Temin, *Taking your medicine*, examines this regulatory history, esp. pp. 4–51.

21 Temin, *Taking your medicine*, pp. 84–6.

22 The quotation, and the evidence supporting this passage, is from R. Merrill, 'Regulation of drugs and devices: an evolution', *Health Affairs*, 13:3 (1994) 47–69, at p. 55.

23 Foote, *Managing the medical arms race*, p. 10.

24 Some of consequences for the hospital industry are examined in P. Arnold, 'The invisible hand in health care: the rise of financial markets in the U.S. hospital industry', in J. Campbell, J. R. Hollingsworth and L. Lindberg (eds), *Governance of the American economy* (Cambridge, Cambridge University Press, 1991), pp. 293–316.

25 Foote, *Managing the medical arms race*, p. 85.

26 This key Reaganite reform is described in W. Brandon, 'Two kinds of Conservatism in US health policy: the Reagan record', in C. Altenstetter and S. Haywood (eds), *Comparative health policy and the new right: from rhetoric to reality* (London, Macmillan, 1991), pp. 165–206.

27 Trajtenberg, *Economic analysis of product innovation*, pp. 45–9. The figure is on p. 48.

28 H. D. Banta, 'The diffusion of the computed tomography (CT) scanner in the United States', *International Journal of Health Services*, 10:2 (1980) 251–69, p. 263.

29 This paragraph relies on Foote, *Managing the medical arms race*, pp. 179–90.

30 On the displacement of herbal medicine see R. L. Caplan, 'The commodification of American health care', *Social Science and Medicine*, 28:11 (1989) 1139–48; on chiropractic see S. C. Martin, 'Chiropractic and the social context of medical technology, 1895–1925', *Technology and Culture*, 34:2 (1993), 808–34. Against the complexity and physical alienation associated with instrumental exploration of the body chiropractic stressed simplicity and direct physical manipulation; the therapy was therefore plunged into a great crisis by the attempt of some practitioners to introduce a technological innovation – a machine to measure the temperature of the spine.

31 P. Starr, *The social transformation of American medicine* (New York, Basic, Books, 1982), p. 124.

32 Cited from A. Heidenheimer, "Professional knowledge and state policy in comparative historical perspective: law and medicine in Britain, Germany and the United States', *International Social Science Journal*, 61 (1989) 529–53, at p. 535.

33 Stevens, *In sickness and in wealth*, p. 282.

34 S. Strickland, *Politics, science and dread disease: a short history of United States medical policy* (Cambridge, Mass., Harvard University Press, 1972), on cancer, and p. 265 for President Nixon's remark; on the artificial heart see T. Preston, 'The artificial heart', in D. Dutton (ed.), *Worse than the disease: pitfalls of medical progress* (Cambridge, Cambridge University Press, 1988), pp. 91–126.

35 R. Rettig, 'Medical innovation duels cost containment', *Health Affairs*, 13:3 (1994) 7–27, at p. 19.

36 Preston, 'The artificial heart', pp. 91–126.

37 Strickland, *Politics, science, and dread disease*, pp. 209–10 sums up these forces.

38 On the FDA see Merrill, 'Regulation of drugs and devices', and Temin, *Taking Your Medicine*, esp. pp. 18–57.

39 M. Peterson, 'The limits of social learning: translating analysis into action', *Journal of Health Politics, Policy and Law*, 22:4 (1997) 1076–114 takes the transformation of expertise as a major theme. My own emphasis is heavily infuenced by Peterson's work, cited here and elsewhere.

40   L. Silk and D. Vogel, *Ethics and profits: the crisis of confidence in American business* (New York, Simon and Schuster, 1996).

41   M. Peterson, 'Political influence in the 1990s: from iron triangles to policy networks', *Journal of Health Politics, Policy and Law*, 18:2 (1993), 395–438; Peterson, 'Institutional change and health politics of the 1990s', *American Behavioral Scientist*, 36:6 (1993) 782–801; J. Walker, *Mobilizing interest groups in America: patrons, professions and social movements* (Ann Arbor MI, Michigan University Press, 1991), esp. pp. 9–11, 49 and 53.

42   Rettig, 'Medical innovation duels cost containment', p. 19.

43   Rettig, 'Medical innovation duels cost containment', p. 20.

44   See the table in Navarro, *Dangerous to your health*, p. 34.

45   For an early summary of international experience see M. Drummond (ed.), *Economic appraisal of health technology in the European Community* (Oxford, Oxford University Press, 1987).

46   The intellectually underdeveloped character of assessment is a main theme of J. McKinlay, 'From "Promising Report" to "Standard Procedure": seven stages in the career of a medical innovation', *Milbank Memorial Fund Quarterly*, 59:3 (1981) 374–411.

47   D. Durenberger and S. Foote, 'Technology and health reform: a legislative perspective', *Health Affairs*, 13:3 (1994) 197–205, at p. 202.

48   Rettig, 'Medical innovation duels cost containment', p. 16.

49   Durenberger and Foote, 'Technology and health reform', p. 202.

50   This relies on J. Eisenberg, 'Health services research in a market–oriented health care system', *Health Affairs*, 17:1 (1998) 98–108; and C. Kahn, 'The AHCPR after the battles', *Health Affairs*, 17:1 (1998) 109–10.

51   A. Garber, 'Can technology assessment control health spending?', *Health Affairs*, 13:3 (1994) 115–26, at p. 124.

52   Rettig, 'Medical innovation duels cost containment', p. 21.

53   F. Andersson, 'Why is the pharmaceutical industry investing increasing amounts in health economic evaluation?', *International Journal of Technology Assessment in Health Care*, 11:4 (1995) 750–61. Andersson's answer is that the investment brings returns in bargaining with regulators.

54   The significance of regulatory standards in controlling market entry, in the US and elsewhere, is described in D. Vogel, 'The globalisation of pharmaceutical regulation', *Governance* 11:1 (1998) 1–22, at p. 9.

55   Rettig, 'Medical innovation duels cost containment', p. 21.

56   R. Schicke, 'Trends in the diffusion of selected medical technology in the Federal Republic of Germany', *International Journal of Technology Assessment in Health Care*, 4 (1988) 395–405, at p. 400.

57   On intellectual traffic with Germany see T. Bonner, *American doctors and German universities: a chapter in the history of international relations 1870–1914* (Lincoln NB, University of Nebraska Press, 1963), esp. pp. 23–67.

58   For a summary: C. Trebilock, *The industrialization of the continental powers, 1780–1914* (Harlow, Longman, 1981), pp. 46–8.

59   This relies on Liebenau, 'Paul Ehrlich as a commercial scientist.'

60   Liebenau, 'Paul Ehrlich as a commercial scientist', p. 73 for the quotation.

61   On pharmaceuticals and chemicals in Germany see J. Pickstone, 'Medicine,

society and the state', in R. Porter (ed.), *The Cambridge illustrated history of medicine* (Cambridge, Cambridge University Press, 1996), pp. 304–41, at p. 326.

62 This relies on L. Hancher, *Regulating for competition: government, law and the pharmaceutical industry in the United Kingdom and France* (Oxford, Clarendon Press, 1990), p. 38.

63 Tarabusi and Vickery, 'Globalization in the pharmaceutical industry, part 1', p. 93.

64 D. Göpffarth and B. Milbrandt, 'Das Gesundheitswesen als Beschäftigungs und Wachstumsfaktor', *Zeitschriften für Gesundheitswissenschaften*, 6:3 (1998) 233–47, at p. 237.

65 S. Kirchberger, 'Health care technology in the Federal Republic of Germany', *Health Policy*, 30 (1994) 163–205, at p. 172.

66 Göpffarth and Milbrandt, 'Das Gesundheitswesen als Beschäftigungs und Wachstumsfaktor', p. 238.

67 The story of the lithotripter is told by S. Kirchberger, 'The process of diffusion of the lithotripter in the Federal Republic of Germany', in B. Stocking (ed.), *Expensive health technologies: regulatory and administrative mechanisms in Europe* (Oxford, Oxford University Press, 1988), pp. 54–9.

68 On the history of the CT scanner see S. S. Blume, *Insight and industry: on the dynamics of technological change in medicine* (Cambridge, Mass., MIT Press, 1992).

69 Advisory Council on Science and Technology, *A report on medical research and health* (London, HMSO, 1993), pp. 8 and 26.

70 The estimate is from 1995 by the then Under Secretary for Health: 'The pharmaceutical industry, the health service and the future', *Healthcare Parliamentary Monitor*, 6 March (1995) 3.

71 On dental technology see Schicke, 'Trends in the diffusion of selected medical technology', pp. 396–8.

72 H. Aaron and W. Schwartz, *The painful prescription: rationing hospital care* (Washington DC, Brookings Institution, 1984), p. 76.

73 Aaron and Schwartz, *The painful prescription*, p. 89, emphasis added.

74 L. Payer, *Medicine and culture: notions of health and sickness in Britain, the US, France and West Germany* (London, Gollancz, 1989).

75 I base this on the Datamonitor figures reported in tabular form in the *Independent on Sunday*, 21 November (1993) 4.

76 Schicke, 'Trends in the diffusion of selected medical technology', pp. 397–8. Schicke uses these figures to point a contrast with the more modest growth of orthodox medical technology assistants, but in my view they indicate the startling growth of a peculiarly German style of technology – the complex artifacts of bath and water treatment.

77 Both these observations are from Schicke, 'Trends in the diffusion of selected medical technology', p. 396, who also gives some figures.

78 See for instance the case studies in H. Held, 'Medical technology in the Federal Republic of Germany', in Stocking (ed.), *Expensive medical technologies*, pp. 116–21.

79 This paragraph relies heavily on B. Stocking, 'Medical technology in the United Kingdom', in Stocking (ed.), *Expensive medical technologies*, pp. 157–77.

80   M. Wright, 'The comparative analysis of industrial policies: policy networks and sectoral governance structures in Britain and France', *Staatswissenschaften and Staatspraxis*, 2:4 (1991) 503–33, at p. 513.

81   The regulatory environment of the Thalidomide tragedy is described in J. Abraham, *Science, politics and the pharmaceutical industry* (London, UCL Press, 1995), pp. 61–4.

82   Wright, 'Comparative analysis of industrial policies', p. 521.

83   Hancher, *Regulating for competition*, pp. 106–50 is authoritative on the development of drug safety policy.

84   A. Maynard and K. Bloor, 'Regulating the pharmaceutical industry', *British Medical Journal*, 315 (1997), 200–1 (20 July) summarise the arrangements and the evidence from economic evaluations.

85   Hancher, *Regulating for competition*, p. 197.

86   I rely on Hancher, *Regulating for competititon*, pp. 197–211; Maynard and Bloor, 'Regulating the pharmaceutical industry'.

87   Wright, 'Comparative analysis of industrial policies', pp. 525–6.

88   This relies on Kirchberger, 'Health care technology', esp. pp. 177–82, and on J.-M. Graf von der Schulenburg, 'Economic evaluation of medical technologies: from theory to practice – the German perspective', *Social Science and Medicine*, 45:4 (1997) 621–33.

89   Kirchberger, 'The process of diffusion of the lithotripter', at p. 59.

90   Graf von der Schulenburg, 'Economic evaluation of medical technologies', p. 627.

91   This relies also on Kirchberger, 'Health care technology', esp. pp. 183–4.

92   This relies on: 'Eur-Assess project subgroup report on coverage', *International Journal of Technology Assessment in Health Care*, 13:2 (1997) 320–7, at p. 323; Vogel, 'The globalisation of pharmaceutical regulation', at pp. 11–14; J. Abraham and M. Charlton, 'Controlling medicines in Europe: the harmonisation of toxicology assessed', *Science and Public Policy*, 22:6 (1995) 354–62, esp. p. 357 on the ICH.

93   This from Foote, *Managing the medical arms race*, p. 186.

94   M. L. Burstall, 'Europe after 1992: implications for pharmaceuticals', *Health Affairs*, 10:3 (1991) 157–71, sketches the history.

95   'Eur-assess project group report on coverage', p. 321.

96   S. J. Treece, 'An evaluation of medicines regulation', *Medical Law International*, 2:4 (1997) 315–36 provides a sketch of the system.

97   This relies on Eur-assess, 'Project subgroup report on coverage', p. 322.

98   This relies on J. Greenwood and K. Ronit, 'Established and emergent sectors: organized interests at the European level in the pharmaceutical industry and the new biotechnologies', in J. Greenwood, J. R. Grote and K. Ronit (eds), *Organized interests and the European Community* (London, Sage, 1992), pp. 69–83; and J. Greenwood, 'The pharmaceutical industry: a European business alliance that works', in J. Greenwood (ed.), *European business alliances* (Prentice Hall, Hemel Hempstead, 1995), pp. 39–48.

99   Tarabusi and Vickery, 'Globalization in the pharmaceutical industry, part I', p. 82, provide some figures to support these assertions.

100 J. Mohan, 'The internationalisation and commercialistion of health care in Britain', *Environment and Planning A*, 23:1 (1991) 853–67.

101 Cabinet Office, Advisory Council for Applied Research and Development, *Medical equipment*, London, HMSO, 1986.

102 House of Lords, Select Committee on Medical Technology, *Priorities in medical research, volume 1 – report*, HL Paper 54–1, March 1988, p. 42.

103 J. Hutton and K. Hartley, 'The influence of health service procurement policy on research and development in the UK medical capital equipment industry', *Research Policy*, 14:4 (1985) 205–11, from which these details are taken; quotation at p. 207.

104 These developments are summarised in Department of Health, *The Government's response to the ACOST report on medical research and health* (London, Department of Health, 1993), pp. 3–4 – otherwise, a remarkably anodyne document.

105 Quoted in Department of Health, *Press release*, 95\45, 30 January 1995.

106 House of Lords, *Priorities in medical research*, p. 42.

107 Association of British Health-Care Industries, *Exporting health care*, issue 1, summer 1996, p. 2.

108 A reorganisation of these arrangements inside the DTI is reported in Association of British Health-Care Industries, *Exporting health care*, issue 5, June 1998, p. 1.

109 Association of British Health-Care Industries, *Exporting health care*, issue 4, November/December 1997, describes some of these.

110 Association of British Health-Care Industries, *Exporting health care*, issue 4, November/December 1997.

111 Association of British Health-Care Industries, *Exporting health care*, issue 2, Autumn/Winter 1996, p. 2. The words are those of Sir Duncan Nichol. A small sign of the private/public fusion which is involved in this exercise is the fact that the newsletter quoted here is published by the trade association on behalf of the DTI.

112 Association of British Health-Care Industries, *Exporting health care*, issue 2, Autumn/Winter 1996, p. 2.

113 M. Kenny, *Biotechnology: the university-industrial complex* (New Haven CT, Yale University Press, 1986), p. 242.

114 The most important statement of this argument has come from Majone, and the most accessible source of his case is: G. Majone (ed.), *Regulating Europe* (London, Routledge, 1996), part 1 of which reprints the most important of Majone's papers.

115 U. Beck, *Risk society: towards a new modernity*, trans. M. Ritter (London, Sage, 1992). I discuss the possibilities of using Beck's account in Chapter 6.

116 Abraham, *Science, politics and the pharmaceutical industry*, pp. 246–7.

6

Transforming the
health care state

A puzzle restated

It is time to return to our opening puzzle – one created by the particular case of
health policy in the United Kingdom. The puzzle lay in the incongruity between
the language used to talk about health care reform and the actual substance of
reform. In the later 1980s and early 1990s, the UK, like many other advanced
industrial nations, introduced radical changes in the way it organised health
care. Indeed, one of the striking features of the reforms introduced after the
publication of the White Paper of 1989[1] was their radical and decisive nature
– by contrast with Germany, where the Blüm reforms of the same year were
whittled away by the power of private interests, and by contrast with the US
where not even the mandate of a presidential victory could save the Clinton
proposals. There was a great reform wave in health care across the advanced
industrial world, and the UK rode the crest of it.

The origins of that reform wave could be traced to the end of the long boom
– the end in the middle of the 1970s of the thirty glorious years when the
advanced capitalist economies had enjoyed more-or-less unbroken expansion.
After the middle of the 1970s the international economic system became more
unstable and difficult to manage and, while individual nations could still enjoy
considerable success, that success had to be won in an increasingly tough competitive environment. During the long boom almost every advanced capitalist
economy had greatly increased its spending on health care. Now, in tougher
times, the priority was to tighten belts. That is why health care reform was
dominated by a language of cost containment. It seemed to follow from this
that the most radical reforms would take place in those health care systems
where the problem of containment was most acute. That expectation made the
British experience in the late 1980s and early 1990s unfathomable. In those
years Britain underwent major institutional changes in health care. But as far
as cost containment was concerned the evidence about Britain since the foundation of the National Health Service was compelling in a way rare in social

inquiry: the UK had an outstanding record in delivering cheap, cost-effective health care; and that record was due to the command and control system of the NHS, the very elements that were being modified by the Conservative government's reforms. If cost containment was so important, why was Britain, a leader in cost containment, also a leader in institutional reform? The subsequent history of reform only deepens the puzzle, for the Conservative reforms of the late 1980s and early 1990s were succeeded by another wave of reforms when the new Labour government was elected in 1997. Why should a system apparently so good at delivering on a key policy priority – cost containment – be so unstable? Either the policy-making system was highly irrational in the outcomes it produced, or something deeper than the search for cost containment was at work.[2]

The puzzle deepened as soon as the matter was considered comparatively. If cost containment was a priority, and if command and control systems were successful in delivering cost containment, we might have expected an international drift of health care reform in the direction of command and control arrangements. If cost containment mattered so much, surely the systems most effective at the job – the command and control systems exemplified by the UK – should be a model for others? But not only did the most successful command and control system, the UK, begin to tinker with its controls; the drift of policy was almost universally in the direction of more market-based arrangements. Indeed, the situation was more paradoxical still. The greatest single failure in cost containment is acknowledged to be the US. Taking advice from Americans about health care cost containment is like having lessons in seamanship from the crew of the Titanic. Yet many of the key policy entrepreneurs in the reform wave, like the economist Alain Enthoven, were American; and many of the key policy innovations were American inspired. The analysis of health policy in the US – especially by political scientists – has focused on the apparent inability of the American state to produce a viable package of health care reform.[3] That package is plainly needed for, whatever virtues it may have, the American health care system patently fails to deliver two important things: effective cost containment and health care coverage for all the American people. In these two critical senses it is demonstrably inferior to systems like those of Germany and the UK, financed as they are on principles of solidarity that reject the actuarial calculations of commercial insurance markets. But the focus on these American failures risks obscuring a key feature of health care policy in the advanced capitalist world in the 1990s: the extent to which the US is a creative policy pioneer. In the great reforms of the 1960s that introduced Medicare and Medicaid the US was plainly a laggard trying, only partly successfully, to catch up on the advances towards universal coverage made by Europeans. It is understandable that American analysts of health policy should in the 1990s have been deeply concerned with the inability of the American political system purposively to address the nation's health care problems and to be concerned, in particular, with the calamity of the Clinton health care reform proposals. But these concerns obscure the pioneering character of the US health care system in the 1990s. Thirty years ago Amercia was struggling to adapt to policy innovations in health care on the other side of the Atlantic; in the 1990s the European (and Antipodean) systems were trying to adapt health care systems originally built on ideologies of solidarity to resurgent market ideologies. These latter ideologies originated in many instances in the US. One of the building blocks of the European systems, solidaristic financing aimed at securing some kind of universal coverage, began to be compromised. Inside the US itself, the image of stasis conveyed by failures like the Clinton attempt at health care reform was also misleading. The most striking feature of the American health care system in recent years has been its protean character: economic forces are constantly reshaping delivery systems; the individual states are laboratories engaged in a wide range of reform experiments;[4] and regulatory agencies in the federal state have been major sources of policy innovation. For better or worse the US, once a laggard, is now a pioneer: many of its institutional innovations are being copied and, in the name of selectivity and market responsiveness, some of the key features of European systems – notably solidaristic financing designed to ensure universal coverage – are being compromised.

One possible response to these observations is to deny that they constitute a puzzle at all. This is in part what Jacobs does in his analysis of the fate of 'market' reforms in the UK, Sweden and the Netherlands. He argues that an analysis of the goals of these reforms, and of the reality of implementation, suggests that there is not convergence, but divergence:

> I contend that, far from converging, these three countries mapped out *divergent* paths. Focusing on developments in the late 1980s and early 1990s, my argument is that each of the three reform schemes took a distinct approach to the common problems confronting Western health systems. Comparative analysts have concentrated too closely on common policy instruments, while ignoring a contrast of policy goals. In addition, the common rhetoric of market reform obscures gaps between market plans and actual implemented change.[5]

Jacobs' argument identifies a common dilemma that we face in comparative analysis: since comparison is essentially about the study of differentiation, we constantly have to choose between emphasising the similarities or the differences between nations. There are indeed systematic differences, for instance in the way consumption regimes are being reorganised. Freeman's recent work reminds us that command and control systems like the UK generally reform in the search for more micro-efficiency, while corporatist systems like Germany tend to reform in the search for more macroeconomic control, for instance through imposing global budgets.[6] But in this book convergence rather than divergence dominates the story for one obvious reason: because the US is part of the story. Brown expresses the point exactly:

> Many other comparable nations want to learn from the United States the ins and outs of managed care, managed competition, diagnosis-related groups (DRGs), medical practice guidelines, and kindred strategic innovations ... The United States is highly inventive in all respects except the truly important ones – affordability and universal coverage – and other nations look here for innovations to install at the edges of sound and solid systems.[7]

This brief statement of the apparent disjunction between the formal policy priority of cost containment and the actual drift of policy also begins to hint at the solution to our opening puzzle. It must be obvious that the form and direction of health care policy are responding to some forces deeper than the pressure for cost containment alone. The very simple model of health care policy outlined in Chapter 1 now begins to make sense of what these forces amount to. That model, to recapitulate, has three key components. First, health care policy is conceived as involving the government of three different, but connected, arenas: governing the vast system of health care consumption; governing the structure of professionalism – especially of the key group, doctors; and governing an industrial economy of health. These three systems of government respond to pressures inside health care institutions. But now we see the second element of our simple model: the governing process is also connected to wider political and economic environments. This elementary insight becomes particularly important when considered in the light of the history of health care institutons. For historical reasons, in advanced capitalist democracies the institutions of states and health care systems are wound round each other in relations of symbiosis: that is, they have grown together and they feed off each other, sometimes in a supportive and sometimes in a destructive way. These notions of entanglement and symbiosis lie behind the idea of the *health care state*. And they lead in turn naturally to the third element of the model, *embeddedness*: to the way the health care states examined in this book are embedded in democratic political arrangements and capitalist economic arrangements. The British story – and for that matter the American story and the German story – is thus in part about the connections between health care policy and capitalist democracy.

The rest of this chapter now does something simple: it revisits the features identified above – the three arenas, the notion of embeddedness, the very idea of the health care state – in the light of the evidence assembled in the preceding chapters.

Three systems of politics

Three separate, though related, processes are taking place in the government of the health care state.

The *government of consumption* arises from some obvious features of health care consumption in the modern capitalist state: the scale of resources allocated to health care, and the fact that the consumption process is collectivised. In the half-century or so up to the end of the First World War a combination of advances in basic science, technological innovations and reforms in institutional practices – especially in hospitals – transformed the therapeutic efficacy of curative medicine, turning it from a danger to the patient into a highly desirable good. A famous reported remark of Henderson's encapsulates the change: it was only after 1910 or 1912 that a random patient with a random condition choosing a physician at random had more than one chance in two of benefiting from the encounter.[8] The very breakthroughs that converted medicine from a menace to a benefit also created systems of medical care which consumed large amounts of society's resources. Collective financing in health care, which had typically functioned historically to provide income maintenance in sickness for parts of the working class, now expanded to cover the costs of this care for manual workers, and then expanded beyond the core of this class. Thus began the process of collectivising consumption. The great expansion of health care provision which occurred across most of the advanced capitalist world in the years of the long boom accelerated this process of collectivisation. The scale and sophistication of modern scientific medicine for the most part put it out of the reach of the pocket of individual consumers. Out-of-pocket payments for care, though still significant, were dwarfed by collective means of financing. Third-party payment became the key to financing health care consumption. Viewed thus, there is a commonality between health care systems normally thought of as very different: in particular, the US, usually pictured as a health care system governed by principles of market individualism, shares the commitment to the collectivisation of consumption – though, of course, some of the most important third-party payers are commercial insurers. (Even in the US, however, let us remind ourselves once again that after the health care reforms of the mid-1960s state agencies now account for nearly half of all spending on care.)

Collectivisation meant that the structure and government of the institutions of third-party payment were central to the politics of consumption. To take only the most obvious instance: the fact that the dominant third-party payer in the history of the NHS was the central state meant that, virtually from the foundation of the service, consumption issues were part of high politics, the object of struggle between the elite in the core executive and the stuff of partisan debate in parliament and beyond. In both Germany and the US, access to collective consumption was heavily influenced by the stratified institutions of labour markets. Germany, although it achieved universalism in the post-war years, regulated the terms of access to health care through labour market institutions. In the US, as the cost of care rose beyond the means of all but the super-rich, access became primarily a function of labour market location: the excluded were, by and large, not the poor or the old but those who worked in particular segments of the labour market (notably for small firms, especially in the service sector.) This direct connection with the labour market – and therefore with labour costs in an era of intense international competition – has also been part of the clue to the incessant interest in both Germany and the US in reforming methods of health care financing. The attack on solidaristic modes of financing outside the US is not in the main an attempt to shift the immediate cost of care onto the shoulders of the individual health care consumer but to expose solidaristic financing to modes of collectivisation organised through commercial insurance markets. It attempts this partly by restricting the range of consumption financed on solidaristic principles and partly by obiliging solidaristic financiers to behave more like operators in commercial insurance markets. The effects on solidaristic modes of financing are well illustrated by the German case in the manner described in Chapter 3: the free choice of funds for workers introduced in the 1993 law has led to competition for members, desertion of funds with high-risk memberships (and therefore high premiums) for funds that in effect practise risk selection, and pressure on funds to displace their solidaristic practices by more commercial calculations.[9] There is now convincing German survey evidence that members are shifting to funds with lower premiums, and that the very process is reinforcing the pressures on solidarity: those moving are better educated, better off, with lower than average health risks – and the movement is thus accentuating the process of risk selection, widening the divide between funds with high-risk and low-risk members.[10]

Björkman and Altenstetter catch the drift of policy in their summation of health reforms to the mid-1990s:

> reform policies in countries with diverse health care systems are increasingly leading towards a common 'middle ground'. For example, there is a widespread attempt in many countries to define a 'basic benefits package' – a list of core health services to which everyone in society is entitled ... Likewise, several countries with insurance-based health care systems have recently introduced adjustment mechanisms to allow competition among insurers. Such a mechanism adjusts the income of insurers by taking into account variations in characteristics of subscribers, which are known to influence health care costs through differential patterns of need and therefore usage of health care services.[11]

As this passage also shows, there are powerful conflicting pressures in solidaristic systems, conflicts exemplified by the recent history of the German system. At the same time as ideologies of competition are eroding solidaristic practices, states are acquiring the authority to oblige third-party payers to shift resources in partial compensation for differences in risk structures.

The politics of collective consumption overlapped with the second system of politics, that of *professional government*, for the very good reason that the key professional group, doctors, were also critical to determining both the shape and level of consumption. But there is much more to the system of professional government than this. Since at least the publication of Alford's classic study the examination of medical government has been dominated by the issue of how far managers, variously identified, have challenged the entrenched position of doctors in the health care systems of the advanced capitalist world.[12] Important though this issue remains, the amount of attention it has attracted has obscured an even more pervasive source of tension, one created by the historical sequencing of professional development. The medical professions examined in this book – notably in their mode of occupational organisation and their legitimising ideologies – are either pre-democratic creations (the UK), are substantially the result of the workings of anti-democratic politics (Germany) or are the result of attempts to shore up medical authority against a populist, challenging culture (the US). What we observe in the case of the three systems of medical government examined here, therefore, is a process by which these non-democratic creations have encountered the democratic politics of the post-war world – and, indeed, encountered systems of democratic politics where deference, including deference to professional authority, has been in decline. That process has produced pressures external to the profession, and challenges created by internal social and cultural change. Perhaps the single most obvious effect produced by the tensions between modern democratic politics and the traditional system of medical government is the way the regulatory contract governing medical professionalism is being reshaped: in the direction of more elaborately codified systems of rules, in the direction of more elaborately organised systems of institutional control, and in the direction of more direct state intervention, often in the form of juridified regulatory systems.

The reshaping power of democracy is also evident in the case of the third system of politics examined in this book, though it is a reshaping limited by the fact that what is at issue in the *government of production* is control over property rights, including intellectual property rights. The government of production has three particularly important features. First, it introduces a wide range of actors from the corporate private sector into the health policy arena, since the production and distribution of the artifacts of medical care are dominated by private firms; that is a feature which unites the three systems examined here, and which is replicated across all modern capitalist states, irrespective of their mode of medical government or the way they finance health care consumption. Second, the geographical range of this part of the health arena is unusually broad. While consumption struggles, and struggles over the government of doctors, are carried on in the main within the boundaries of nations, the production networks in health care are internationally, sometimes globally, organised: the markets are international in character and, as we saw in the last chapter, the systems of industrial governance also have a cross-national scale. Finally, there is a particularly problematic relationship between the government of production and the wider setting of democratic politics, for reasons that will be immediately obvious to any reader of Lindblom: the production process takes place within a legal setting which assigns rights over property to private interests (either individuals or corporate bodies); the distribution of these rights is highly unequal; and the exercise of these property rights (for instance to produce and market artifacts that might be dangerous to health, of dubious therapeutic efficacy, or economically wasteful) has historically been exercised without much control by the democratic state. Lindblom might have been thinking about the medical technology industries when he wrote these words about the politics of polyarchy (his label for the kind of democratic elitism possible under capitalist democracy):

> in any private enterprise system, a large category of major decisions is turned over to businessmen, both small and larger. They are taken off the agenda of government. Businessmen thus become a kind of public official and exercise what, on a broad view of their role, are public functions. The significant logical consequence of this for polyarchy is that a broad area of public decision making is removed from polyarchal control. Polyarchal decision making may of course ratify such an arrangement or amend it through governmental regulation of business decision making. In all real-world polyarchies a substantial category of decisions is removed from polyarchal control.[13]

A short way to characterise the health care state, therefore, is to say that it developed as an oligarchic set of institutions which empowered a narrow range of professional and corporate elites. These historically engrained features have been subjected to pressure from four directions: from social change; from cultural change; from economic change; and from institutional change. Some of these changes are traceable to factors internal to health care institutions, some to features external to those institutions. What is remarkable, however, is that while the substantive policy problems faced by the three systems examined here are very different, the direction of change in all three 'systems of politics' is strikingly similar. In a nutshell, closely integrated oligarchies dominated by professional and corporate interests, operating with a substantial degree of independence from the core institutions of the state, are being replaced: by looser, more open, more unstable networks; by networks in which professional and corporate elites still exercise great power but in a more contested environment than hitherto; and by an institutional setting in which the core institutions of the state exercise much tighter surveillance and control than hitherto. This is the sense in which to speak about the rise of the market and the retreat of the state is a great oversimplification. There has indeed been a turning to some market solutions, notably in the government of consumption. But the turn to new modes of government has actually strengthened the core institutions of the state, and accentuated one of the defining features of the health care state – the intertwining of the institutions of the health care system and the state itself.

The *social* changes which have brought about these altered circumstances are many, but perhaps the most significant is the changed social profile of consumption. The changes over the thirty years or so of the long boom did more than merely increase the volume of resources devoted to health care, though that was indeed significant. One of the most momentous consequences of the collectivisation of consumption was to extend systems of third-party payment beyond the core of the working class. Behind this change lies one of the most insistent pressures for changes in the government of consumption – the demands of more affluent health care consumers for a differentiated service. It is this pressure – explored by Saltman and von Otter in their work on the command and control systems of governing consumption in northern Europe[14] – which helps explain much of the pressure for reform in a British system so good at the business of cost containment: the price of effective cost containment was a quality of service, and a speed of service, unacceptable to middle-class consumers. As the class profile of those covered by private health shows, the middle class have responded by 'exiting' from the command and control system, at least for a range of elective treatments.

These social changes are in a rather obvious way connected to the impact of *cultural* change. This has been one of the main themes of the preceding chapters, both in the management of consumption and in the management of professionals. It is not just that the institutions and practices of the health care state originated in undemocratic political circumstances, but that the cultures that supported professional authority were marked by high levels of confidence in professional expertise – the essential foundation of deference to the profession. There has been a demonstrable change in the confidence with which citizens view important public institutions, and that has extended to the institution of medicine.[15] An added factor in this cultural change is the altered expectations and attainments of women who, for obvious reasons, have had a disproportionate contact with health care institutions. As we saw in Chapter 3, there have been demonstrable changes in the condition of women, measured by rising educational attainments and by rising participation in the workforce, which affect the kind of attitudes they bring to health care institutions. These cultural changes are also behind what Giesen has called the medical malpractice crisis – 'characterized by a sharp increase in the number of patients seeking recovery at law for injuries suffered as a result of the negligent provision of medical care and by a correspondingly steep increase in the insurance premiums which doctors have to pay'.[16]

Economic change has had more obvious effects still. The construction of the health care state, especially in the post-war years, involved acts of great generosity in the expenditure of resources. That is the economic thread which most obviously joins the three countries examined here during the years of the long boom. The end of the long boom was probably the single most important recent event in the history of the health care state: important because it brought to an end the more-or-less untroubled economic expansion that funded growing spending on health care; and important in a more subtle way because it destroyed the confidence in a future of untroubled prosperity that itself underpinned the expansion of health care services.

Institutional change refers to the impact of the sheer scale of modern health care systems, and to the complexity of the institutional forms of delivery. The great rise in health care spending in the years of the long boom did not simply increase the scale of resources given to health care. It also had profound effects on the character of the institutions of delivery. One of the most obvious consequences was to magnify the scale of organisations: this is reflected in the sheer size of institutions like hospitals, in the internal complexity of their division of labour (consider the multiplication, for instance, of health care professions) and in the way the complex advanced technologies of health care interacted with these organisational factors. It also helps account for a feature of the health care policy process identified by Alford over two decades ago: the fact that it is almost perpetually consumed by projects of institutional reform, by the language of crisis, and by waves of fashion, sometimes favouring more, sometimes favouring less, centralisation. Institutional change, and especially growth in institutional size, has produced changes in the political character of health care policy by making more difficult the maintenance of small, homogenous policy-making communities. It has greatly elongated the process of policy delivery by extending and elaborating the division of labour in health care. And the insoluble problem – how best to organise this complex instititutional world – means that the competing interests in health care can, in addressing this problem, more-or-less continuously manoeuvre around it. 'Crises' in health care are precipitated by the struggles between the great competing interests, and solutions to the insoluble problems of institutional complexity represent attempts by those competing interests to solve both substantive problems and the problem of how to practice symbolic manipulation of patients/consumers.[17]

All this, though, is only to focus on the impact of institutional change *within* health care systems. These changes reflect one aspect of the embedded nature of health care institutions: the way they are subject to influences from the wider political and economic environment. But embeddedness also entails something else: the capacity of health care institutions to have a shaping influence on their environment.

Embeddedness revisited[18]

Casual usage of the notion of embeddedness would suggest that health care policy is the recipient of influences from its environment – and it is. But that is an inadequate usage of the notion. To be embedded, if the organic metaphor is to be pursued consistently, is to experience influences that can flow two ways: from the embedded, as much as to it. That is exactly the importance of the notion here. I have pursued at some length the importance of shaping influences from outside health care institutions in the preceding chapters. But the significance of the health care state also resides in its transformative influence on its surrounding environment. It is not just that health care institutions are big, or that health care issues are important. It is that size and importance mean that the surrounding political system, while helping reshape health care institutions, is itself being reshaped by those very institutions. There are four particularly important ways in which this is happening with the institutions of the health care state: through their role as players in the wider governing process; through their impact on the structure of the policy making system; through their effect on economic statecraft; and through their effect on the form and substance of mobilised political alliances. Each is here examined in turn.

The fact that the institutions of the health care system and of the state are wound round each other means that health care agencies are major players in the wider governing process. Political reputations can be made or broken by success or failure in the health care arena: consider the contrasting cases of President Clinton, whose authority as president was greatly damaged by the failure of the Clinton health reforms reforms in 1994, and the (less important) case of Kenneth Clarke whose political career was greatly enhanced by association with the successful passage of the British internal market reforms. More generally, the sheer size of health care systems means that the agencies of the health care state are major bureaucratic actors. Something of this emerged, in particular, in our chapter on the government of medical technology, where it was obvious that the importance of regulatory agencies was not confined to health care – they were major players in regulatory games, and even in larger processes like the creation of more unified regulatory systems across the European Union.

In the administration of the state, health care institutions also have major roles. Because of the central historical importance of the medical profession, they have been pioneers in managing and incorporating professional elites in the policy-making process. More important still they, alongside defence industries, are key ways in which the impact of science and technological innovation is felt within government. Indeed, one of the most striking features of the preceding chapter is the extensive evidence of a 'medical-industrial' complex in the modern state, linking corporate, professional and bureaucratic elites.[19]

That consideration links to the third way in which the health care state is a shaping, rather than a shaped, institution. The very scale of the resources now allocated to health care, and the fact that many of these resources draw on the most socially and technologically advanced parts of the economy, make health care a vital resource for the modern state. The lesson of the preceding chapter is that the medical technology industries have emerged as important instruments of economic statecraft in the modern industrial state: because of the extent to which health care goods and services are now an important tradeable group of commodities in the advanced capitalist world; and because of the extent to which governments, acknowledging this importance, have begun to use health care as a contribution to industrial policy. Health care policy also impinges on modern economic statecraft because of its consequences for the wider conduct of fiscal policy and for the condition of the public finances. Perhaps the most graphic illustration of this is provided by the US – graphic precisely because we so rarely think of the US as a system in which the state provides an important role in financing health care. The escalating cost of health care has meant that Medicare is a dominant influence on the US federal budget. Thus health care budgeting is central to the wider federal budgetary process, both in the processual sense and, more substantively, in the sense that the problems of federal finance in recent years have in large measure been a reflection of problems in containing the size of Medicare bill.[20] A similar story of the importance of health care spending for the public purse can, of course, be told about the UK. Even where the cost is not integrated into the public purse, as in Germany, the impact of health care insurance premiums on the wider conduct of industrial policy is profound.

To all this we should add the fourth set of influences that come out of the health care system: its effect on the wider shaping of political alliances. For over two decades now the reform of health care policy has been a dominant concern of the advanced industrial states – in the case of two countries examined here, the US and Germany, there have been repeated efforts to try to reform health care institutions; in the case of the UK arguments over reform became central to electoral partisanship from the early 1980s. In short, in terms of the self-constructed tasks of statesmanship the reform of health care policy has been a major task – and its success or otherwise a major index of success or failure. That consideration has been reinforced by the impact of the problems of health care policy on public perceptions of the competence of governments. One of the most striking features of the democratic politics of the systems considered here is the extent to which health care issues over time have climbed the democratic agenda: witness the seemingly perpetual cycle of attempts at health care reform in al three countries examined in these pages. That in turn reflects some of the structural features of the policy-making system outlined earlier, notably the extent to which what was historically an enclosed, oligarchic policy-making system broke down and was replaced by more open, contested arrangements. And, of course, it also reflected the impact of some of the changes identified earlier in the substance of policy, notably the way the increase in the scale of resources devoted to health care increased the stakes in the struggles for distribution of resources.

This increase in the stakes has connected to a wider impact still, on patterns of political mobilisation and electoral struggle. The sheer scale of employment in the health care arena has made the occupational politics of this arena a vital part of the modern electoral process. In each of the three countries examined the numbers employed in health care are huge: just look back for a moment to Table 1.5. In some instances this is magnified by the concentration of numbers in particular regions: that is an important source of the sort of analysis referred to by Mohan, for instance, in his account of the way the concentration of certain kinds of health care services in the south east of England had a major influence on the reforms of UK health care policy in the 1990s.[21] In short, the health care workforce, not to mention the beneficiaries of the consumption of health care, have had to be integrated into the electoral calculations of modern politicians.

The effects of the health care system on wider patterns of political mobilisation and organisation are more profound still. This continues a historically established pattern, for as we saw in earlier chapters the organisation of, for instance, the medical profession was a prototype for effective pressure group organisation. What is remarkable in recent decades is the way the sheer scale of health care policy has fashioned important political groupings which have then spilled over from the conventional field of health care. The most obvious instance of this is provided by Morone, who points to the way in which the 'grey' lobby in the US, now one of the most important in American politics, is virtually the creation of the original Medicare legislation in the mid 1960s.[22] The consumption politics of health care is particularly important as a source of mass mobilisation. It is increasingly a *mass* politics in a number of critical respects: in the scale of numbers involved, given the universal demand for health care; in the fact that payment systems are largely collectivised; and, as a result of this collectivisation, in the way the kind of access individuals have to means of collectivisation – for instance whether through principles of citizenship or through private insurance markets – is becoming a major determinant of the access groups enjoy to a highly valued set of goods and services.

This has interacted with one of the characteristic features of the changing health status of populations in advanced industrial societies: the way chronic disease has increasingly supplanted acute conditions, as curative medicine becomes more effective at dealing with acute ailments.[23] The political significance is that acute ailments, by their transient character, are a poor foundation for political mobilisation. Chronic diseases, by contrast, are providing the foundation for the creation of new groups, making this social arena one of the most buoyant parts of the pressure group world.[24] The successful pioneers in this respect have been Aids groups, notably in the US, with their capacity to borrow many of the features of new social movements and use them for health care lobbying: the integration between the group as a species of political mobilisation and a particular kind of subculture; the use of the most innovative means of mass communication; and the use of celebrity support in order to make that mass publicity more effective still.

This last observation re-emphasises the particular significance of 'embeddedness'. The case of political organisation and mobilisation is a very good instance of the way the embedded character of the health care state makes it both a patient and an agent: ensures that it is both transformed by, but also helps transform, the environment. The changing character of democratic politics has undoubtedly had an important impact on the shape of the health care state. It is obvious that much of the new open and contested character of the health care domain has to do with with the changing nature of Schumpeterian democracy, notably with the difficulty of preserving a democratic model where citizens are restricted to choosing between competing elites. But it is equally the case that this changing character has a great deal to do with what has been happening to the institutions of the health care state itself. That catches both the idea of embeddedness and the intertwining which is central to the notion of the health care state.

The same is true of the economic impact of the health care state. The chapter on medical technology made plain that the health care industries were being shaped by the process of globalisation – but were also contributing independently to that very process. What happens in health care is not a function of some mechanical effects transmitted by wider institutional systems. It is the result of attempts at creative institution building and policy shaping. These themes form a part of the last section of this chapter, to which we now turn.

Death or transfiguration?

The solution to the puzzle which prompted this book, and with which we opened this chapter, is now in broad terms obvious. The search for cost containment is certainly important, but it is important for two rather different reasons: it is significant in its own right since, in the wake of the great post-war expansion in health care spending and the end of the long boom, all health care systems have been forced to make it a policy priority; but it is also important as a symptom of fundamental changes in the politics of the health care state. This latter reason explains why systems that actually seem rather good at cost containment – such as the British command and control system – have nevertheless been weakened rather than strengthened in the age of cost containment. These considerations also begin to answer, in an unsurprising way, the question posed at the head of this section: the health care state is indeed not dying, but it is being transfigured, in some instances by purposive policy change and in others by structural responses to pressures coming from within and from outside health care systems.

At the root of these changes lies the fact that the fate of health care institutions is implicated in the fate of democratic politics in the advanced capitalist world. What happens in health care is affected by the surrounding environment of democratic politics; but precisely because of the size and strategic location of health care institutions the way they develop in turn significantly affects that surrounding democratic environment. In the wider democratic environment the institutions and cultural patterns that supported elitist Schumpeterian democracy have in recent decades come under intense pressure: the key institution of Schumpeterian democracy, the political party, has ceased to dominate quite as hitherto either the political identities or the participatory opportunities of citizens; rising levels of education, and changing occupational patterns, have created a citizenry which is more politically competent and questioning; new modes of political organisation and mobilisation have drawn citizens into activities in single-issue groups; within government, enclosed policy-making communities have been increasingly transformed into more open, unstable policy networks.

The institutions of the health care state were bound to come under increasing pressures in democratic political systems because, as I have sought to show in the preceding pages, they were the product of oligarchic political arrangements. But the wider changes in the surrounding democratic environment summarised above – which weakened the elitist democracy developed after the Second World War – have intensified these pressures. They leave us with three particularly striking sets of changes corresponding to three arenas of health care government examined in this book. I take them in reverse order to that used in earlier chapters for reasons that should become clear when we reach the account of the government of consumption.

The most striking development of the *government of production* in health care is the increasing integration of the industrial government of health care into the wider government of the modern industrial state. Some areas of the control of the medical technology industries are slowly succumbing to democratic politics. As an arena where private property rights – whether to physical or intellectual property – have been dominant, the government of production until recently resembled a polyarchic arrangement of the sort classically described by Lindblom: the capacity of democratic institutions to control innovation, investment, production or sales was limited both by the privileges of private property and by imbalances in the distribution of expertise and regulatory resources between firms and states. The rising interest in technology assessment in health care and the growth of regulatory regimes in the wake of safety scandals are signs of the way this polyarchic structure is being eroded. The limited extent of that erosion is a sign of the continuing imbalance of resources between agencies of democratic control and the institutions of polyarchy. But another reason for the limited incursion of democratic control is connected to the increasingly important role played by the health care production industries in the wider industrial economy. The importance of these industries limits the control capacities of democratic states, because those states, in managing their industrial economies, also have to promote indigenous medical technology industries in a competitive world. The most rational strategy for a nation is to promote technological innovation in health care as strenuously as possible, but to export the results of innovation to other jurisdictions. That is something of the strategy, for instance, that characterises some in niche markets: for instance, the Swiss in pharmaceuticals or the Danes in the world hearing-aid industry.[25] But that is characteristically a strategy open only to niche producers. Beyond the world of the niche producer there exists the stress and tension between the pressures of democracy and the constraints of market competition.

Whether we view the changed environment of production in optimistic or pessimistic terms turns in part on how we view the culture of modernity. It is possible to write an account of what is summarised above in Beck's language of reflexive modernity. The economy of health has indeed a kind of self-referential quality. It is demonstrably driven in part by its own industrial imperatives: by the forces of global competition and by the incentive structures of modern scientific research communities. And much of the popular challenge to this – from patients seeking empowerment, from new political movements seeking a voice in the health production process – has precisely the character of reflexity identified in Beck's strange, mesmeric nightmare: it directly challenges the rationality of science and the arithmetic of risk assessment. But it only mounts a partial challenge. In part it simply demands more technology and more say in the allocation of the miracles of modern medical science: consider the account in Chapter 5 of the attitudes of some modern patient movements, like the Aids lobby, to the curative possibilities of technology. More narrowly, it is not at all clear that the history of modern medical technology conforms to Beck's picture of growing catastrophic risk. On the contrary: what is produced in the health care economy now is safer and more efficiacious than ever before. It is safer at least in part precisely because democratic politics has challenged the self-referential quality of scientific production, albeit only to a limited extent. The Thalidomide disaster, an episode that realised exactly Beck's notion of catastrophic collective risk, was turned into a scandal by the agents of pluralist politics – and, thus constructed as a scandal, became the occasion for the more effective public regulation of risk.[26]

The most striking development in *professional government* is the reshaping of systems for governing the medical profession. Doctors were the linchpin of the health care state as it developed historically. They were the first great interest in health care to achieve effective organisation; and as mass consumption of

health care developed in the wake of the transformation of the curative efficacy of medicine, they emerged as the managers of the consumption process.
The characteristic mode of doctor government was an oligarchy protected
from democratic politics by the ideologies and practices of self-regulation.
This state of affairs came about in part because of the profession's cultural
ascendancy, and in part because the historical timing of the development of
systems of professional government meant that institutions were established
before, or apart from, democratic politics, In retrospect, we can see that
oligarchic professional government in medicine was the most likely casualty of
democratic politics, and so it has proved. But recall that this oligarchic system
was a linchpin of the whole system of health care government; its weakening
has created serious problems of control, which have shown themselves most
notably in the *government of consumption*.

The collectivisation of health care consumption, we have already noted,
is one of the most important features of modern health care policy across
the advanced industrial world, and is a shaping influence on the politics of
consumption. It has made third-party payers major political actors; and in
the choice it has opened up – essentially between collectivisation based on
solidaristic principles and collectivisation based on the principles of commercial markets in insurance – it has created a major political fault line. These
two developments – the rise in the political significance of third-party payers,
and the choice between solidaristic and commercially based financing – are
associated with the changes in medical government. It is obvious that the
government of consumption is about resource allocation: about collectively
allocating the societal resources needed to fund consumption, and then about
allocating the resources – the health care goods and services – created by that
collectively raised finance. As it is now a truism to say, at heart this is a
rationing process. Rationing has always existed in health care, but the hegemony of the medical profession shaped the rationing process in particular
directions. The cultural authority of doctors meant that they were able to
ration health care resources in the name of medical judgement, defusing the
politically explosive implications of making decisions that involved pain, fear
and often death. The rise of rationing as an issue in health care – a rise which
is observable in all the three systems considered in this book, and in a wide
range of others – is a sign that the mechanism for defusing this politically
explosive process no longer functions effectively.[27]

Rationing is the issue which most obviously connects the three arenas of
health care politics examined in this book, and it promises to be an important
influence in the continuing transformation of the health care state. The
system of production in health, precisely by virtue of its dazzling intellectual
virtuosity, perpetually offers new rationing choices. One of the great achieve-
ments of curative medicine – shifting the balance of sickness from the acute to
the chronic – has in the process greatly expanded the proportion of citizenry

with claims to long-term treatment of conditions which are incurable under present technology. Meanwhile, the process of innovation in medical technology, fuelled by a mixture of economic forces and the incentive structures of scientific professionalism, continually offers expanded therapeutic choices. At the most intellectually exciting boundaries of research, such as those occupied by new work in genetics, fresh developments are raising issues for the collective organisation of consumption, whether organised on solidaristic or commercial lines, because of the possibilities offered to predict and screen for health conditions long before they show themselves in the individual patient. Innovation in health care is so locked into the modern industrial economy of innovation that there is no possibility of its cessation short of the destruction of that wider economy – probably an inconceivable eventuality, and certainly an undesirable one. The health care state will be, more than ever, about the management of the rationing choices continually being opened up by the systems of innovation. These choices have to be made in a world where the control systems exercised by the old medical oligarchies have been weakened, and where it is increasingly difficult to manipulate the consuming citizen by either cultural or institutional mystification.

All this rationing has to take place in the light of an obvious, but overwhelmingly important, consideration: the cultural and physical significance of ill health in modern industrial society. Most citizens now have dazzling levels of material comfort and security by comparison with what their predecessors experienced even a couple of generations ago; that is particularly true of the three societies examined in this book. In such societies encounters with health care institutions now take on a particular intensity, for they constitute an important remaining area of great anxiety, and potentially even worse. With the possible exception of childbirth, all our encounters with the health care system are to some degree unpleasant, involving anxiety, discomfort, pain and, at the end of it all, the final unpleasantness of death. Before we die – indeed usually shortly before we die – most of us make great demands on the health care state.

These circumstances originate in one of the key historical moments of the transition to modernity. In the half-century before the First World War the focus of health care shifted from the external to the internal. In the first half of the nineteenth century the public health movement was a powerful and vigorous force. In its focus on problems like sanitation it drew inspiration from an alliance of medicine and civil engineering. The therapeutic revolution robbed public health of vigour and put most creativity into curative medicine. In Freeman's words: 'In the course of the twentieth century, the expert gaze was to move from the external to the internal, from the boundary between individuals and their environments (sanitation) to the boundaries between people (the management of infection and contagion)'.[28] In the 1980s and 1990s the intractability of the problems of cost containment stimulated once again a widespread revival of interest in managing the public health environment and preventing the onset of illness by encouraging healthy lifestyles. Desirable though all this may be, it is more a hindrance than a help to cost containment. Klein puts it with characteristic directness: 'Even if policies of prevention and social engineering were to be successfully introduced, their very success in extending life expectancy would create new demands for alleviating the chronic degenerative diseases of old age. In short, no policy can ensure that people will drop dead painlessly at the age of 80, not having troubled the health services previously.'[29] There is no escape from rationing, nor from pain, fear and finally death.

Notes

1   *Working for patients*, Cm 555 (1989).
2   Of course, the two observations may be true: the subterranean forces may be a source of policy irrationality. I have attempted a solution to a related problem – the rise of market ideologies in health care – along these lines in Moran, 'Explaining the rise of the market in health care' in W. Ranade (ed.), *Markets and health care: a comparative analysis* (London, Longman, 1998), pp. 17–33, with an emphasis on embeddedness which resembles the argument of this chapter.
3   Notably, the collection in J. Morone and G. Belkin (eds), *The Politics of health care reform: lessons from the past, prospects for the future* (Durham NC, Duke University Press, 1994). The recent work of Theda Skocpol is also an extended exploration of the failure of the US to develop either a welfare or a health care state: notably, Skocpol, *Protecting soldiers and mothers: the political origins of social policy in the United States* (Cambridge, Mass., Belknap Press, 1992); and *Boomerang: Clinton's health security effort and the turn against government in U.S. politics* (New York, Norton, 1996).
4   There is a striking study of seven state pioneers in reform in P. Paul-Sheehan, 'The states and health care reform: the road travelled and lessons learned from seven that took the lead', *Journal of Health Politics, Policy and Law*, 23:2 (1998) 319–61.
5   A. Jacobs, 'Seeing difference: market health reforms in Europe', *Journal of Health Politics, Policy and Law*, 23:1 (1998) 1–33.
6   R. Freeman, 'Competition in context: the politics of health care reform in Europe', *International Journal for Quality in Health Care*, 10:5 (1998) 395–401.
7   L. Brown, 'Exceptionalism as the rule? U.S. health policy innovation and cross-national learning', *Journal of Health Politics, Policy and Law*, 23:1 (1998) 35–51.
8   I have seen this remark quoted in several places, but only have one attributed citation: M. Field in his introduction to his collection, *Success and crisis in national health systems: a comparative approach* (London, Routledge, 1989), pp. 3–4, cites L. Henderson, 'The physician and patient as a social system', *New England Journal of Medicine*, 212: 18 (1935) 819–23. However, the words do not appear in the original. I therefore take this to be a piece of apocrypha about the legendary Henderson.

9   J. Müller and W. Schneider, 'Entwicklung der Mitgliederzahlen, Beitragssätze, Versichertenstrukturen und RSA-Transfers in Zeiten des Kassenwettbewerbs', *Arbeit und Sozialpolitik*, 52: 3/4 (1998) 10–32.

10 The survey evidence is reported and analysed in H. Andersen and J. Schwarze, 'GKV'97: Kommt Bewegung in die Landschaft? Eine empirische Analyse der Kassenwahlenentscheidungen', *Arbeit und Sozialpolitik*, 52:9/10 (1998) pp. 11–23.

11 J. Björkman and C. Altenstetter, 'Globalized concepts and localized practice: convergence and divergence of health policy reforms', in Altenstetter and Björkman (eds), *Health policy reform, national variations and globalization* (London, Macmillan, 1997), pp. 1–16, at p. 3.

12 R. Alford, *Health care politics: ideological and interest group barriers to reform* (Chicago IL, University of Chicago Press, 1975).

13 C. Lindblom, *Politics and markets: the world's political-economic systems* (New York, Basic Books, 1977), p. 172.

14 R. Saltman and C. von Otter, *Planned markets and public competition: strategic reform in northern European health systems* (Buckingham, Open University Press, 1992).

15 This is most obvious in the US. We do not have such clear cut evidence for elsewhere, but for evidence of growing public dissatisfaction with health care delivery (including GPs) in the UK, see the surveys cited in R. Baggot, *Health and health care in Britain* (Basingstoke, Macmillan, 1998, 2nd edn), pp. 305–7. I am convinced that this generalisation is correct, however, and less by direct survey evidence about longtitudinal trends and more by the the bulk of contextual and circumstantial evidence indicating a transformation over the last half-century in the political and social context of doctoring.

16 D. Giesen, 'Medical malpractice and the judicial function in comparative perspective', *Medical Law International*, 1:1 (1993) 3–16, at p. 3.

17 The opening words of this sentence are almost a direct quotation from Alford, *Health care politics*, p. 249; and the debt of this passage to Alford, notably to Chapters 2 and 8, will be plain.

18 After I thought out the idea of embeddedness I read Peter Evans' fine book, *Embedded autonomy: states and industrial transformation* (Princeton NJ, Princteon University Press, 1995). I read it in the hope that it would provide clues to help me develop the idea, but to no avail. In part, I think, this is because my usage of embeddedness differs from that of Evans; in part because I have not been able to think out as creatively as him the implications of different forms of embeddedness.

19 For an earlier argument see S. Wohl, *The medical industrial complex* (New York, Harmony Books, 1984).

20 The way this is connected to Medicare as an entitlement regime is succinctly described in C. Weissert and W. Weissert, *Governing health: the politics of health policy* (Baltimore MD, Johns Hopkins University Press, 1996), pp. 33–5.

21 J. Mohan, *A national health service? The restructuring of health care in Britain since 1979* (Basingstone, Macmillan, 1995), pp. 73–100.

22 J. Morone, Introduction to Morone and Belkin, *Politics of health care reform*, pp. 1–7 at p. 2.

23 This statement glosses – I think defensibly – a complex picture, one which changes depending on the geographical range covered by generalisations. For exemplifications of this see R. Saltman and J. Figueras, *European health care reform: analysis of current strategies* (Copenhagen, World Health Organization, 1997), pp. 13–29.

24 This is a central finding of Wood's forthcoming book comparing patient organisations in the UK and the US: B. Wood, *Patient power? Patients' associations and health care in Britain and America* (Buckingham, Open University Press, 1999).

25 On the Danish example see P. Lotz, 'Demand as a driving force in medical innovation', *International Journal of Technology Assessment in Health Care*, 9:2 (1993) 174–88.

26 U. Beck, *Risk society: towards a new modernity*, trans. M. Ritter (Sage, London, 1992), esp. pp. 19–102. Beck's conception of the character of risk in modern society is carefully elaborated here, and it stresses the rise of what might be called collectivised risks. His paradigmatic case is the risk to life and health from nuclear power. But the Thalidomide case is thus particularly revealing because it had precisely the socialised, invisible quality which Beck sees as the characteristc feature of modern risk. Thalidomide was a drug taken by pregnant women on medical advice; its catastrophic effects were initially invisible; and its victims, the innocents in the womb, were in no position to take precautionary measures.

27 These issues are discussed at greater length in S. Harrison and M. Moran, 'Resources and rationing: managing supply and demand in health care', in G. Albrecht, R. Fitzpatrick and S. Scrimshaw (eds), *The handbook of social studies in health and medicine* (New York, Sage, forthcoming).

28 R. Freeman, *Health care policy in Europe* (Manchester, Manchester University Press, forthcoming).

29 R. Klein, *The politics of the National Health Service* (London, Longman, 1989, 2nd edn), p. 182.

Index